Learning Windows Server Containers

Build and deploy high-quality portable apps faster

Srikanth Machiraju

BIRMINGHAM - MUMBAI

Learning Windows Server Containers

First published: April 2017

Production reference: 1260417

Published by Packt Publishing Ltd.
Livery Place
35 Livery Street
Birmingham
B3 2PB, UK.

ISBN 978-1-78588-793-2

www.packtpub.com

Credits

Author

Srikanth Machiraju

Copy Editors

Safis Editing
Dipti Mankame

Reviewer

Romeo Mlinar

Project Coordinator

Judie Jose

Commissioning Editor

Kartikey Pandey

Proofreader

Safis Editing

Acquisition Editor

Rahul Nair

Indexer

Pratik Shirodkar

Content Development Editor

Abhishek Jadhav

Graphics

Kirk D'Penha

Technical Editor

Gaurav Suri

Production Coordinator

Shantanu N. Zagade

Foreword

Containers have become an elegant way to virtualize system level services in the recent past. Coupled with microservices which provide well-bounded, self-contained, application services, containers bring a revolutionary shift to the way solutions are built and deployed on computer infrastructure. Docker has been a favorite way to build containers and container clusters on open source. The ability to pack hundreds or even thousands of these containers into a physical machine provides a great way to deploy services in an optimal and scalable fashion. The ability to use different operating systems in each of the containers (such as, Linux, Windows) along with any needed functionality packed together is a convenience that contributes to building modular systems. Microsoft Windows and Azure cloud platforms have matured over time and plays a critical role in building systems addressing the needs of digital transformation currently underway in enterprise IT systems across the world. Whether it is the enterprise application that handles millions (or billions) of mobile users or one that handles zillions of IoT sensors (connected cars, refrigerators, or whatever you have), it can now be built using Windows as a platform using the containers model and hosted on Azure cloud to provide the necessary scale.

Deployment and frequent releases is another area which has been revolutionized by container technology. DevOps, the practice that bring together development, deployment, and operations into a seamless continuum by making *infrastructure as code* a reality, is a part of the agile way of building solutions today. By using the concept of containers, enterprise IT teams can effortlessly and efficiently deploy solutions to immutable infrastructure.

This book deals with all the above aspects and is a timely addition to the windows and Azure developer's toolkit to understand windows containers and their usage in building different types of systems. The integration of DevOps into the subject brings a well thought out addition that helps in implementing cutting edge application development practices.

The author is a well-seasoned developer and architect, who has significant experience building modern enterprise solutions for large customers and his practical approach in dealing with this complex subject shines through in every page of this book. Bringing his consulting background and enormous technical prowess to the task, he has detailed out approach to application development with windows containers which will help developers, architects and operation teams in building modern cloud based enterprise scale applications.

Starting with an introduction to containers and microservices, the author takes a developer on a profound journey that covers from building a simple *Hello World* container to advanced practical usage, such as building complex enterprise applications using SQL Server, Redis Cache, storage volumes, VSTS for continuous build and deployment, resource management, and insights.

Ritesh Modi

Senior Technology Evangelist

Microsoft India

About the Author

Srikanth Machiraju is an ardent techie, DevOps practitioner, and developer consultant on Microsoft Azure and .NET technologies. He works for Microsoft Global Services, Modern Apps team, Hyderabad India. Over the past 9 years he has worked as a lead consultant for design and development of cloud-based application, migrating legacy applications to cloud, corporate trainer on Azure technologies, and speaker at various user group meetings on Microsoft Technologies. He loves to teach and evangelize best practices and patterns in application development. He continues to explore building modern, smart, and cloud-born applications with more reachability and integration using Azure, IoT devices, Artificial Intelligence, deep learning, parallelism, and enterprise level security. When away from work he loves to cook for his family, explore and review new food joints, watch movies, swim, and play Xbox.

He is also working on another artwork called Developing Bots using Microsoft Bot Framework which is due for release by end of 2017. The book focuses on building smart and intelligent bots using Microsoft Bot framework and Azure Cognitive Services.

I would like to thank my family, specially my wife Sonia Madan for being unconditionally supportive throughout the journey of this book. I would also like to thank my mentors Vineet Bhatia and Phani Tipparaju from BrainScale for their guidance throughout my career without learning from them this achievement would not have been possible. It is the people above and many more I may not have listed here inspired me learn, achieve, and feel obligated to pass the knowledge and learnings to the willing.

About the Reviewer

Romeo Mlinar has been working as Microsoft Senior System Engineer. Professionally connected with computer technology for more than a decade. Passionately devoted with Microsoft products and technology, for instance, system center, planning and design of Active Directory, as well as Windows Server services, devoting special attention to virtualization (Hyper-V), which is his recent preoccupation. He bears large number of Microsoft industrial certificates. Since 2012, he is Microsoft's Most Valuable Professional (MVP) for Cloud and Datacenter Management. He is a regular speaker at various IT conferences in the region and abroad. Also, he is an IT Pro and Edu IT Pro User Group lead in Zagreb, Croatia. He spends his free time with people from the IT world, acquiring new knowledge, eagerly sharing it with others, while at the same time enjoying his life with his family.

He blogs at: `http://blog.mlinar.biz/`.

He was also a reviewer on *Hyper-V 2016 Best Practices* written by Romain Serre and Benedict Berger.

> *I would like to thank my wife Ana and to my lovely son Vito, for their kind and full support, their understanding, and encouragement. Without you guys I could not have followed my passion. You are the source of my inspiration and happiness.*

www.PacktPub.com

For support files and downloads related to your book, please visit www.PacktPub.com.

Did you know that Packt offers eBook versions of every book published, with PDF and ePub files available? You can upgrade to the eBook version at www.PacktPub.com and as a print book customer, you are entitled to a discount on the eBook copy. Get in touch with us at service@packtpub.com for more details.

At www.PacktPub.com, you can also read a collection of free technical articles, sign up for a range of free newsletters and receive exclusive discounts and offers on Packt books and eBooks.

https://www.packtpub.com/mapt

Get the most in-demand software skills with Mapt. Mapt gives you full access to all Packt books and video courses, as well as industry-leading tools to help you plan your personal development and advance your career.

Why subscribe?

- Fully searchable across every book published by Packt
- Copy and paste, print, and bookmark content
- On demand and accessible via a web browser

Customer Feedback

Thanks for purchasing this Packt book. At Packt, quality is at the heart of our editorial process. To help us improve, please leave us an honest review on this book's Amazon page at: https://www.amazon.com/dp/1785887939.

If you'd like to join our team of regular reviewers, you can e-mail us at: customerreviews@packtpub.com. We award our regular reviewers with free eBooks and videos in exchange for their valuable feedback. Help us be relentless in improving our products!

Table of Contents

Preface

Containers is the next breakthrough in building modern and cloud based applications, comparing it with its predecessors like VM virtualization one would realize that containerization is the fastest, most resource-efficient, scalable, and secure way of building application hosting environments we know so far. *Learning Windows Server Containers* take you through a long and profound journey of building containerized ASP.NET applications on latest windows server platforms using Docker command line and Docker REST API. The book shows you how to build and ship containers from one environment to other with less hassle during the continuous integration and delivery process. You will learn to build containerized applications using scalable storage containers, cache containers with isolation levels like in VMs. The book helps you build an ecosystem of container hosts, manage composite container deployments, and resource governance.

What this book covers

Chapter 1, *Exploring Virtualization*, teaches you different virtualization levels, challenges with each type of virtualization, containers as a virtualization platform, and benefits of running containerized applications, tooling support, other container platforms available in market today.

Chapter 2, *Deploying First Container*, teaches you to set up development environment, understand the Docker terminology, installing images from Docker Hub, create custom windows container images using Docker CLI and authoring Dockerfile.

Chapter 3, *Working with Container Images*, will introduce you to common container management tasks such as listing the containers, start/stop, cleaning up unused containers or images using Docker CLI on Windows Server environment.

Chapter 4, *Developing Container Applications*, teaches you to create and deploy ASP.NET Core Web applications using Visual Studio 2015, .NET Core, and C# to Windows Server 2016 Core as Windows Container using PowerShell and Docker CLI.

Chapter 5, *Deploying Container Applications*, teaches you to create Windows Server Container environment on Azure using Azure Resource Manager templates and Azure PowerShell, configure remote management for container hosts, deploy container applications remotely as Windows Containers and Hyper-V containers, configuring software load balancer and so on.

Chapter 6, *Storage Volumes*, talks about building file based storage based containers using Docker volumes and relational database containers using Microsoft SQL Server.

Chapter 7, *Redis Cache Containers*, teaches you to create persistent Redis Cache containers using Redis and storage volumes.

Chapter 8, *Container Network*, introduces you to Windows Container networks, different networking modes, building custom container networks using different networking modes and deploying containers on custom networks.

Chapter 9, *Continuous Integration and Delivery*, teaches you to build continuous integration and deployment pipelines for container applications using Visual Studio Team Services (TFS Online) on Azure, Docker Hub, and Git. You will learn to create a create a custom build server for building, packaging and releasing containers to windows container hosts.

Chapter 10, *Manage Resource Allocation and REST API*, teaches you to manage container resource utilization, create and manage containers using Docker REST API via Postman and C#, image optimization strategies and monitoring options available for containers and container hosts.

Chapter 11, *Composite Containers and Clustering*, teaches you to orchestrate multiple container deployments using Docker Compose, set up scaling for multicontainer environments and authoring Docker Compose service definition. Also, you will learn the concepts of cluster management using Docker Swarm and Azure Container Service.

Chapter 12, *Nano Server*, serves as an introduction to Windows Nano Server, building custom Nano Server images using PowerShell, deploying containers on Nano Server, working with Nano containers, and configuring Nano Server using PowerShell DSC.

What you need for this book

This book assumes basic knowledge of PowerShell, C#, .NET, ASP.NET 5, cloud computing, and Azure. The book will help your setup development environment on desktop operating system like Windows 10 (with Anniversary update) and deploying container applications on VMs running on-premise and on Azure. To practice building containerized applications on an on-premise environment like Windows 10, the host machine should have Hyper-V feature enabled. The book shows building virtual environments using Windows 10 built-in feature called Hyper-V but you can try any other desktop virtualization software like VMware or virtual box. The book also uses Visual Studio 2015 for application development, if you have hands-on experience working with Visual Studio 2015 it will easy to execute the samples. Following is the basic hardware configuration for running Hyper-V and Visual Studio 2015:

- CPU: 1.6 GHz or faster processor, 4 cores
- 64-bit processor with Second Level Address Translation (SLAT) – (for Hyper-V only)
- CPU support for VM Monitor Mode Extension (VT-c on Intel CPU's) – (for Hyper-V only)
- Minimum of 8 GB RAM
- Disk space: 80 GB

Apart from the these, you will also need an Azure subscription for creating container environments on Azure. Microsoft offers a free subscription which can be used for 30 days in-case you do not have a paid subscription. The software requirements for the book are as follows:

- Visual Studio 2015 (Community Edition or above)
- Windows 10 with Anniversary update
- SQL Server Management Studio
- Redis Desktop Manager
- Postman

Internet connectivity is required to install any packages for application development, download images (ISO files) for windows server 2016 or source code from GitHub repository.

Who this book is for

The primary target audience for this book would be developers who would like to use Windows Server Containers to build portable apps that can run anywhere (laptop, server, and public or private cloud) without little or no changes to the code. Developers will be able to build and ship high-quality applications. As Windows Containers has a broad impact on developers and administrators alike, this book will also help IT professionals or DevOps Engineers prepare infrastructure which is easy to use and maintain. IT professionals will be able to optimize resource utilization by increasing the density of applications per machine. The concepts discussed in this book also help DevOps develop a container mindset, establish practices around publishing developed code as containers from development environment to production easily.

Conventions

In this book, you will find a number of text styles that distinguish between different kinds of information. Here are some examples of these styles and an explanation of their meaning.

Code words in text, database table names, folder names, filenames, file extensions, pathnames, dummy URLs, user input, and Twitter handles are shown as follows: "The `remove()` method finds the first instance of the element (passed an argument) and removes it from the list."

Any command-line input or output is written as follows:

```
docker search microsoft
```

New terms and **important words** are shown in bold. Words that you see on the screen, for example, in menus or dialog boxes, appear in the text like this: "Click on **Test Connection** and ensure the connection is successful."

Warnings or important notes appear in a box like this.

Tips and tricks appear like this.

Reader feedback

Feedback from our readers is always welcome. Let us know what you think about this book-what you liked or disliked. Reader feedback is important for us as it helps us develop titles that you will really get the most out of.

To send us general feedback, simply e-mail `feedback@packtpub.com`, and mention the book's title in the subject of your message.

If there is a topic that you have expertise in and you are interested in either writing or contributing to a book, see our author guide at `www.packtpub.com/authors`.

Customer support

Now that you are the proud owner of a Packt book, we have a number of things to help you to get the most from your purchase.

Downloading the example code

You can download the example code files for this book from your account at `http://www.packtpub.com`. If you purchased this book elsewhere, you can visit `http://www.packtpub.com/support` and register to have the files e-mailed directly to you.

You can download the code files by following these steps:

1. Log in or register to our website using your e-mail address and password.
2. Hover the mouse pointer on the **SUPPORT** tab at the top.
3. Click on **Code Downloads & Errata**.
4. Enter the name of the book in the **Search** box.
5. Select the book for which you're looking to download the code files.
6. Choose from the drop-down menu where you purchased this book from.
7. Click on **Code Download**.

Once the file is downloaded, please make sure that you unzip or extract the folder using the latest version of:

- WinRAR / 7-Zip for Windows
- Zipeg / iZip / UnRarX for Mac
- 7-Zip / PeaZip for Linux

You can download the latest code samples from the code repository belonging to this book from the author's code repository at `https://github.com/vishwanathsrikanth/learningwsc`.

The code bundle for the book is also hosted on Packt's GitHub repository at `https://github.com/PacktPublishing/Learning-Windows-Server-Containers`. We also have other code bundles from our rich catalog of books and videos available at `https://github.com/PacktPublishing/`. Check them out!

Errata

Although we have taken every care to ensure the accuracy of our content, mistakes do happen. If you find a mistake in one of our books-maybe a mistake in the text or the code-we would be grateful if you could report this to us. By doing so, you can save other readers from frustration and help us improve subsequent versions of this book. If you find any errata, please report them by visiting `http://www.packtpub.com/submit-errata`, selecting your book, clicking on the **Errata Submission Form** link, and entering the details of your errata. Once your errata are verified, your submission will be accepted and the errata will be uploaded to our website or added to any list of existing errata under the Errata section of that title.

To view the previously submitted errata, go to `https://www.packtpub.com/books/content/support` and enter the name of the book in the search field. The required information will appear under the **Errata** section.

Piracy

Piracy of copyrighted material on the Internet is an ongoing problem across all media. At Packt, we take the protection of our copyright and licenses very seriously. If you come across any illegal copies of our works in any form on the Internet, please provide us with the location address or website name immediately so that we can pursue a remedy.

Please contact us at `copyright@packtpub.com` with a link to the suspected pirated material.

We appreciate your help in protecting our authors and our ability to bring you valuable content.

Questions

If you have a problem with any aspect of this book, you can contact us at `questions@packtpub.com`, and we will do our best to address the problem.

1
Exploring Virtualization

In this highly competitive and rapidly changing world, for enterprises to be at the leading edge a highly reliable, cost effective, and infinitely scalable IT infrastructure is required. It is very important for enterprises to adapt to changing customer needs, fail fast, learn, and reinvent the wheel. Ever since hardware costs have come down the emphasis has shifted to making the most out of the capital investments made on physical infrastructure or reducing the amount of investments to build or rent new infrastructure. This fundamentally means running more applications/services out of the existing IT landscape.

Virtualized infrastructure solves the preceding problems and it caters to all the IT needs of a modern enterprise. Virtualization provides an abstraction over compute, storage, or networking resources and provides a unified platform for managing the infrastructure. Virtualization facilitates resource optimization, governance over costs, effective utilization of physical space, high availability of **line-of-business** (**LOB**) applications, resilient systems, infinite scalability, fault-tolerance environments, and hybrid computing.

The following are a few more features of virtualization:

- Virtualization is a software which when installed on your IT infrastructure allows you to run more **virtual machines** (**VMs**) in a single physical server, thereby increasing the density of machines per square feet of area
- Virtualization is not just for enabling more computers, it also allows collaborating all storage devices to form a single large virtual storage space, which can be pooled across machines and provisioned on demand
- It also provides benefits of hybrid computing by enabling you to run different types of **operating systems** (**OSes**) in parallel, therefore catering to large and varied customers
- It centralizes the IT infrastructure and provides one place to manage machines and cost, execute patch updates, or reallocate resources on demand
- It reduces carbon footprint, cooling needs, and power consumption

Cloud computing is also an implementation of virtualization. Apart from virtualizing the hardware resources, the cloud also promises to offer rich services such as reliability, self-service, and Internet level scalability on a pay-per-use basis.

Due to reduced costs, today's VMs offered by public or private cloud vendors are highly powerful. But are our applications or services utilizing the server capacity effectively? What percentage of compute and storage are the applications actually using? The answer is very low. Traditional applications are not so resource heavy (except a few batch processing systems, big data systems with heavy scientific calculations, and gaming engines that fully utilize the PC's power). In order to provide high scalability and isolation to the customers we end up running many instances of the application in each VM with 10%-30% utilization. And also it takes substantial amounts of time to procure a machine, configure it for the application and its dependencies, make it ready to use, and of course the number of VMs that you can run on your private data center is limited to the physical space you own. Is it really possible to further optimize resource utilization but still have the same isolation and scalability benefits? Can we get more throughput out of our IT infrastructure than we get today? Can we reduce the amount of preparation work required to onboard an application and make it ready to use? Can we run more services using the same physical infrastructure? Yes, all of this is possible, and containerization is our magic wand.

Containerization is an alternative to VM virtualization from which enterprises can benefit from running multiple software components in a single physical/virtualized machine with the same isolation, security, reliability, and scalability benefits. Apart from effective utilization, containerization also promotes rapid application deployment capabilities with options to package, ship, and deploy software components as independent deployment units called **containers**.

In this chapter, we are going to learn:

- Levels of virtualization
- Virtualization challenges
- Containerization and its benefits
- Windows Server Containers
- Hyper-V Containers
- Cluster management
- Terminology and tooling support

Microsoft's history of virtualization

Microsoft's journey with VM/hardware virtualization began with its first hypervisor called **Hyper-V**. In the year 2008, Microsoft released Windows Server 2008 and 2008 R2 with Hyper-V role, which is capable of hosting multiple VMs inside a physical machine. Windows Server 2008 was available in different flavors such as **Standard**, **Enterprise**, and **Datacenter**. They all differ in the number of VMs or **guest OS** that can be hosted for free per server. For example, in Windows Server 2008 Standard edition you can run one guest OS for free and new guest OS licenses have to be purchased for running more VMs. Windows Server 2008 Datacenter edition comes with unlimited Windows guest OS licenses.

 Often when talking about virtualization we use words such as **host OS** and guest OS. Host OS is the OS running on a physical machine (or VM if the OS allows nested virtualization) that provides the virtualization environment. Host OS provides the platform for running multiple VMs. Guest OS refers to the OS running inside each VM.

At about the same time, Microsoft also shipped another hypervisor called Hyper-V Server 2008 with a limited set of features, such as Windows Server Core, CLI, and Hyper-V role. The basic difference between a server with role and Hyper-V versions is the licensing norms. Microsoft Hyper-V Server is a free edition and it allows you to run a virtualized environment by using existing Windows Server licenses. But of course you would miss the other coolest OS features of full Windows Server as host OS, such as managing the OS using neat and clean GUI. Hyper-V can only be interacted via remote interfacing and a CLI. Hyper-V server is a trimmed down version for catering to the needs of running a virtualized environment.

In the year 2008, Microsoft announced its cloud platform called **Windows Azure** (now **Microsoft Azure**), which uses a customized Hyper-V to run a multitenant environment of compute, storage, and network resources using Windows Server machines. Azure provides a rich set of services categorized as **Platform as a Service** (**PaaS**) and **Infrastructure as a Service** (**IaaS**) using the virtualized infrastructure spread across varied geographical locations.

In August 2012, Windows Server 2012 and 2012 R2 bought significant improvements to the server technology, such as improved multitenancy, private virtual LAN, increased security, multiple live migrations, live storage migrations, less expensive business recovery options, and so on.

Windows Server 2016 marks a significant change in the server OSes from the core. Launched in the second half of the year 2016, Windows Server 2016 has noteworthy benefits, especially for new trends such as containerization and thin OS:

- **Windows Server 2016 with Windows Server Containers and Hyper-V Containers**: Windows Server 2016 comes with a container role that provides support for containerization. With containers role enabled applications can be easily packaged and deployed as independent containers with a high degree of isolation inside a single VM. Windows Server 2016 comes with two flavors of containers: Windows Server Containers and Hyper-V Containers. Windows Server Containers run directly on Windows Server OS while Hyper-V Containers are the new thin VMs that can run on a Hyper-V. Windows Server 2016 also comes with enhanced Hyper-V capabilities such as nested virtualization.
- **Windows Server 2016 Nano Server**: Nano Server is a scaled down version of Windows Server OS, which is around 93% smaller than the traditional server. Nano Servers are designed primarily for hosting modern cloud applications called microservices in both private and public clouds.

Other virtualization platforms from Microsoft:

- Microsoft also offers a hosted virtualization platform called **Virtual PC** acquired from Connectix in 2003. Hosted virtualization is different from regular hypervisor platforms. Hosted virtualization can run on a 32/64-bit system such as traditional desktop PCs from Windows 7 OS and above, whereas the traditional hypervisors run on special hardware and 64-bit systems only.
- A few more virtualization solutions offered by Microsoft are hosted virtualizations called Microsoft Virtual Server 2005 for Windows Server 2003, **Application Virtualization (App-V)**, **MED-V** for legacy application compatibility, terminal services, and **virtual desktop infrastructure (VDI)**.

Understanding virtualization levels

Depending on how the underlying infrastructure is abstracted away from the users and the isolation level, various virtualization technologies have evolved. The following sections discuss a few virtualization levels in brief, which eventually lead to containerization.

Hardware/platform/server virtualization

During the pre-virtualization era, a physical machine was considered a singleton entity that could host one operation system and could contain more than one application. Enterprises that run highly critical businesses or multitenant environments need isolation between applications. This limits from using one server for many applications. Hardware virtualization or VM virtualization helped to scale out single physical servers as they host multiple VMs within a single server where each VM can run in complete isolation. Each VM's CPU and memory needs can be configured as per the application's demand.

A discrete software unit called hypervisor or **Virtual Machine Manager** (**VMM**) runs on top of virtualized hardware and facilitates server virtualization. Modern cloud platforms, both public and private, are the best examples of hardware virtualization. Each physical server runs an operation system called host OS, which runs multiple VMs each with their own OS called guest OS. The underlying memory and CPU of the host OS is shared across the VMs depending on how the VMs are configured while creating. Server virtualization also enables hybrid computing, which means the guest OS can be of any type, for example, a machine running Windows with Hyper-V role enabled can host VMs running Linux and Windows OSes (for example Windows 10 and Windows 8.1) or even another Windows Server OS. Some examples of server virtualization are VMware, Citrix XenServer, and MS Hyper-V.

In a nutshell, this is what platform virtualization looks like:

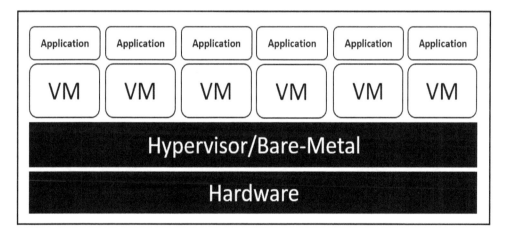

Storage virtualization

Storage virtualization refers to pooling of storage resources to provide a single large storage space, which can be managed from a single console. Storage virtualization offers administrative benefits such as managing backups, archiving, on demand storage allocation, and so on.

For example, Windows Azure VMs by default contain two disk drives for storage, but on demand we can add any number of disk drives to the VM within minutes (limited to the VM tier). This allows instant scalability and better utilization since we are only paying for what we use and expand/shrink as per demand.

This is what storage virtualization looks like:

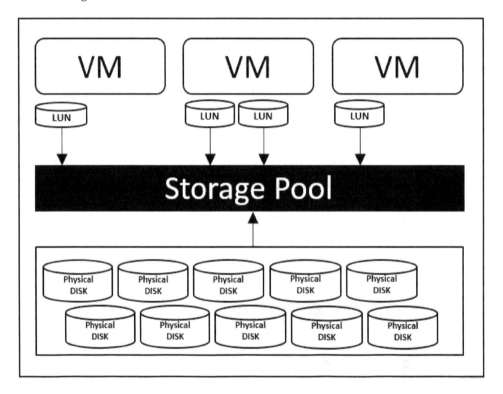

Network virtualization

Network virtualization is the ability to create and manage a logical network of compute, storage, or other network resources. The components of a virtual network can be remotely located in the same or different physical networks across different geographical locations. Virtual networks help us create custom address spaces, logical subnets, custom network security groups for configuring restricted access to a group of nodes, custom IP configuration (few applications demand static IPs or IPs within a specific range), domain defined traffic routing, and so on.

Most of the LOB applications demand logical separation between business components for enhanced security, isolation, and scalability needs. Network virtualization helps build the isolation configuring subnet level security policies, restrict access to logical subnets or nodes using **access control list** (**ACL**), and restrict inbound/outbound traffic using custom routing without running a physical network. Public cloud vendors provide network virtualization on pay per use basis for small to medium scale business who cannot afford running a private IT infrastructure. For example, Microsoft Azure allows you to create a virtual network with network security boundaries, secure VPN tunnel to connect to your personal laptops, or on-premise infrastructure, high bandwidth private channels, and so on using pay-per-use pricing. You can run your applications on cloud with tight security among nodes using logical separation without even investing on any network devices.

OS virtualization

The topic of this book is associated with OS virtualization. OS virtualization enables the kernel to be shared across multiple processes inside a single VM with isolation. OS virtualization is also called user-mode or user-space virtualization as it is one level up from the kernel. Individual user-space instances are called containers. The kernel provides all the features for resource management across containers.

This is highly helpful while consolidating a set of services spread across multiple servers into a single server. Few benefits of OS virtualization are high security due to reduced surface of contact for a breach or viruses, better resource management, easy migration of applications or services across hosts, and also instant and dynamic load balancing. OS virtualization does not require any hardware support, so it is easy to implement than other technologies. The most recent implementations of OS virtualization are Linux LXC, Docker, and Windows Server Containers.

This is what OS virtualization looks like:

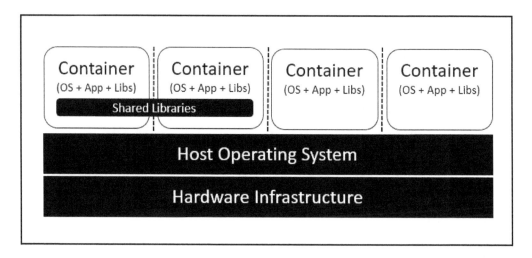

 Today's containers are not yet cross platform, which means a Linux container cannot be directly ported to Windows. Containers being an OS virtualization are tied up to the kernel features, this makes it difficult to pursue cross platform portability.

Limitations of virtualization

There are a few limitations with the hardware or VM virtualization, which leads to containerization. Let's look at a few of them.

Machine turn up time

VMs run a fully-fledged OS. Every time a machine needs to be started, restarted, or shut down it involves running the full OS life cycle and booting procedure. A few enterprises employ rigid policies for procuring new IT resources. All of this increases the time required by the team to deliver a VM or to upgrade an existing one because each new request should be fulfilled by a whole set of steps. For example, a machine provisioning involves gathering the requirements, provisioning a new VM, procuring a license and installing OS, allocating storage, network configuration, and setting up redundancy and security policies.

Every time you wish to deploy your application you also have to ensure application specific software requirements such as web servers, database servers, runtimes, and any support software such as plugin drivers are installed on the machine. With teams obliged to deliver at light speed, the current VM virtualization will create more friction and latency.

Low resource utilization

The preceding problem can be partially solved by using the cloud platforms, which offer on-demand resource provisioning, but again public cloud vendors come up with a predefined set of VM configuration and not every application utilizes all allocated compute and memory.

In a common enterprise scenario every small application is deployed in a separate VM for isolation and security benefits. Further for ensuring scalability and availability identical VMs are created and traffic is balanced among them. If the application utilizes only 5-10% of the CPU's capacity, the IT infrastructure is heavily underutilized. Power and cooling needs for such systems are also high, which adds up to the costs. Few applications are used seasonally or by limited set of users, but still the servers have to be up and running. Another important drawback of VMs is that inside a VM OS and supporting services occupy more size than the application itself.

Operational costs

Every IT organization needs an operations team to manage the infrastructure's regular maintenance activities. The team's responsibility is to ensure that activities such as procuring machines, maintaining **SOX Compliance**, executing regular updates, and security patches are done in a timely manner. The following are a few drawbacks that add up to operational costs due to VM virtualization:

- The size of the operations team is proportional to the size of the IT. Large infrastructures require larger teams, therefore more costs to maintain.
- Every enterprise is obliged to provide continuous business to its customers for which it has to employ redundant and recovery systems. Recovery systems often take the same amount of resources and configuration as original ones, which means twice the original costs.
- Enterprises also have to pay for licenses for each guest OS no matter how little the usage may be.

Application packaging and deployment

VMs are not easily shippable. Every application has to be tested on developer machines, proper instruction sets have to be documented for operations or deployment teams to prepare the machine and deploy the application. No matter how well you document and take precautions in many instances the deployments fail because at the end of the day the application runs on a completely different environment than it is tested on which makes it riskier.

Let us imagine you have successfully installed the application on VM, but still VMs are not easily sharable as application packages due to their extremely large sizes, which makes them misfit for DevOps type work cultures. Imagine your applications need to go through rigorous testing cycles to ensure high quality. Every time you want to deploy and test a developed feature a new environment needs to be created and configured. The application should be deployed on the machine and then the test cases should be executed. In agile teams, release happens quite often, so the turnaround time for the testing phase to begin and results to be out will be quite high because of the machine provisioning and preparation work.

Choosing between VM virtualization or containerization is purely a matter of scope and need. It might not always be feasible to use containers. One advantage, for example, is in VM virtualization the guest OS of the VM and the host OS need not be the same. A Linux VM and a Windows VM can run in parallel on Hyper-V. This is possible because in VM virtualization only the hardware layer is virtualized. Since containers share the kernel OS of the host, a Linux container cannot be shipped to a Windows machine. Having said that, the future holds good things for both containers and VMs in both private and public clouds. There might be cases where an enterprise opts to use a hybrid model depending on scope and need.

Introduction to containerization

Containerization is an ability to build and package applications as shippable containers. Containers run in isolation in a user-mode using a shared kernel. A kernel is the heart of the operating system which accepts the user inputs and converts/translates them as processing instructions for CPU. In a shared kernel mode containers do the same as what VMs do to physical machines. They isolate the applications from the underlying OS needs. Let's see a few key implementations of this technology.

A few key implementations of containers

Some of the key implementations of containers are as follows:

- The word *container* has been around since 1982 with the introduction of chroot by Unix, which introduced process isolation. **Chroot** creates a virtual root directory for a process and its child processes, the process running under chroot cannot access anything outside the environment. Such modified environments are also called **chroot jails**.

- In 2000, a new isolation mechanism for FreeBSD (a free Unix like OS) was introduced by R&D Associates, Inc.'s owner, Derrick T. Woolworth, it was named jails. Jails are isolated virtual instances of FreeBSD under a single kernel. Each jail has its own files, processes, users, and super accounts. Each jail is sealed from other jails.

- Solaris introduced its OS virtualization platform called **zones** in the year 2004 with Solaris 10. One or more applications can run within a zone in isolation. Inter-zone communication was also possible using network APIs.

- In 2006, Google launched **process containers**, a technology designed for limiting, accounting, and isolating resource usage. It was later renamed to **control groups** (**cgroups**) and merged into the Linux kernel 2.6.24.

- In 2008, Linux launched its first out-of-the-box implementation of containers called **Linux containers** (**LXC**) a derivative of OpenVZ (OpenVZ developed an extension to Linux with the same features earlier). It was implemented using cgroups and **namespaces**. The cgroups allow management and prioritization for CPU, memory, block I/O, and network. Namespaces provided isolation.

Docker

Solomon Hykes, CTO of **dotCloud** a PaaS (Platform as a Service) company, launched Docker in the year 2013, which reintroduced containerization. Before Docker, containers were just isolated processes and application portability as containers across discrete environments was never guaranteed. Docker introduced application packaging and shipping with containers. Docker isolated applications from infrastructure, which allowed developers to write and test the applications on traditional desktop OS and then easily package and ship it to production servers with less trouble.

Docker architecture

Docker uses client-server architecture. The **Docker daemon** is the heart of the Docker platform, and it should be present on every host, as it acts as a server. The Docker daemon is responsible for creating the containers, managing their life cycle, creating and storing images, and many other key things around containers. Applications are designed and developed as containers on developer's desktop and packaged as **Docker images**. Docker images are read-only templates that encapsulate the application and its dependent components. Docker also provides a set of base images that contain a pretty thin OS to start application development. **Docker containers** are nothing but instances of Docker images. Any number of containers can be created from an image within a host. Containers run directly on the Linux kernel in an isolated environment.

The Docker repository is the storage for Docker images. Docker provides both public and private repositories. Docker's public image repository is called **Docker Hub**, anyone can search the images in the public repository from Docker CLI or a web browser, download the image, and customize as per the application's needs. Since public repositories are not well suited for enterprise scenarios, which demand more security, Docker provides private repositories. Private repositories restrict access to your images for users within your enterprise; unlike Docker Hub, private repositories are not free. **Docker registry** is a repository for custom user images, users can pull any publicly available image or push to store and share across other users. The Docker daemon manages a registry per host too, when asked for an image the daemon first searches within the local registry and then the public repositories aka Docker Hub. This mechanism eliminates downloading images from the public repository each time.

Docker uses several Linux features to deliver the functionality. For example, Docker uses namespaces for providing isolation, cgroups for resource management, and union filesystem for making the containers extremely lightweight and fast. **Docker client** is the command-line interface, which is the only user interface for interacting with the Docker daemon. The Docker client and daemon can run out of a single system serving as both client and server. When on the server, users can use the client to communicate with the local server. Docker also provides an API that can be used to interact with remote **Docker hosts**. This can be seen in the following image:

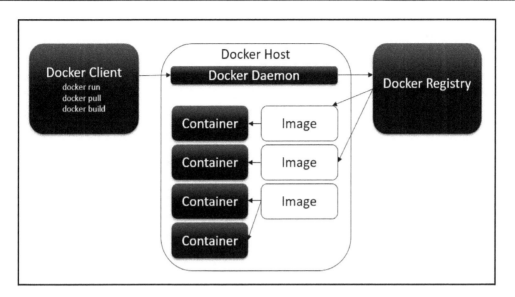

Development life cycle

The Docker development life cycle can be explained with the help of the following steps:

1. Docker container development starts with downloading a base image from Docker Hub. Ubuntu and Fedora are a few images available from Docker Hub. An application can be containerized post application development too. It is not necessary to always start with Dockerizing the application.

2. The image is customized as per application requirement using a few Docker-specific instructions. These sets of instructions are stored in a file called Dockerfile. When deployed the Docker daemon reads the Dockerfile and prepares the final image.

3. The image can then be published to a public/private repository.

4. When users run the following command on any Docker host, the Docker daemon searches for images on the local machine first and then on Docker Hub if the images are not found locally. A Docker container is created if the image is found. Once the container is up and running, `[command]` is called on the running container:

```
$ docker run -i -t [imagename] [command]
```

Docker's success stories

Docker made enterprises life easy, applications can now be contained and easily shipped across hosts and distributed with less friction between teams. Docker Hub today offers 450,000 images publicly available for reuse. A few of the famous ones are ngnix web server, Ubuntu, Redis, swarm, MySQL, and so on. Each one is downloaded by more than 10 million users. **Docker Engine** has been downloaded 4 billion times so far and still growing. Docker has enormous community support with 2,900 community contributors and 250 meet up groups. Docker is now available on Windows and Macintosh. Microsoft officially supports Docker through its public cloud platform Azure.

eBay, a major e-commerce giant, uses Docker to run their same day delivery business. eBay uses Docker in their **continuous integration** (**CI**) process. Containerized applications can be easily moved from a developer's laptop to test and then production machines seamlessly. Docker also enables the application to run alike on developer machines and also on production instances.

ING, a global finance services organization, faced nightmares with constant changes required to its monolithic applications built using legacy technologies. Implementing each change involved a laborious process of going through 68 documents to move a change to production. ING integrated Docker into its continuous delivery platform, which provided more automation capabilities for test and deployment, optimized utilization, reduced hardware costs, and saved time.

The road ahead for Dockers

Up to Docker release 0.9, containers were built using LXC, which is a Linux centric technology. Docker 0.9 introduced a new driver called **libcontainer** alongside LXC. The libcontainer is now a growing open source, open governed, non-profit library. The libcontainer is written using *Go language* for creating containers using Linux kernel API without relying on any close coupled features such as user-spaces or LXC. This means a lot to companies trending towards containerization. Docker has now moved out of being a Linux centric technology, in the future we might also see Docker adapting other platforms discussed previously, such as **Solaris Zones**, BSD jails, and so on. Libcontainer is openly available with contributions from major tech giants such as Google, Microsoft, Amazon, Red Hat, VMware, and so on. Docker being at its core is responsible for developing the core runtime and container format. Public cloud vendors such as Azure and AWS support Docker on their cloud platforms as first class citizens.

Introduction to Windows Server Containers

Windows Server Containers is an OS virtualization technology from Microsoft that is available from Windows Server 2016 onwards. Windows Server Containers are lightweight processes that are isolated from each other and have a similar view of the OS, processes, filesystem, and network. Technically speaking, Windows Server Containers are similar to Linux containers, which we discussed earlier. The only difference being the underlying kernel and workloads that run on these containers. The following image describes Windows Server Containers:

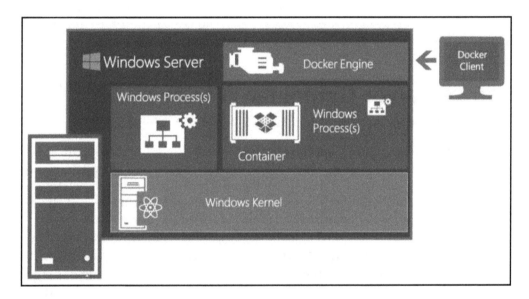

A little background

Here's a little background about Windows Server Containers:

- Microsoft's research team worked on a program called **Drawbridge** for bringing the famous container technologies to Windows Server ecosystem
- In the year 2014, Microsoft started working with Docker to bring the Docker technology to Windows
- In July 2015, Microsoft joined **Open Container Initiative** (**OCI**) extending its support for universal container standards, formats, and runtime

- In 2015, Mark Russinovich, CTO at Microsoft Azure, demonstrated the integration of containers with Windows
- In October 2015, Microsoft announced the availability of Windows Server with containers and Docker support in its new Windows Server 2016 Technical Preview 3 and Windows 10

Microsoft adapted Docker in its famous Windows Server ecosystem so developers can now develop, package, and deploy containers to Windows/Linux machines using the same toolset. Apart from support for the Docker toolset on Windows Server, Microsoft is also launching native support to work with containers using PowerShell and Windows CLI. Since OS virtualization is a kernel level feature there is no cross platform portability yet, which means a Linux container cannot be ported to Windows or vice versa.

Windows Server Container versions

Windows Server Containers are available on the following OS versions:

- **Windows Server 2016 Core (no GUI)**: A typical Windows Server 2016 server with minimal installation. The Server Core version reduces the space required on disk and the surface of attack. CLI is the only tool available for interacting with the Server Core, either locally/remotely. You can still launch PowerShell using the `start powershell` command from the CLI. You can also call `get-windowsfeature` to see what features are available on Windows Server Core.
- **Windows Server 2016 (full GUI)**: This is a full version of Windows Server 2016 with standard **Desktop Experience**. The server roles can be installed using **Server Manager**. It is not possible to convert Windows Server Core to full Desktop Experience. This should be a decision taken during installation only.
- **Windows 10**: Windows Server Containers are available for Windows 10 Pro and Enterprise versions (insider builds 14372 and up). The containers and Hyper-V/virtualization feature should be enabled before working with containers. Creating container and images with Windows 10 will be discussed in following chapters.
- **Nano Server**: Nano Server is a headless Windows Server 30 times or 93% smaller than the Windows Server Core. It takes far less space, requires fewer updates, high security, and boots much faster than the other versions. There is a dedicated chapter in this book on working with Nano Servers and Windows Containers.

The most important part is that Windows Server Containers are available in two flavors, Windows Server Containers and Hyper-V Containers. All of the previously mentioned OS types can run Windows Server Containers and Hyper-V Containers. Both the containers can be managed using Docker API, Docker CLI, and PowerShell.

Hyper-V Containers

Hyper-V Containers are a special type of container with a higher degree of isolation and security. Unlike Windows Server Containers, which share the kernel, Hyper-V Containers do not share kernels and instead each container runs its own kernel, which makes them special VMs. The following image represents Hyper-V Containers:

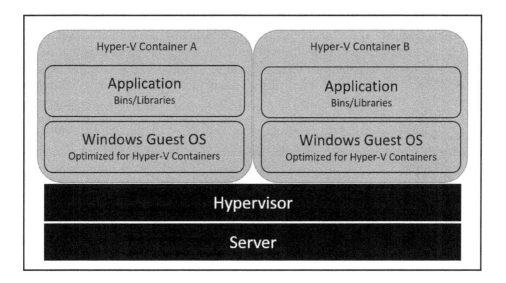

Why another container type?

The following are some of the other container types:

- Windows Server Containers run as isolated containers on a shared kernel. In a single tenant environment or private clouds this is not a problem, since the containers run in a trusted environment. But Windows Containers are not ideal for a multitenant environment. There could be security or performance related issues such as noisy neighbors or intentional attacks on neighboring containers.

- Since Windows Container shares the host OS, patching the host OS disrupts the normal functioning of applications hosted in the OS.

This is where Hyper-V Containers make perfect sense. Windows OS consists of two layers, kernel mode and user-mode. Windows Containers share the same kernel mode, but virtualize the user-mode, to create multiple container user-modes, one for each container. Hyper-V Containers run their own kernel mode, user-mode and container user-mode. This provides an isolation layer among Hyper-V Containers. Hyper-V Containers are very similar to VMs, but they run a stripped down version of an OS with a non-sharable kernel. In other words, we can call this a nested virtualization, a Hyper-V Container running within a virtual container host running on a physical/virtual host.

The good news is that Windows Server Containers and Hyper-V Containers are compatible. In fact, which container type to use is a deployment time decision. We can easily switch the container types once the application is deployed. Hyper-V Containers also have a faster boot time, faster than the Nano Server. Hyper-V Containers can be created using the same Docker CLI commands/PowerShell commands using an additional switch that determines the type of the container. Hyper-V Containers run on Windows 10 Enterprise (insider builds), which enables developers to develop and test applications on native machines to production instances, either as Windows Containers or Hyper-V Containers. Developers can directly ship the containers to Windows Server OS without making any changes. Hyper-V Containers are slower than Windows Containers as they run a thin OS. Windows Containers are suitable for general purpose workloads in private clouds or single tenant infrastructure. Hyper-V Containers are more suitable for highly secure workloads.

Containers terminology

Windows Container terminology is very much similar to Docker. It is important to understand the terminology before teams start working on containers as it makes it easy to communicate across developer and operation teams. Windows Containers contain the following core terms.

Container host

A **container host** is a machine that is running an OS that is supported by Windows Containers, such as Windows Server 2016 (full/Core), Windows 10, and Nano Server. Hyper-V Containers hosts are required to have nested virtualization enabled, since the containers have to be hosted on a VM.

Container OS image

Container OS images or base images are the very first layer that makes up every container; these images are provided by Microsoft. Two of the images available today are `windowsservercore` and `nanoserver`.

OS image provides the OS libraries for the container. Developers can create Windows Server Containers by downloading the base image and adding more layers as per the application needs. OS images are nothing but `.wim` files that get downloaded from **OneGet**, a PowerShell package manager for Windows. OneGet is included in Windows 10 and Windows Server 2016 versions. Base OS images are sometimes huge, but Microsoft allows us to download the file once and save it offline for reusing without Internet connection or within an enterprise network.

Container images

Container images are created by users deriving from base OS image. Container images are read-only templates that can be used to create containers. For example, a user can download Windows Server Core image install IIS and the application components, and then create an image. Every container made out of this image comes with IIS and the application preinstalled. You can also reuse prebuilt images that come preinstalled with MySQL, nginx, node, or Redis by searching from the remote repository and customize as per your needs. Once customized, it can be converted to an image again.

Container registry

Container registry is a repository for prebuilt images. Windows Server 2016 maintains a local repository as well. Every time a user tries to install an image it first searches for a local repository and then the public repository. Images can also be stored in a public repository (Docker Hub) or private repository. Base OS images have to be installed first before using any prebuilt images such as MySQL, nginx, and so on. Use `docker search` to search the repository.

Dockerfile

Dockerfile is a text file containing instruction sets that are executed in sequential order for preparing a new container image. Docker instruction sets are divided into three categories, instructions for downloading a base OS image, for creating the new image, and finally instructions on what to run when new containers are created using the new image. Dockerfile goes as an input to the Docker build step, which creates the image. Users can also use PowerShell scripts within the instruction sets.

Benefits of containers

The following are a few benefits of containerization:

- **Monolithic apps to microservices**: Microservices is an architecture pattern in which a single monolithic application is split into thin manageable components. This promotes having focused development teams, smoother operations, and instant scalability at each module. Containers are ideal deployment targets for microservices. For example, you can have a frontend web app run in an individual container and other background services such as e-mail sending process, thumbnail generator, and so on, run in separate containers. This makes them update individually, scale as per load, and better resource management.
- **Configuration as code**: Containers allow you to create, start, stop, and configure containers using clean instruction sets. Integrating code as part of the application build system enables a lot of automation options. For example, you can create and configure containers as part of your CI and CD pipelines automatically so that development teams can ship increments at a faster pace.
- **Favors DevOps**: DevOps is a cultural shift in the way operations and developer teams work together seamlessly to validate and push increments to production systems. Containers help faster provisioning of dev/test environments for running various intermediate steps such as unit testing, security testing, integration testing, and so on. Many of these might need preplanning for infra procurement, provisioning, and environment setup. Containers can be quickly packaged and deployed using an existing infrastructure.

- **Modern app development with containers**: Many new open source technologies are designed using containers or microservices in mind, so that when applications are built using these technologies they are inherently container aware. For example, ASP.NET Core/ASP.NET 5 applications can be deployed to Linux/Windows alike because ASP.NET Core is technically isolated from web servers and the runtime engine. It can run on Linux with net core as a runtime engine and **Kestrel** as a web server.

Windows Server Containers on Azure

Azure has grown by leaps and bounds to become a top class public cloud platform for on demand provisioning of VMs or pay-per-use services. With the focus shifting towards resource optimization and microservices, Azure also provides a plethora of options for running both LXC and Windows Containers on Azure.

Windows Server 2016 Core with containers image is readily available on Azure. Developers can log in to the portal and create a Windows Server 2016 Core machine and run containers within minutes. It comes preinstalled with Docker runtime environment. Users can download the **Remote Desktop Client** from the portal and run Docker native commands using Windows CLI or PowerShell. Windows Server Containers are the only option on Azure, it does not support Hyper-V Containers. In order to use Hyper-V Containers on premise, a container host is required.

Azure Container Service (**ACS**) is a PaaS offering from Microsoft, which helps you create and manage a cluster of containers using orchestration services such as Swarm or DC/OS. ACS can be used as a hosted cluster environment, managed using your favorite open source tools or APIs. For example, you can log in to the portal and create a **Docker Swarm** by filling a few parameters such as **Agent count**, **Agent virtual machine size**, **Master count**, and **DNS prefix for container service**. Once the cluster is created it can be managed using your favorite tool set such as Docker CLI or API in this case.

Azure also provides ready to deploy **Azure Resource Manager** (**ARM**) templates to automate provisioning of Windows Server Core with containers. Azure ARM templates can be used for deploying dev/test Docker Swarm on Azure within minutes. ARM (JSON) templates are great tools to integrate with your continuous build and deployment process. Azure also provides prebuilt Docker images such as MySQL, MongoDB, Redis, and so on, as shown in the following screenshot:

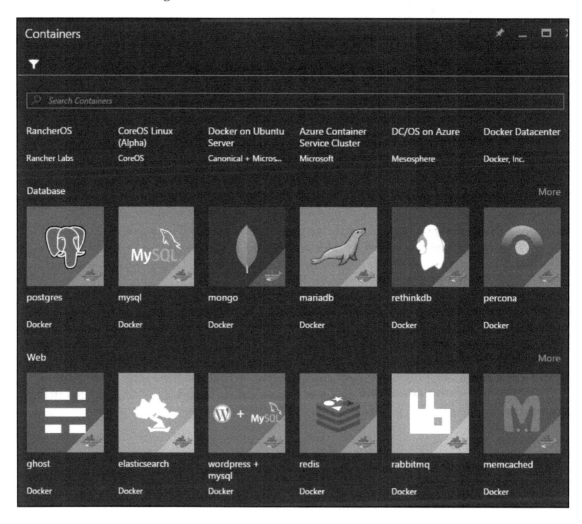

Azure provides a free trial account for a period of one month. Microsoft offers you $200 for a 30-day period, which helps you learn anything on Azure.

Comparing containerization and VM virtualization

Containers, or VMs, intend to solve a common problem of resource wastage, manual efforts in resource procurement, and high costs for running monolithic applications. Comparing VMs with containers is ideal since each share their own set of pros and cons, a few comparisons are:

- **Virtualization layer**: Containers are very different from virtualization by design. VM virtualization is at a hardware level, which allows multiple VMs to run in parallel on a single hardware, whereas the containers run out of a single host OS as if each container is running in its own OS. This design has a disadvantage of disallowing containers to be of varied OS. But this can be easily overcome by using a hybrid computing model combining VM and container virtualization.

- **Size**: VMs are heavyweight, whereas containers are extremely light. VMs contain the complete OS, kernel, system libraries, system configuration files, and all the directory structure required by the OS. Containers only contain application specific files, which makes it extremely lightweight and easily sharable. Also a VM that is not being utilized or if it is running some background process eats memory, which restricts the number of VMs than can run on the host. Containers occupy very less space and they can be easily suspended/restarted due to their extremely low boot timings.

- **Portability**: The same size constraints are a huge disadvantage for VMs. For example, developers writing code cannot test the applications as if they are running in production instances. But with containers it is possible since containers run alike on developer machines and production servers. Since containers are lightweight they can easily be shared by uploading to any shared storage. This can be partially overcome by using modern thin server OS such as Nano Server or Windows Server Core, which we will discuss in following chapters.

- **Security**: Undoubtedly VMs have an upper hand here due to the isolation at the very bottom level. Containers are more vulnerable to OS level attacks; if the OS is compromised all the containers running it will also be compromised. That being said, it is possible to make a container highly secure by implementing proper configuration. In a shared or multitenant environment noisy neighbors could also create potential attacks by demanding more resources, affecting the other containers running on the machine.

Cluster management

The microservices architecture influences application packaging and transferring across hosts/environments at a faster pace, as a result enterprises adapting to containerization face problems with increasing number of containers. Containers created new administration challenges for enterprises, such as managing a group of containers or a cluster of container hosts. A **container cluster** is a group of nodes, each node is a container host and it has containers running inside. It is important for enterprises/teams to facilitate manage the containers hosts and facilitate communication channels across container hosts.

Cluster management tools help operations teams or administrators to manage containers and container hosts from single management consoles. They assist in moving containers from one host to another, control resource management (CPU, memory, and network allocation), executing workflows, scheduling jobs/tasks (jobs/tasks is a set of steps to be executed on a cluster(s)), monitoring, reliability, scalability, and so on. Now that you know what clusters are, let's see the variety of offerings available on the market today and the core values offered by each one. Cluster management will be discussed in more detail in following chapters.

Docker Swarm

Swarm is a native cluster management solution from Docker. Swarm helps you manage a pool of containers hosts as a single unit. Swarm is delivered as an image called Docker Swarm image. Docker Swarm image should be installed on a node and the container hosts should be configured with TCP ports and TLS certificates to connect to the swarm. Swarm provides an API layer to access the container or cluster services so that developers can build their own management interface. Swarm follows **Plug and Play** (**PnP**) architecture, so most of the components of swarm can be replaced as per needs. A few of the cluster management capabilities provided by swarm are:

- Discovery services for discovering images using public/private hosts or event list of IPs
- **Docker Compose**, which can be used for orchestrating multicontainer deployment in a single file
- Advanced scheduling for strategically placing containers on selective nodes depending on the ranking/priority and filtering nodes

Kubernetes

Kubernetes is a cluster manager from Google. Google was the first company to introduce the concept of container clusters. Kubernetes has many amazing features for cluster management. A few of them are:

- **Pods**: Kubernetes pods are used for logically grouping containers. Pods are scheduled and managed as independent units. Pods can also share data and communication channels. On the down side if one container in a pod dies, the whole pod dies. This might be valid in the cases of these containers being interdependent or closely coupled.

- **Replication controllers**: Replication controllers ensure reliability across hosts. For example, let's say you always want three pod units/pods of the backend service, replication controllers ensure that three pods are running by checking their health on a regular basis. If any pod doesn't respond, replication controllers immediately spin up another instance of pod and therefore ensure reliability and availability.

- **Labels**: Labels are used to collectively name a set of pods so that teams can operate them as collective units. Naming can be done using environments such as dev, staging and production, or using geographical locations. Replication controllers can be used to collectively migrate collection of pods across nodes, grouping them by labels.

- **Service proxy**: Within a huge container cluster, you would need a neat and clean mechanism to resolve pods/container hosts using labels or name queries. Service proxy helps you resolve requests to a single logical set of pods using label-driven selectors. In the future you might see custom proxies that resolve to a pod based on custom configuration. For example, if you want to serve your premium customers using one set of frontend pods that are configured for quick response times and basic customers using another set of frontend pods, you can configure the environment accordingly and route traffic based on smart domain driven decisions.

DC/OS

DC/OS is another distributed kernel OS built using Apache Mesos for cluster management. Apache Mesos is a cluster manager that integrates seamlessly with container technologies such as Docker for scheduling and fault tolerance. Apache Mesos is in fact a generic cluster management tool that is also used in big data environments such as Hadoop and Cassandra. It also gels well with several batch scheduling, PaaS platforms, long-running applications, and mass data storage systems. It provides a web dashboard for cluster management.

Apache Mesos's complex architecture, configuration, and management makes it difficult to adapt directly. DC/OS makes it easy and significantly straightforward. DC/OS runs on top of Mesos and does the job of what kernel does on your laptop OS, but over a cluster of machines. It provides services such as scheduling, DNS, service discovery, package management, and fault tolerance over a collection of CPUs, RAM, and network resources. DC/OS is supported by a wealth of developer community, rich diagnostics support, and management tools using GUI, CLI, and API.

ACS, which was discussed previously, has a reference implementation for DC/OS. Within a few clicks Azure makes it easy to build a DC/OS cluster on the cloud and makes it ready to deploy applications. The same sets of services are provided for on premise data centers or private clouds using Azure Stack (Azure Stack is an OS provided by Microsoft for managing private clouds). You also get an additional benefit of integrating with other rich sets of services provided by Azure for increasing the agility and scalability.

Two other cluster managers that are not discussed here are Amazon EC2 Container Service, which is built on top of Amazon EC2 instances and uses shared state scheduling services, and CoreOS Tectonic, which is Kubernetes as a service on AWS (Amazon's cloud offering).

Tooling support

Microsoft has released an amazing set of tools for working with Windows Containers for both application developers and IT administrators. Let's look at a few of them.

Visual Studio Tools for Docker

Visual Studio Tools for Docker comes with Visual Studio 2015, which helps you deploy ASP.NET Core apps as containers to Windows Container/LXC hosts. It comes with context options for Dockerizing an existing application. These tools also provide rich debugging functionalities to debug code from containers. By just pressing *F5* you can run and debug applications using local Docker containers and then push to production Windows Server machines with containers with a single click.

Visual Studio Code

Visual Studio Code is another source code editor by Microsoft that is available for free. Visual Studio Code also runs on non-windows OSes such as Linux and OS X. It includes support for debugging, GIT, IntelliSense, and code refactoring. **Docker Toolbox** extension is also available for Visual Studio Code. Auto code completion makes it easy to author Docker and Docker Compose files.

Visual Studio Online

Not just for application deployment, Microsoft also provides automation capabilities through its cloud repository, **Visual Studio Online** (**VSO**) or **Visual Studio Team Services** (**VSTS**). VSO provides lots of features to automate, build, and deploy to container hosts or a cluster. VSO provides predefined build steps to convert an application into a Docker image during build. It also provides ARM templates for one-click deployment and service endpoints to private Docker repositories for accessing existing images from VSTS as part of your build. Pretty cool, isn't it?

Docker for Windows

For simulating a Docker environment on developer systems we can use **Docker for Windows**. Docker for Windows uses Windows Hyper-V features to provide the Docker Engine on Windows and Linux kernel-specific features for the Docker daemon. Since Docker for Windows uses Hyper-V with containers features it runs only on 64-bit Windows 10 Pro, Enterprise and Education Build 10586 or later. VMware, VirtualBox, or any other hosted virtualization software cannot run in parallel with Docker for Windows. Docker for Windows can be used to run containers, build custom images, share drives with containers, configure networks, and allocate container specific CPU and RAM memory for performance or load testing.

Docker Toolbox for Windows

For PCs that do not meet the requirements of Docker for Windows, there is an alternative solution called **Docker Toolbox for Windows**. Unlike Docker for Windows, Docker Toolbox do not run natively, instead they run on a customized Linux VM called a Docker Machine. Docker Toolbox for Windows runs on 64-bit Windows 7, 7.1, 8, and 8.1 only. Docker Machine is specially customized to run as a Docker host. Once it is installed the host can be accessed from Windows using Docker client, CLI, or PowerShell. Docker Toolbox for Windows comes with a plethora of options to run and manage Docker containers, images, Docker Compose, **Kitematic**, a GUI for running Docker on Windows, and Macintosh. Docker Toolbox for Windows also needs virtualization to be enabled. Boot2Docker, an emulator for Windows, is now deprecated.

Who else is working with containers?

The heat is on! It is not just Docker, Linux, and Microsoft in the race anymore, with enterprises witnessing the benefits of containerization and the pace at which adaptability is growing more companies have started putting in effort to the build new products or services around containers. A few of them are listed in the following sections.

Turbo

Windows Containers, which we have learned so far run on a kernel modified to adapt containers, **Turbo** allows you to package applications and their dependencies into lightweight, isolated virtual environments called containers. Containers can then be run on any Windows machine that has Turbo installed. This makes it extremely easy to adapt for Windows.

Turbo is built on top of Spoon VMs. **Spoon** is an application virtualization engine that provides lightweight namespace isolation of the Windows Core OS features such as filesystem, registry, process, network, and threading. These containers are portable, which means no client is required to run. Turbo can containerize from simple desktop applications to complex server objects such as Microsoft SQL Server. Turbo VMs are extremely light and also possess streaming capabilities. Teams can share Spoon VMs using a shared repository called **Turbo Hub**.

Rocket

Docker is no longer the only container available on Linux. CoreOS developed a new container technology called **Rocket**, which is quite different from Docker in architecture. Rocket does not have a daemon process; Rocket containers (called **App Containers**) are created as child processes to the host process, which are then used to launch the container. Each running container has a unique identity. Docker images are also convertible to **App Container Image** (a naming convention used for Rocket images). Rocket runs on a container runtime called **App Container Runtime**.

Summary

In this chapter we covered the following points:

- VMs help create isolated environments, each with guest OS. Software applications or services can run inside a VM with complete isolation from another VM.
- Hypervisors can run discrete VMs such as Linux and Windows together.
- VMs suffer from portability and packaging due to the huge size and intense orchestration needs.
- Containerization helps run software systems as isolated processes inside a machine. Containers increase the density of applications per machine, and also provide application packaging and shipping capabilities.
- Windows Server 2016 supports containerization using kernel features such as filesystems, namespaces, and registry.
- Windows Server 2016 runs two types of containers, Windows Server Containers and Hyper-V Containers. Windows Server Containers share OS kernels, whereas Hyper-V Containers run their own OS.
- Nano Server is a deeply refactored version of Windows Server, which is 93% smaller, remotely-administered, and ideal for microservices.
- Microsoft Azure supports cluster management solutions such as DC/OS and swarm.

2
Deploying First Container

Containerization helps you build software in layers, containers inspire distributed development, packaging, and publishing in the form of containers. Developers or IT administrators just have to choose a base OS image, create customized layers as per their requirements, and distribute using public or private repositories. Microsoft and Docker together have provided an amazing toolset that helps you build and deploy containers in no time. It is very easy to set up a dev/test environment as well. Microsoft Windows Server OS or Windows 10 Desktop OS comes with **Plug and Play** (**PnP**) features for running Windows Server Containers or Hyper-V Containers. Docker Hub, a public repository for images, serves as a huge catalog of customized images built by community or Docker enthusiasts. The images on Docker Hub are freely available for anyone to download, customize, and distribute.

In this chapter, we will learn how to create and configure container development environments. We will learn how to use images from Docker Hub to create containers and also understand how to create our own images from scratch using the Windows base OS images. We will be using both Docker CLI and PowerShell commands together to create our first image and container.

The following are a few more concepts that you will learn in this chapter:

- Preparing a Windows Server Containers environment
- Pulling images from Docker Hub
- Installing base OS images
- Creating custom images using Docker client
- Creating our first container
- Authoring Dockerfiles
- Managing Docker Service

Preparing the development environment

In order to start creating Windows Containers, you need an instance of Windows Server 2016 or Windows 10 Enterprise/Professional edition (with **Anniversary update**). Irrespective of the environment, the PowerShell/Docker commands described in this chapter for creating and packaging containers/images are the same. If you already have the environment configured, you can directly skip to the *Windows Server Containers development* section. The following are the options we have for setting up a Windows Server Container development environment:

- **Windows 10**: Using Windows 10 Enterprise or Professional edition with Anniversary update you can create Hyper-V Containers by enabling the containers role. Docker or PowerShell can be used to manage the containers. We will learn how to configure the Windows 10 environment in the following section.

 Windows 10 only supports Hyper-V Containers created using `nanoserver` base OS image; it does not support Windows Server Containers.

- **Windows Server 2016**: There are two options for working with containers on Windows Server 2016:
  - You can download the Windows Server 2016 ISO from here (`https://www.microsoft.com/en-in/evalcenter/evaluate-windows-server-technical-preview`) and install it on a VM running on Hyper-V or VirtualBox. For running Windows Server 2016 the host machine should have Hyper-V virtualization enabled. Additionally, for the containers to access the Internet, ensure that the network is sharable between the host and Hyper-V VMs.
  - Windows Azure provides a readymade instance of Windows Server 2016 with containers configured. This so far is the easiest option available.

In this chapter, I will be using Windows Server 2016 with containers enabled on Azure to create and manage Window Server Containers.

Containers on Windows 10

The following steps explain how to set up a dev/test environment on Windows 10 for learning container development using Hyper-V Containers. Before continuing further, ensure that you're running Windows 10 Professional/Enterprise version with Anniversary update. For validating Windows Edition on Windows 10, click **Start** and type `This PC`, and then right-click on **This PC** and click on **Properties**. Check the Windows Edition section for the Windows 10 edition. If your PC shows Windows 10 Enterprise or Professional, you can download and install the Anniversary update from here (`https://support.microsoft.com/en-us/help/12387/windows-10-update-history`).

If you do not have any of the above, please proceed to the following section, which explains how to work with containers using the Windows Server 2016 environment on Azure and on-premises. Follow these steps to configure Hyper-V Containers on Windows 10:

1. Click on **Start** menu and type `powershell`. Right-click **Windows PowerShell** and click on **Run as administrator**.

2. Run the following command to install the containers feature on Windows 10:

   ```
   Enable-WindowsOptionalFeature -Online -FeatureName containers -All
   ```

   The preceding command gives the following output:

   ```
   PS C:\WINDOWS\system32> Enable-WindowsOptionalFeature -Online -FeatureName containers -All

   Path          :
   Online        : True
   RestartNeeded : False
   ```

3. Run the following command to install the Hyper-V Containers feature on Windows 10. We will only be using Windows Server Containers in this chapter; we will learn about working with Hyper-V Containers in following chapters:

   ```
   Enable-WindowsOptionalFeature -Online -FeatureName
   Microsoft-Hyper-V -All
   ```

4. Restart the PC by running the following command:

   ```
   Restart-Computer -Force
   ```

5. Run the following command to update the registry settings:

```
Set-ItemProperty -Path 'HKLM:SOFTWARE\Microsoft\Windows
NT\CurrentVersion\Virtualization\Containers'
-Name VSmbDisableOplocks -Type DWord -Value 1 -Force
```

6. Although PowerShell can be used to manage and run containers, Docker commands give a full wealth of options for container management. Microsoft PowerShell support for Windows Container development is still a work in progress, so we will mix and match PowerShell and Docker as per the scenarios.

   Run the following set of steps one by one to install and configure Docker on Windows 10:

```
Invoke-WebRequest "https://master.dockerproject.org/windows/
amd64/docker-1.13.0-dev.zip" -OutFile "$env:TEMP\docker-1.13.0
-dev.zip"
-UseBasicParsing
Expand-Archive -Path "$env:TEMP\docker-1.13.0-dev.zip"
-DestinationPath $env:ProgramFiles
$env:path += ";c:\program files\docker"
[Environment]::SetEnvironmentVariable("Path", $env:Path + ";
C:\Program Files\Docker", [EnvironmentVariableTarget]::Machine)
dockerd --register-service
```

7. Start the **Docker Service** by running the following command:

```
Start-Service docker
```

8. In order to develop Windows Server Containers, we need any Windows base OS image, such as windowsservercore or nanoserver. Since Windows 10 supports Nano Servers only, run the following command to download the nanoservercore base OS image (we have a dedicated chapter for learning development using Nano Server images). The following command might take some time depending on your bandwidth; it downloads and extracts the nanoserver base OS image, which is 970 MB in size, approximately:

```
docker pull microsoft/nanoserver
```

At the time of writing, Windows 10 can only run Nano Server images. Even though the windowsservercore image gets downloaded successfully, running containers using this image will fail due to incompatibility with the OS.

9. Ensure that the images are successfully downloaded by running the following command:

```
docker images
```

The preceding command gives the following output:

Now you are ready to start container development on Windows 10, you can directly skip to the *Windows Server Containers development* section to start creating Windows Containers.

Windows Server Containers on-premise

This section will help you to download and install Windows Server 2016 on a VM using a hosted virtualization software such as Hyper-V or VirtualBox. Windows Server 2016 comes with two installation options, Windows Server 2016 Core and Windows Server 2016 full feature, as shown in the following screenshot:

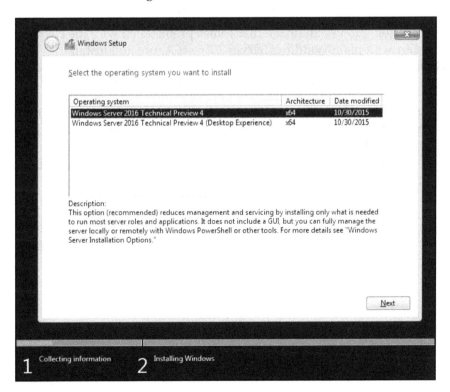

Windows Server 2016 Core is a *no GUI* version of Windows with minimalistic server features and bare minimum size, whereas the full version is the traditional server OS and it comes with all features installed. No matter which installation option you choose, you will be able to install and run Windows Server Containers. You cannot change the *no GUI* version to full version post installation, so make sure you are choosing the right option during installation.

You can download the Windows Server ISO from here `https://www.microsoft.com/en-in/evalcenter/evaluate-windows-server-technical-pr eview` (make sure you copy the *activation key* as well from here) and set up a hosted virtualization software such as VirtualBox or Hyper-V. Once you start installing from the ISO, you will be presented with the following screen, which lets you select full installation with Desktop Experience or just the core with **command-line interface** (**CLI**). Once the installation is complete, you can use the steps mentioned in the *Containers on Windows 10* section to configure containers on Windows Server 2016.

For the remainder of this chapter, we will be using a prebuilt image available on Azure.

Windows Server Containers on Azure

On Azure we are going to use an image that comes preinstalled with the containers feature. You can also start with plain Windows Server 2016 on Azure and install the Windows **Containers** role from add/remove Windows features and then install Docker Engine or use the steps mentioned in the *Containers on Windows 10* section.

In this chapter, we are going to create Windows Server 2016 VM on Microsoft Azure. The name of the image on Windows Azure is `Windows Server 2016 with Containers Tech Preview 5`. Microsoft Azure does not support Hyper-V Containers on Azure. However, you can deploy these container types when running Windows Server 2016 on premises or on Windows 10.

 For creating a VM on Azure you will need an Azure account. Microsoft provides a free account for beginners to learn and practice Azure for $200/30 days. More details regarding creating a free account can be found here `https://azure.microsoft.com/en-in/free/`.

Container options on Windows Server 2016 TP5

Windows Server 2016 supports two types of containers: Windows Server Containers and Hyper-V Containers. You can run either of these containers on Windows Server 2016. But for running Hyper-V Containers, we would need a container host that supports Hyper-V nested virtualization enabled, which is not mandatory for Windows Server Containers.

Create Windows Server 2016 TP5 on Azure

Azure VMs can be created using a variety of options such as **Service Management Portal** (`https://manage.windowsazure.com`), PowerShell, or Azure CLI. We will be using the new Azure portal (code name **Ibiza**) for creating an Azure VM.

Please follow these steps to create a new Windows Server 2016 Containers VM:

1. Log in to the Azure Management portal `https://portal.azure.com`.
2. Click on **+New** and select **Virtual Machines**.
3. Click on **See All** to get a full list of VMs.
4. Search using text `Windows Server 2016` (with double quotes for full phrase search).
5. You will find three main flavors of Windows Server 2016, as shown in the following screenshot:

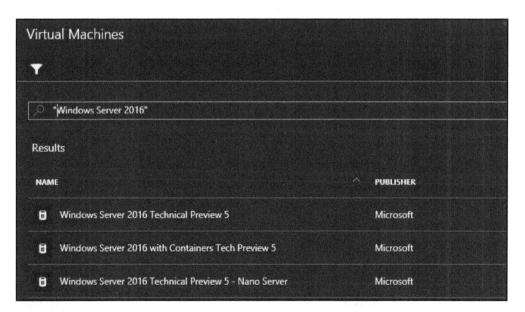

6. Click **Windows Server 2016 with Containers Tech Preview 5** and then click **Create** on the new blade.

7. Select **Resource Manager** as the deployment model.

8. Fill in the parameters as follows:

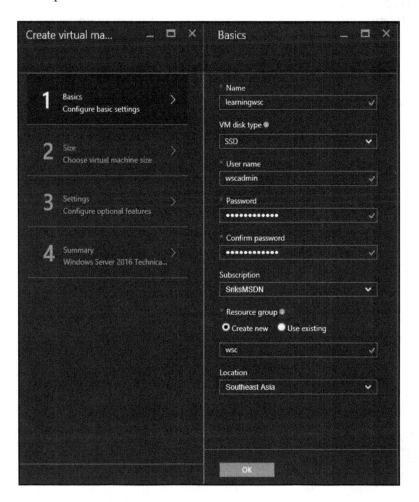

9. Basic settings:

- **Name**: The name of the VM or the host name.
- **VM disk type**: SSD.
- **User name**: Administrator account username of the machine. This will be used while remotely connecting to the machine using RDP.
- **Password**: Administrator password.

- **Confirm password**: Repeat administrator password.
- **Subscription**: Select the Azure subscription to be used to create the machine.
- **Resource group**: Resource group is a group name for logically grouping resources of a single project. You can use an existing resource group or create a new one.
- **Location**: The geographical location of the Azure data center. Choose the nearest available to you.

10. Click **OK**.
11. Select **Size** and click on **DS3_V2**. For this exercise, we will be using **DS3_V2 Standard**, which comes with four cores and **14 GB** memory.
12. Select **DS3_V2 Standard** and click **Select**:

13. Click on **Settings**. The **Settings** section will have most of the parameters pre-filled with defaults. You can leave the defaults, unless you want to change anything, and then click **OK**.

14. Check a quick summary of the selections made using the **Summary** tab and click **OK**. Azure will start creating the VM. The progress will be shown on a new tile added to the dashboard screen, as shown in the following screenshot:

Azure might take a couple of minutes or more to create the VM and configure extensions. You can check the status on the newly created dashboard tile.

Installing base OS images and verifying installation

The following steps will explain how to connect to an Azure VM and verify whether the machine is ready for Windows Server Container development:

1. Once the VM is created and running, the status of the VM on the tile will be shown as **Running**:

We can connect to Azure VMs primarily in two ways using RDP and remote PowerShell. In this sample, we will be using RDP to connect to the Azure VM.

2. Select the tile and click on the *connect* icon. This downloads a remote desktop client to your local machine, as shown in the following screenshot:

 If you are using any browser other than IE 10 or Edge, please check for the .rdp file in the respective downloads folder.

3. Double-click the .rdp file and click **Connect** to connect to the VM.
4. Enter the username and password used while creating the VM to log in to the VM.
5. Ignore the **Security Certificate Warning** and click on **Yes**.
6. Ensure that the containers feature is installed by running the following command:

```
Get-WindowsFeature -Name Containers
```

This should show **Installed** in the **Install State** of containers, as shown in the following screenshot:

```
PS C:\Users\wscadmin> Get-WindowsFeature -Name Containers

Display Name                                        Name                    Install State
------------                                        ----                    -------------
[X] Containers                                      Containers                  Installed
```

7. Ensure that the Docker client and engine is installed using the following commands on PowerShell CLI and verify the version:

    ```
    docker version
    ```

    The preceding command gives the following output:

    ```
    PS C:\Users\wscadmin> docker version
    Client:
      Version:       1.12.0
      API version:   1.24
      Go version:    go1.6.3
      Git commit:    8eab29e
      Built:         Thu Jul 28 23:54:00 2016
      OS/Arch:       windows/amd64

    Server:
      Version:       1.12.0
      API version:   1.24
      Go version:    go1.6.3
      Git commit:    8eab29e
      Built:         Thu Jul 28 23:54:00 2016
      OS/Arch:       windows/amd64
    ```

`docker info` provides the current state of the Docker daemon, such as the number of containers running, paused or stopped, the number of images, and so on, as shown in the following screenshot:

```
PS C:\learningwsc-chapter1\hellodocker> docker info
Containers: 0
 Running: 0
 Paused: 0
 Stopped: 0
Images: 7
Server Version: 1.12.0
Storage Driver: windowsfilter
 Windows:
Logging Driver: json-file
Plugins:
 Volume: local
 Network: nat overlay null
Swarm: inactive
Security Options:
Kernel Version: 10.0 14300 (14300.1045.amd64fre.rs1_release_svc.160705-1059)
Operating System: Windows Server 2016 Datacenter Technical Preview 5
OSType: windows
Architecture: x86_64
CPUs: 2
Total Memory: 3.5 GiB
Name: learningwsc
ID: DEFU:I7ST:JY2S:E3ZG:PCXX:J7PY:JQE4:FELG:PDOT:Z3SL:6RCD:MNQ4
Docker Root Dir: C:\ProgramData\docker
Debug Mode (client): false
Debug Mode (server): false
Registry: https://index.docker.io/v1/
Insecure Registries:
 127.0.0.0/8
```

Windows Server Containers development

If you have an environment ready for executing Windows Server Containers, you can start from here to learn how to create containers from existing images or create new images.

Pulling images from Docker Hub

In this section, we will use an existing Docker image to create a new container. Docker Hub is a public repository for storing Docker images. Docker images can be made up of Linux base OS or windowsservercore OS. Since OS kernels are completely different, containers made up of Linux cannot be installed on Windows and vice versa. At this point we cannot differentiate by looking at the name if the base OS is made up of Linux/Windows.

If you try to install or pull a Linux image on Windows, it might fail with an error as follows:

```
PS C:\WINDOWS\system32> docker pull microsoft/aspnet
Using default tag: latest
latest: Pulling from microsoft/aspnet

52747b744e22: Extracting [===================================================>]  37.19 MB/37.19 MB
a3ed95caeb02: Download complete
bcdfa5245946: Download complete
50df7d9be93c: Download complete
5fc529821ea0: Download complete
1c84e9c72d61: Download complete
661d126a35e4: Download complete
727dae7c5697: Download complete
8794f7667054: Download complete
9ea879a105dc: Download complete
failed to register layer: re-exec error: exit status 1: output: Failed to OpenForBackup failed in Win32: open \\?
gramData\docker\windowsfilter\21c5255232ad21d0baea127fa088edc4da1ca3cc04e1aa161bbef122c51d500f\usr\share\man\man3
::gettext.3pm.gz: The filename, directory name, or volume label syntax is incorrect. (0x1f) \\?\C:\ProgramData\do
ndowsfilter\21c5255232ad21d0baea127fa088edc4da1ca3cc04e1aa161bbef122c51d500f\usr\share\man\man3\Locale::gettext.3
```

Microsoft has also published a few docker images starting with `microsoft/` that are made up of both Linux and `windowsservercore` base. Follow these steps to search and create a new container using a `windowsservercore`-based image called `microsoft/iis`:

1. Run the following command to search images starting with `microsoft`:

   docker search microsoft

   This will list containers containing the word `microsoft`, as shown in the following screenshot:

```
PS C:\Users\wscadmin> docker search microsoft
NAME                                      DESCRIPTION                                       STARS
ATED
microsoft/aspnet                          ASP.NET is an open source server-side Web ...     474
microsoft/dotnet                          Official images for working with .NET Core..      248
mono                                      Mono is an open source implementation of M...     182
microsoft/azure-cli                       Docker image for Microsoft Azure Command L...     62
microsoft/nanoserver                      Nano Server base OS image for Windows cont...     27
microsoft/iis                             Internet Information Services (IIS) instal...     27
microsoft/mssql-server-2014-express-windows   Microsoft SQL Server 2014 Express installe... 27
microsoft/windowsservercore               Windows Server Core base OS image for Wind...      16
microsoft/oms                             Monitor your containers using the Operatio...      5
microsoft/dotnet-preview                  Preview bits for microsoft/dotnet image            5
microsoft/dotnet35                                                                           4
microsoft/sample-nginx                    Nginx installed in Windows Server Core and...      3
microsoft/applicationinsights             Application Insights for Docker helps you ...      3
microsoft/sample-node                     Node installed in a Nano Server based cont...      2
microsoft/sample-redis                    Redis installed in Windows Server Core and...      2
microsoft/sample-mongodb                                                                     1
microsoft/sqlite                          SQLite installed in a Windows Server Core ...      1
microsoft/sample-dotnet                   .NET Core running in a Nano Server container       1
microsoft/dotnet-nightly                  Preview bits of the .NET Core CLI                  1
microsoft/sample-httpd                    Apache httpd installed in Windows Server C...      1
microsoft/sample-mysql                    MySQL installed in Windows Server Core and...      1
berlius/microsoft-malmo                   Microsoft-malmo - artificial intelligence ...      0
microsoft/sample-python                   Python installed in Windows Server Core an...      0
microsoft/sample-golang                   Go Programming Language installed in Windo...      0
microsoft/sample-ruby                     Ruby installed in a Windows Server Core ba...      0
PS C:\Users\wscadmin>
```

2. Now let's try pulling an image called `microsoft/iis`, which is a Windows Server Core image with `windowsservercose` as base OS image and it comes installed with IIS web server. Run the following command to pull the image on to the container host:

   docker pull microsoft/iis

The `docker pull` command is used to download the images from remote repositories. By default, Docker will search for images on Docker Hub. Once downloaded, Docker maintains a local cache of images:

```
PS C:\Users\wscadmin> docker pull microsoft/iis
Using default tag: latest
latest: Pulling from microsoft/iis

1239394e5a8a: Already exists
847199668046: Pull complete
4b1361d2706f: Pull complete
Digest: sha256:1d64cc22fbc56abc96e4b7df1b51e6f91b0da1941aa155f545f14dd76ac522fc
Status: Downloaded newer image for microsoft/iis:latest
```

3. Now if you list the local images by typing `docker images`, you should see the `microsoft/iis` image alongside the other base OS images, as shown in the following screenshot:

```
PS C:\Users\wscadmin> docker images
REPOSITORY                        TAG                IMAGE ID
microsoft/iis                     latest             accd044753c1
microsoft/windowsservercore       10.0.14300.1030    02cb7f65d61b
microsoft/windowsservercore       latest             02cb7f65d61b
windowsservercore                 10.0.14300.1000    2b824ea36a88
```

4. Now let's create a new container using the above image. Run the following command to create a new container using `microsoft/iis`:

```
docker run -t -d -p 80:80 microsoft/iis cmd
```

`docker run` can be used to create a new container using an image that is locally available. Docker tries to download the image from the public repository if it is not found locally. The following are the parameters of the preceding command:

- `-t`: This switch is used to let Docker enable a pseudo terminal for this container.
- `-d`: This switch lets Docker know to run the container in detached mode. By design, Docker containers running in detached mode exit as soon as the parent process used to create the container exits.

- -p: This switch is used to configure port mapping from the container host to the new container.

5. Now if you try to reach port 80 of the container host, you should be able to see the default home page of the IIS, as shown in the following screenshot:

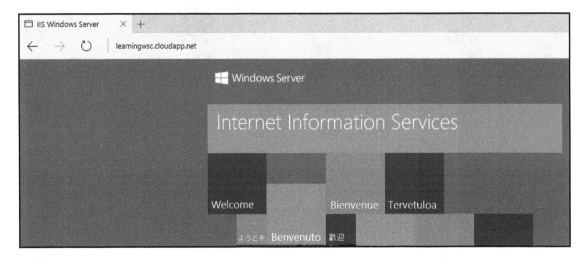

6. You can also check the container running by calling the following command:

```
docker ps -a
```

This shows the running containers:

Hurray! We have successfully created a new container. The new container is running on port 80 (PORTS section) and it is named randomly as elegant_kowalevski by Docker Engine. Docker assigns a unique ID, c8ee2696da3b, for every container; both the ID and names can be used to interact with a running container. We will see more about managing containers in our next chapter.

Preparing a Windows Containers image

A Windows Containers image can be developed primarily in two ways: using PowerShell commands or by using Docker CLI commands. Every Windows Server Container or Hyper-V Container should be created from a base OS image. Windows Server 2016 TP5 comes with two types of base OS images, `windowsservercore` and `nanoserver`. The Windows Server we created on Azure comes with `windowsservercore` installed by default. You can install the `nanoserver` image by running the following command:

```
docker pull microsoft/nanoserver
```

In this chapter, we will use Docker commands to create a Windows Containers image from scratch, which will host default index pages on the IIS web server. First let's check for base OS images installed on our containers host:

```
docker images
```

The preceding command will give the following output:

```
PS C:\Users\wscadmin> docker images
REPOSITORY                     TAG                IMAGE ID        CREATED        SIZE
microsoft/windowsservercore    10.0.14300.1030    02cb7f65d61b    9 weeks ago    7.764 GB
microsoft/windowsservercore    latest             02cb7f65d61b    9 weeks ago    7.764 GB

PS C:\Users\wscadmin> |
```

`windowsservercore` is the base OS image used in the Windows Containers world and it forms the bottom-most layer of a container. As you can see, the image is still heavy on size with 7.75 GB. This additional size hurdle is overcome by a special type of server image called `nanoserver` images. For now, we will only use `windowsservercore`.

If you do not find any image on your container host, you can pull the image from Docker Hub by running the following command:

```
docker pull microsoft/windowsservercore
```

> If you want to search the repository, use `docker search` to get a list of all container images available.

You can list the number of containers running, exited, or paused on any host by using the following command:

```
docker ps
```

The preceding command will give the following output:

```
PS C:\Windows\system32> docker ps
CONTAINER ID        IMAGE            COMMAND          CREATED          STATUS
NAMES
c8ee2696da3b        microsoft/iis    "cmd"            5 minutes ago    Up 4 minutes
 elegant_kowalevski
```

As you can see, running `docker ps` lists the containers and the corresponding image names, status, and so on. The following list explains two methods that can be used to create windows server images:

- Since containers are layered systems, we can start with creating a new container using the base OS image, start customizing the container as per your needs using PowerShell or Windows CLI, and once you are done convert it into an image. Though this sounds simple, this is not quite often how we develop containers. Since we do not maintain a list of steps executed before creating an image, this method is more error prone and not recommended for production scenarios.
- The second and the most preferred way is to write the instructions to prepare an image in a special type of file called Dockerfile. Dockerfile is a set of instructions that follow Docker semantics and they are compiled by Docker Engine while preparing the image. Since we are documenting our configuration as code, it can be easily incorporated in continuous integration or deployment practices.

Running web application in Docker

Now let's start creating our first image using the Dockerfiles approach:

1. Create a folder under `C:\` on Windows Server Containers host machine for storing our image artifacts; let's call it `learningwsc-chapter2`.
2. Create another folder within `learning-chapter2/hellodocker`, which will hold the artifacts for our first image.
3. Open a text editor such as notepad and copy the following contents into the file:

```
FROM microsoft/windowsservercore
MAINTAINER srikanth@live.com
LABEL Description="IIS" Vendor=Microsoft" Version="10?
RUN powershell -Command Add-WindowsFeature Web-Server
COPY index.htm /inetpub/wwwroot/
EXPOSE 80
CMD [ "ping localhost -t" ]
```

4. Save this file as Dockerfile under `learningwsc-chapter2/hellodocker`.
5. Make sure the file is saved without any extension.

 To save a file without any extensions under Windows, just surround the filename with `""`. In this example, save the file as `"Dockerfile"`.

6. Open notepad again and copy the following contents:

```
<h1> Hello from Docker !! </h1>
```

7. Save the file as `index.htm` under `learningwsc-chapter2/hellodocker`. This serves as our simple HTML application.

 Since this book is all about working with Windows Server Containers, the sample applications used to package as containers will be made as simple as possible. However, the same methodologies can be applied for any complex applications. The packaging process is completely decoupled from the application development.

8. Now that we have all the artifacts ready we can build our first Docker image. Press the Windows key on your keyboard and type `PowerShell`.
9. Right-click **Windows PowerShell** and **Run as Administrator**.
10. Navigate to the folder that contains our artifacts, which is in `learningwsc-chapter2/hellodocker`:

```
Cd\
Cd learningwsc-chapter2\hellodocker
```

11. Run the following command to build our first Docker image:

```
docker build -t hellodocker .
```

 Downloading the example code
Detailed steps to download the code bundle are mentioned in the Preface of this book. The code bundle for the book is also hosted on GitHub at: `https://github.com/PacktPublishing/Learning-Windows-Server-Containers`. We also have other code bundles from our rich catalog of books and videos available at: `https://github.com/PacktPublishing/`. Check them out!

12. The output should look as follows:

```
PS C:\learningwsc-chapter2\hellodocker> docker build -t hellodocker .
Sending build context to Docker daemon 3.072 kB
Step 1 : FROM microsoft/windowsservercore
latest: Pulling from microsoft/windowsservercore

Digest: sha256:464ab695bbbfe8f216926c2d2d7e8517c94cb115b094945fb32d7756753be301
Status: Downloaded newer image for microsoft/windowsservercore:latest
 ---> 02cb7f65d61b
Step 2 : MAINTAINER srikanth@live.com
 ---> Running in e564ff909431
 ---> a981a0257815
Removing intermediate container e564ff909431
Step 3 : LABEL Description IIS Vendor Microsoft Version 10?
 ---> Running in 8a933706279e
 ---> ad4f6e87b350
Removing intermediate container 8a933706279e
Step 4 : RUN powershell -Command Add-WindowsFeature Web-Server
 ---> Running in c5da27a9be64

Success Restart Needed Exit Code      Feature Result
------- -------------- ---------      --------------
True    No             Success        {Common HTTP Features, Default Documen...


 ---> 1f7890978070
Removing intermediate container c5da27a9be64
Step 5 : COPY index.htm /inetpub/wwwroot/
 ---> c55e2e864039
Removing intermediate container 18de7a2fec2b
Step 6 : EXPOSE 80
 ---> Running in abcdd1f8498a
 ---> 80b96b5c63a9
Removing intermediate container abcdd1f8498a
Step 7 : CMD [ ping localhost -t ]
 ---> Running in 28f14a8958bb
 ---> 0ca9ca35e8d8
Removing intermediate container 28f14a8958bb
Successfully built 0ca9ca35e8d8
```

13. Ensure that the log ends with `Successfully built [imageidentifier]`, as shown previously. The image identifier here is the unique ID provided to our image by Docker Engine.

14. You should now be able to see your `hellodocker` image in the Docker image list:

```
PS C:\learningwsc-chapter2\hellodocker> docker images
REPOSITORY                      TAG               IMAGE ID         CREATED          SIZE
hellodocker                     latest            0ca9ca35e8d8     3 minutes ago    7.906 GB
microsoft/iis                   latest            accd044753c1     6 weeks ago      7.907 GB
microsoft/windowsservercore     10.0.14300.1030   02cb7f65d61b     3 months ago     7.764 GB
microsoft/windowsservercore     latest            02cb7f65d61b     3 months ago     7.764 GB
```

Creating a container

Perform the following steps in order to create a container:

1. Run the following command on the same PowerShell window to create a Docker container from our `hellodocker` image that we just created:

    ```
    docker run --rm -it -p 80:80 hellodocker cmd
    ```

    This should create a container and connect to it. You should see a new command shell open if creating a new container was successful, as shown in the following screenshot:

2. Verify that the container is successfully installed by accessing port 80 on the container host. You should see the following default page that we created earlier:

    For accessing port 80 on Azure VMs, an endpoint has to be created on the VM using the portal. Additionally, ensure that port 80 is not blocked by the host's firewall settings.

For more details on adding endpoints to the Azure VMs using the new portal, please select the virtual machine and navigate to **Resource group** | **Network security group** | **Inbound security rules** and then click **+Add**. Fill all the fields, which are **Name**, **Priority**, **Source IP**, **Port range**, **Protocol**, **Destination IP**, and set **Action** as **Allow**, and click **OK**. Wait for the VM settings to be updated.

3. You can also open a new PowerShell/command window as an administrator and run the following command to check the running containers:

```
docker ps -a
```

The preceding command will give the following output:

```
PS C:\learningwsc-chapter2\hellodocker> docker ps -a
CONTAINER ID        IMAGE           COMMAND           CREATED          STATUS          PORTS
MES
ad12ba597ae5        hellodocker     "cmd"             55 seconds ago   Up 46 seconds   80/tcp, 0.0.0.
```

Decoding image preparation

Let's understand what just happened. We have authored a Dockerfile that contains the instructions for Docker Engine to prepare an image. Once the image is ready we were able to create a container and run it on a particular port. As you can see all the magic goes into the Dockerfile. Let's understand the Dockerfile line by line. Each Docker line as it executes creates an intermediate container (or layer) and commits it if successful or fails creating the image completely in case of failures.

FROM

This command is used to select the base OS image, for example, in FROM windowsservercore we are starting with windowsservercore as our base OS image. You can use any base image, such as windowsservercore (or nanoserver for Hyper-V Containers) or Linux images (if Linux is the container host). You can also use your own image that you just created as the base for creating another image. As you can see, we are building images using layered structures one on top of another to create customization as we need. This promotes building applications as extensions and makes it extremely easy to distribute customized applications for others to use or extend as they like.

MAINTAINER

MAINTAINER allows you to set the author of the image. When we finally push the image to a public repository such as Docker Hub or a private repository, this information serves as metadata.

LABEL

LABEL can be used to add application-specific metadata to the image in terms of key-value pairs. Each label is just a key value pair that allows us to add more context to the image we are building. Each key-value pair can be separated by a space or backslashes (spaces preferred).

 Separating metadata by backslashes creates one intermediate container for each key-value pair. Since the performance of the container decreases due to many intermediate containers, it is generally not recommended to use backslashes.

RUN

RUN will execute commands in a new layer and commits if they are successful. The resulting image will be used by the next set of statements to add more layers. In this RUN command we are using the Add-WindowsFeature PowerShell command to install IIS on the windowsservercore base OS image. There can be any number of RUN commands in a Dockerfile. For example, RUN powershell Add-WindowsFeature Web-Server instructs Docker to run the following command on Windows PowerShell, which will install IIS, the default web server component on the Windows platform:

```
Add-WindowsFeature Web-Server
```

COPY

The COPY instruction copies the files/folders from the source to the destined location on the intermediate image or layer and commits if the copy is successful. So the commit image will have these files under the destined path whenever a new container is created. There can be any number of COPY instructions in a Dockerfile. It is mandatory for the source to be within the build context (in this case, the current folder or root); we cannot point to files that are remotely located. In the following example, Docker copies the index.htm file from the build context to the /inetpub/wwwroot location on the container, which is the default location for the IIS web server:

```
COPY index.htm /inetpub/wwwroot/
```

EXPOSE

The EXPOSE instruction exposes the port for the container. It informs Docker that the container will be listening on specified ports during runtime. The -p 80:80 flag we used while creating the container will map port 80 of the container host to port 80 of the running container so that all the traffic on port 80 can be forwarded to the container's port, this is called port forwarding. It is not necessary for the container's host port to be the same as that of the container, for example, we can also do -p 5000:80. In this case, we have to reach the container by accessing port 5000 on the container host. For example, in the following instruction Docker exposes port 80 of the container:

```
EXPOSE 80
```

CMD

CMD instructs the Docker Engine to execute the command on the container. There can only be one CMD in a Dockerfile, which can be overridden while creating a container. If there are more CMD commands in a Dockerfile only the last one will be considered. For example, the following command will ping the localhost once the container is successfully created:

```
CMD [ "ping localhost -t" ]
```

Starting and stopping Docker Service

Docker Service on Windows can be started by using the following command:

```
Start-Service docker
```

Docker Service can be stopped by running the following command:

```
Stop-Service docker
```

Summary

In this chapter, we have learnt how to create and configure Windows Server Container and Hyper-V environment on Windows 10 or Windows Server 2016. Windows 10 professional or Enterprise with Anniversary update can be used to run Hyper-V Containers only.

Windows Server 2016 TP5 ISO can be downloaded and configured as VM using VirtualBox or Hyper-V Manager to run Windows Server Containers. We can also use a readily available template on Azure.

Windows Server 2016 has two installation options, Windows Server Core no GUI version and full GUI versions. Both the versions support windows and Hyper-V Containers. To host Hyper-V Containers, the hosting OS should support nested virtualization.

Every Windows Server Container is based off of a base OS image called `windowsservercore`.

Hyper-V Containers use a much smaller version of a base OS image called `nanoserver`.

Windows PowerShell or Docker commands can be used for searching and downloading images from Docker Hub and also creating and managing images or containers. You can deploy containers from pre-existing images available on Docker Hub using PowerShell or Docker commands. You can create custom images using Docker commands and configure networking.

Container image configuration can be authored in a single file called Dockerfile. Dockerfile follows Docker semantics and commands, which the Docker Engine compiles, and then creates a Docker image.

3
Working with Container Images

Windows Containers can be managed using Docker CLI and PowerShell. Docker provides a lot of commands and options to automate most common activities such as creation, update, publishing, and deletion of images and containers. At this point, PowerShell commands for working with Windows Server Containers are still in development, so in this chapter we will be learning Docker commands only. Irrespective of the language choice, be it Docker CLI or PowerShell, communication with local or remote Docker daemons happens using a common REST-based API called **Docker Remote API**. This also means that you can build your own management interface using your favorite languages that interact with the Docker API.

This chapter helps you get acquainted by providing sample usage for the most common commands and attributes for creating Windows Server Containers and images using Docker CLI. In this chapter, readers will also learn how to sign up to Docker Hub and prepare an image for publishing to Docker Hub.

The following topics and corresponding commands will be discussed in this chapter:

- Listing images
- Searching images
- `docker pull`
- `docker run`
- `docker build`
- Docker tags
- `docker commit`
- `docker exec`
- `docker push`
- Cleaning up containers or images

Listing images

The following command can be used to show a full list of Docker containers, irrespective of state. If you want to see only the running containers omit the −a (stands for all) option:

```
docker ps -a
```

The −f or −−filter flags are applicable for the preceding command. −f or −−filter, when used along with docker ps [OPTIONS], the list of containers, will be filtered as per the filtering condition provided along with this flag. For example, the following command shows details of the container matching the name:

```
docker ps --filter name=nostalgic_norman.
```

A few more valid flags for the filter option are exited=0, status=paused, and ancestor=windowsservercore. The following options are also valid while listing images:

- −n: Shows the number of containers in any state
- −l: Shows the latest container created
- −s: Shows total file size

The usage is very similar to the filter flag shown previously.

Searching images

If users want to create a new Windows Server Container, they need not start from scratch. There are ample images that are already built, which you can pick as your starting point. But how do you know which images are available? This is where docker search will be really helpful. The docker search command helps you search images from the docker public repository. It helps you find popular images using the *star rating* and also filtering images by the official flag, which ascertains great quality and trust. docker search is used to search the images from any remote repository. docker search needs a bare minimum of one parameter, which is the Docker image name:

```
docker search [searchcriteria]
```

The following screenshot shows the result of `docker search`:

```
PS C:\Users\wscadmin> docker search microsoft
NAME                                         DESCRIPTION                                     STARS   OFFICIAL   AUTOMATED
microsoft/aspnet                             ASP.NET is an open source server-side Web ...   476                [OK]
microsoft/dotnet                             Official images for working with .NET Core...   259                [OK]
mono                                         Mono is an open source implementation of M...   186     [OK]
microsoft/azure-cli                          Docker image for Microsoft Azure Command L...   62                 [OK]
microsoft/nanoserver                         Nano Server base OS image for Windows cont...   31
microsoft/mssql-server-2014-express-windows  Microsoft SQL Server 2014 Express installe...   29
microsoft/iis                                Internet Information Services (IIS) instal...   27
microsoft/windowsservercore                  Windows Server Core base OS image for Wind...   19
microsoft/oms                                Monitor your containers using the Operatio...   5                  [OK]
microsoft/dotnet-preview                     Preview bits for microsoft/dotnet image         5                  [OK]
microsoft/dotnet35                                                                           4
microsoft/applicationinsights                Application Insights for Docker helps you ...   3                  [OK]
microsoft/sample-nginx                       Nginx installed in Windows Server Core and...   3
microsoft/sample-httpd                       Apache httpd installed in Windows Server C...   2
microsoft/sample-node                        Node installed in a Nano Server based cont...   2
microsoft/sample-redis                       Redis installed in Windows Server Core and...   2
microsoft/sample-mongodb                                                                     1
microsoft/sqlite                             SQLite installed in a Windows Server Core ...   1
microsoft/sample-dotnet                      .NET Core running in a Nano Server container    1
microsoft/dotnet-nightly                     Preview bits of the .NET Core CLI               1                  [OK]
microsoft/sample-mysql                       MySQL installed in Windows Server Core and...   1
berlius/microsoft-malmo                      Microsoft-malmo - artificial intelligence ...   0
microsoft/sample-python                      Python installed in Windows Server Core an...   0
microsoft/sample-golang                      Go Programming Language installed in Windo...   0
microsoft/sample-ruby                        Ruby installed in a Windows Server Core ba...   0
```

By default, the list returns the top 25 images with truncated descriptions. `docker search` also comes with flags or options that help enhance the search criteria. For example, `docker search -no-trunc` helps you to list images with non-truncated image descriptions. Here is an example of `docker search` with no truncation flag for the container, which comes preinstalled with MS SQL Server:

```
docker search --no-trunc microsoft/
mssql-server-2014-express-windows
```

As you can see in the following screenshot, the command will return a full description of the image instead of a truncated one:

```
PS C:\Users\wscadmin> docker search --no-trunc microsoft/mssql-server-2014-express-windows
NAME                                         DESCRIPTION                                                                          STARS
MATED
microsoft/mssql-server-2014-express-windows  Microsoft SQL Server 2014 Express installed in Windows Server Core based containers.  29
```

The `limit` flag limits the search results to a certain number, for example, the following command will return only three Docker images matching the search criteria:

```
docker search microsoft --limit=3
```

The default value for the limit is `25`. This value can only be between 1 and 100:

```
PS C:\Users\wscadmin> docker search microsoft --limit=3
NAME                  DESCRIPTION                                     STARS   OFFICIAL   AUTOMATED
microsoft/aspnet      ASP.NET is an open source server-side Web ...   476                [OK]
microsoft/dotnet      Official images for working with .NET Core...   259                [OK]
microsoft/azure-cli   Docker image for Microsoft Azure Command L...   62                 [OK]
```

`docker search` offers an amazing filtering option called `-- filter`. The `filter` flag accepts a key-value pair as the filtering value. The filtering value is restricted to only three image attributes, such as stars, official repository flag, or automated flag. Each Docker image has a star rating that explains the popularity of the image. Using `docker search` you can filter your search by searching only for popular images using the `filter` flag.

For example:

```
docker search -filter stars=100 microsoft
```

The preceding command returns all the images containing the word `microsoft` and which have got more than hundred stars. You could also mix and match other `search` flags, such as the one shown in the following screenshot, here we are trying to find an image with the name Microsoft that is both official and contains a minimum of five stars:

What are Official Repositories?

Docker Official Repositories are the curated repositories that are expected to have the utmost quality. Official Repositories are also believed to be the providers of base OS images. Ensure security updates.

You could also log in to the Docker Hub (`https://hub.docker.com/explore/`) and use the search box to search for images, as shown in the following screenshot:

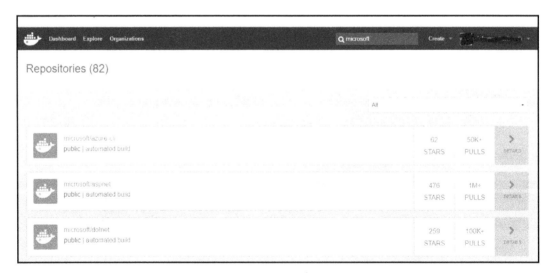

Clicking on the **DETAILS** button will show you how to use the image, sample Dockerfiles, tag or versioning information, and build details. Users are required to register at Docker Hub to log in and search images on Docker Hub.

docker pull

Once you figure out which image you would like to work with, you can download the image locally by using the `docker pull` command:

```
PS C:\Windows\system32> docker pull microsoft/iis
Using default tag: latest
latest: Pulling from microsoft/iis

1239394e5a8a: Already exists
847199668046: Pull complete
4b1361d2706f: Extracting [=>                                    ] 1.081 MB/35.33 MB
```

By default, the latest tag or version is pulled from the Docker Hub.

> Image tagging or versions will be explained in more detail in the following sections.

Docker images are made up of multiple layers; each layer is marked with a unique identifier. When a user types `docker pull`, the Docker daemon downloads layers in parallel and extracts them onto your local computer. Docker is smart enough to pull only those layers that are not present on the local computer.

For example, in the preceding command, `docker pull microsoft/iis`, the image named `microsoft/iis` is made using `windowsservercore` as the base OS, when it is downloaded to the container host the Docker daemon pulls all the layers, but not the `windowsservercore` base OS image. This is because the Docker daemon is intelligent enough to identify the layers or base OS images that are already present on the container host. Each Docker layer is marked with a unique identifier, in the preceding example `windowsservercore` is marked with `UUID 1239394e5a8a` also marked as already exists.

Once the image is successfully downloaded, the Docker daemon prints SHA256 digest onto the screen, which can be used to create containers:

```
PS C:\Windows\system32> docker pull microsoft/iis
Using default tag: latest
latest: Pulling from microsoft/iis

1239394e5a8a: Already exists
847199668046: Pull complete
4b1361d2706f: Pull complete
Digest: sha256:1d64cc22fbc56abc96e4b7df1b51e6f91b0da1941aa155f545f14dd76ac522fc
Status: Downloaded newer image for microsoft/iis:latest
```

Identical Docker images can be tagged or versioned differently using the Docker tagging feature. When different versions of the same image are downloaded Docker stores the common layers only once thus saving a lot of disk space. You can also pull all the tags of a particular image using the following command or any particular version using the following tag option or by using SHA256 digest:

```
PS C:\Windows\system32> docker pull --all-tags microsoft/iis
latest: Pulling from microsoft/iis

Digest: sha256:1d64cc22fbc56abc96e4b7df1b51e6f91b0da1941aa155f545f14dd76ac522fc
windowsservercore-10.0.14300.1030: Pulling from microsoft/iis

Digest: sha256:1d64cc22fbc56abc96e4b7df1b51e6f91b0da1941aa155f545f14dd76ac522fc
Status: Downloaded newer image for microsoft/iis
```

Once the image is downloaded you can list the images using the docker images command, as shown in the following screenshot. As you can see, two versions of microsoft/iis exist on the machine, but with different tags:

```
PS C:\Windows\system32> docker images
REPOSITORY                      TAG                                 IMAGE ID        CREATED         SIZE
microsoft/iis                   latest                              accd044753c1    5 weeks ago     7.907 GB
microsoft/iis                   windowsservercore-10.0.14300.1030   accd044753c1    5 weeks ago     7.907 GB
microsoft/windowsservercore     10.0.14300.1030                     02cb7f65d61b    12 weeks ago    7.764 GB
microsoft/windowsservercore     latest                              02cb7f65d61b    12 weeks ago    7.764 GB
windowsservercore               10.0.14300.1000                     2b824ea36a88    4 months ago    9.354 GB
```

While the Docker daemon is pulling the image from Docker Hub, you can voluntarily end the download by using the *Ctrl + C* option.

docker run

docker run can be used to create an instance of an image from a local or remote repository. The Docker daemon will kick off a new container in its own filesystem, networking, and it contains its own isolated processes. Since the Docker image is made up of layers docker run creates a new writable layer on top of the image. This allows the user to customize the container and commit to create a new customized docker image.

 The Docker daemon will try to pull the image from the remote repository before creating a container if it doesn't find the image on the host.

The syntax for docker run is as follows:

```
docker run [OPTIONS] IMAGE [COMMAND] [ARG..]
```

The docker run command needs an image name at the bare minimum to create a container. run contains the highest number of command-line options, a few of them are listed in the following sections.

Detached versus foreground mode

When you start a container you should be able to decide if you want your container to run in a detached mode or foreground mode. In detached mode, which is the default option, the container exits as soon as the root process that was used to run the container exits. For example, the following command can be used to run a container in detached mode:

```
docker run -d microsoft/iis powershell
```

In foreground mode, when the -d option is not specified and with the -it flag the Docker daemon runs the container and attaches the console to the container's standard input, output, and error streams.

An example for this is as follows:

```
docker run -it microsoft/iis powershell
```

The following are the parameters of the preceding command:

- -i is used to specify interactive mode
- -t is used to attach a pseudo tty
- -a can be used to attach the running container to a particular stream such as standard input, standard output, or standard error streams

In the following command, the Docker daemon flushes only the errors to the interactive console:

```
docker run -a stderr -it microsoft/iis powershell
```

Name

By default, the Docker daemon assigns a random name to the container if it is not specified. Users can name the container by using the -name option for easy identification. The name can be used as one of the identifiers to interact with the running container. Other options to interact with a container are UUID (long and short) and the SHA256 digest value. Use the following command to create a container with a user defined name:

```
docker run -name mycustomwebserver microsoft/iis
```

Isolation technology

The Docker daemon has a very important option called -isolation, which is only applicable in a Windows environment. This option is used to specify the isolation to be used while creating the container. For example, for creating a Hyper-V Container hyperv should be used as the isolation value, as follows:

```
docker run -d --isolation hyperv microsoft/nanoserver powershell
```

The other options available are default and process. The default option is the only supported value for containers running on Linux environments since Linux has only one type of isolation. The process option is the default value on Windows environment, which creates Windows Server Containers with namespace isolation.

To run Hyper-V Containers nested virtualization should be supported on container host, also ensure that the Hyper-V feature is enabled on the container host. The Hyper-V feature can be installed on Windows Server 2016 (on-premise only, Azure does not support Hyper-V Containers yet) by navigating to **Server Manager** | **Add Roles and Features** wizard and selecting the **Hyper-V** option. On Windows 10 you can enable Hyper-V by navigating to **Control Panel** | **Add or Remove Windows Programs** and enable **Hyper-V**.

Overriding Dockerfile image defaults

In `Chapter 2`, *Deploying First Container,* we have used a Dockerfile to create a Docker image that contains a series of commands to the Docker daemon for creating an image. The `docker run` command allows you to override a few docker commands set by the Dockerfile developer that are part of the Dockerfile except commands such as `FROM`, `MAINTAINER`, `RUN`, and `Add`. The commands or options that can be overridden using the `docker run` command are `CMD`, `EXPOSE`, `ENTRYPOINT`, `ENV` (environmental variables), `HEALTHCHECK`, `TMPFS`, `VOLUME`, `USER`, and `WORKDIR`.

For example, you can use the `-p` option to map a containers port or range of ports to similar or dissimilar ports or ranges of ports on the container's host. The image developer might have exposed a few ports for the container using the Dockerfile using the `EXPOSE` command. You can also use the `--expose` option to add to the list of ports used by the `EXPOSE` command in the Dockerfile:

```
docker run -p 80:80 microsoft/iis
```

Dockerfile's `CMD` instruction is used as a default for the container. The defaults can be an executable with parameters such as `CMD [cmd, ping localhost]` or just a set of arguments for the `ENTRYPOINT`. You can also extend the `CMD` option (with arguments) for an image by prepending `docker run` with the command that should be run when the container is started as shown in the following snippet. The following command opens the PowerShell CLI and prints the date from the container once the container is successfully started overriding the `CMD` instruction in the Dockerfile:

```
docker run microsoft/windowsservercore powershell Get-Date
```

docker build

Docker images can be built in two ways. One way is to author a Dockerfile with instructions to prepare the image and use the `docker build` command to create an image. The second way, which will be discussed in the following section, is to create a container using a base OS image such as `windowsservercore`, connect to the container using an interactive command line such as PowerShell or Windows Command Prompt, customize the container using automation scripts such as PowerShell or any other tools (since Windows Server Core does not have a UI any customization can only be done via scripts) and then convert to an image using the `docker commit` command. In this section, we will be learning how to create an image using the `docker build` command.

`docker build` is used to create an image using a Dockerfile; the two main elements for creating an image are the Dockerfile and a build context. Build context is the folder and its contents are specified in the `Path` or `URL` option. `URL` can also be a remote repository such as GitHub. In the following command, the image is built using the root or current folder as the build context. In this example, the build context is inferred using the `.` symbol. The `-t` option is used to give the image a name and optionally the tag name, if nothing is mentioned the latest is used as the default tag.

Build context

For example, in the following screenshot the contents of the preceding folder will used when executed using `.` as the context, dot here refers to current folder. Alternatively you can also point to any local or remote folder path:

```
PS C:\learningwsc\chapter3\hellodocker> dir

    Directory: C:\learningwsc\chapter3\hellodocker

Mode                LastWriteTime         Length Name
----                -------------         ------ ----
-a----        9/13/2016   3:09 PM             37 .ReadMe
-a----         9/3/2016   3:54 PM            267 Dockerfile
-a----        9/13/2016   3:02 PM         126289 image.jpg
-a----        9/13/2016   3:06 PM            167 index.htm
```

Build Docker image

The Docker image name is slash separated and it contains only lowercase characters, digits, and separators. Separators are defined as a period, one or more underscores, or one or more dashes:

```
PS C:\learningwsc\chapter3\hellodocker> docker build -t mycustomwebserver .
Sending build context to Docker daemon 186.4 kB
Step 1 : FROM microsoft/windowsservercore
 ---> 02cb7f65d61b
Step 2 : MAINTAINER srikanth@live.com
 ---> Using cache
 ---> 2665d75ad7aa
Step 3 : LABEL Description IIS Vendor Microsoft Version 10?
 ---> Using cache
 ---> da8c9fa8e227
Step 4 : RUN powershell -Command Add-WindowsFeature Web-Server
 ---> Running in 01886de498e8

Success Restart Needed Exit Code        Feature Result
------- -------------- ---------        --------------
True    No             Success          {Common HTTP Features, Default Documen...


 ---> bd4f26842c50
Removing intermediate container 01886de498e8
Step 5 : COPY index.htm /inetpub/wwwroot/
 ---> 72d7e7b185cb
Removing intermediate container a4a1332824f2
Step 6 : EXPOSE 80
 ---> Running in df88dfedfc12
 ---> f9aeea6abf3f
Removing intermediate container df88dfedfc12
Step 7 : CMD [ ping localhost -t ]
 ---> Running in da10a8729a28
 ---> e6ab161f613e
Removing intermediate container da10a8729a28
Successfully built e6ab161f613e
```

The recommended image name format is
`[username]/[imagename]:[tag]`, this makes it easy to push to the Docker public repository and easily identifiable using the tagging information.

Docker builds the image incrementally; at every instruction the Docker daemon creates an intermediate container with a writable layer on the image, makes changes as per the instruction, and commits back to create an updated image and then deletes the intermediate container. This repeats for every step until the last one, in every step the updated image will be used to create updates.

You can also point to the Dockerfile placed elsewhere using the `-f` or `--file` option. This can be helpful when you want to point at different Dockerfiles based on the release version of the application such as `dockerfile.debug` and `Dockerfile.release`.

The build context is sent to the Docker daemon irrespective of whether the Docker daemon is local or remote. The Dockerfile can refer to any file within the build context in the instructions such as `ADD`, `COPY`, or `RUN`. You can also build images using remote build contexts such as GitHub. This enables automation with continuous integration and delivery. For example, a development team working on a feature can push the developed code to GitHub or any other repository on a regular basis, post a check-in and successful run of tests; a continuous integration process can kick in which compiles the developed code, build a docker image with the GitHub repository as the build context, and publish the image to Docker Hub. You can also use GitHub's branching feature while building an image targeting a particular branch. You can also extend this further by integration with the continuous delivery process, which deploys the image built in the previous step from to test or staging environments automatically. Since containers are light weight processes the entire cycle from development to testing will be drastically smaller than the conventional process. The next few chapters will explain orchestrating automated builds and deployments to production environments using Docker images in detail.

dockerignore

While building an image Docker uses entire contents of the folder as the build context. If you want the Docker daemon to ignore any specific file you can use the `dockerignore` file option. The Docker daemon recognizes a special type of file in the build context with the filename as `.dockerignore`, which can be used to let the daemon ignore files from the build context. Multiple files or directories can also be excluded from the build context using regular expressions as follows:

`*` . (extension)	`*` can be used as a match all pattern. For example: • `*.md` ignores all the files with the `.md` extension • `*READ*.md` ignores all the files that have `READ` in the filename and have `.md` as the extension • `*/READ.md` ignores the `READ.md` file in the immediate sub directory • `*/*/READ.md` ignores the `READ.md` file in the sub directory two levels below

!	! can be used as an exclusion from the ignore list. All the preceding pattern matching can be used to match a file or directory from the exclusion list. For example, !README.* will exclude any file that starts with README and has any extension.
?	? can be used to match single characters. For example, !web.release.v?.config will exclude any file with a name like web.release.v1.config.
#	# can be used to include comments in a .dockerignore file For example, # this line will be ignored.

Docker tags

Tagging helps developers to version images. An image can contain any number of tags. Developers or operators using the image can download/pull a particular version using the tag name. A tag name can consist of numbers, lowercase or uppercase alphabets, underscores, periods, and dashes. The following command creates a new image with v1.0 as the tag name and learningwsc/mycustomwebserver as the image name where learningwsc is the Docker Hub username and mycustomwebserver is the name of my image:

```
docker build -t learningwsc/mycustomwebserver:v1.0 .
```

The Docker daemon is intelligent enough to avoid downloads of redundant layers when working with multiple tags of the same image. When the users download the image with a tag, docker checks for existing layers on the host machine and the differential set of the image, or say only the latest layers are downloaded, this makes software really thin and easily portable.

If not specified the latest is used as the default tag. Tagging information of an image is also available from the Docker Hub web portal. It is always good practice to tag your images before pushing the image to Docker Hub.

 The latest tag does not mean that it is the latest build. Latest simply means the last build/tag that was pushed without any tag/version name specified.

docker commit

As explained in the previous sections, there are primarily two ways to create an image. While Dockerfile and `docker build` together allows us to create an image using a completely scripted approach, `docker commit` allows us to convert an existing container to an image. It also gives you an option to update the existing container's Dockerfile using the command-line arguments.

For example, the following set of commands create a container from scratch and then convert the container into a redistributable image. In this example, we will install a Redis on our container and convert it into an image to reuse in the following chapters:

1. Create a container using the following command. This creates an instance of Windows Server Core and opens an interactive shell (since we used `-it` flags) with PowerShell (you can also use `CMD` in the place of PowerShell):

   ```
   docker run -it microsoft/windowsservercore powershell
   ```

2. Now we can start customizing our container. Use the following command to download Redis for Windows on to the `C` drive:

   ```
   Invoke-WebRequest -Method Get -Uri
   https://github.com/MSOpenTech/redis/releases/
   download/win-2.8.2400/Redis-x64-2.8.2400.zip
   -OutFile c:\redis.zip
   ```

   Redis is an open source in-memory data structure that can be used as a database, cache, and message broker. The distinguishing benefits of Redis from other cache providers are support for data structures such as hashes, lists, sets, and sorted sets. It also has built-in replication, command-line clients for interacting with servers, transactions support, and so on. For more details, visit `http://redis.io/documentation`

3. Run the following command on the container to unzip the package:

   ```
   Expand-Archive -Path c:\redis.zip -DestinationPath c:\redis
   ```

4. Run the following command on the container to start Redis server. This starts **Redis server** on port `6379` by default and waits for connections. You can shut down the server by using the *Ctrl + C* option from the keyboard:

   ```
   cd redis
   .\redis-server.exe
   ```

The preceding command gives the following output:

We have a Redis server ready and functional. Use the following command to create an image using the container. Before we run the following command we have to stop the container. Docker does not allow creation of images using the running containers. Press *Ctrl* + *C* to shut down Redis server and return to the command shell.

5. Exit from the container using the following command. This should close the interactive session with the container and set the context back on the container host:

    ```
    exit
    ```

6. Ensure that the container is stopped using the following command. This prints out a list of running containers. The container we just created should not be part of this list:

    ```
    docker ps
    ```

7. You can also check if the container is stopped using the following command. This command lists all the containers irrespective of the state:

    ```
    docker ps -a
    ```

The preceding command gives the following output:

```
PS C:\Windows\system32> docker ps -a
CONTAINER ID        IMAGE                    COMMAND        CREATED             STATUS
RTS                 NAMES
7542f093e262          microsoft/windowsservercore   "powershell"   About an hour ago   Exited (0) 47 minutes ago
                    furious_kalam
```

As you can see, the status of our container is `Exited`.

8. The `docker commit` command is used to create an image using an existing container referred to using container ID or name of the container. Container ID can be obtained from the above command. You can also use the container name, for example, `furious_kalam` in the following example:

   ```
   docker commit [containerid] [imagename]
   ```

   An example for this is as follows:

   ```
   docker commit 7542f093e262 vishwanathsrikanth/mycacheserver
   ```

   This prints out a `SHA56` digest, as shown in the following screenshot, which can also be used as an identifier for the image:

```
PS C:\Windows\system32> docker commit 7542f093e262 vishwanathsrikanth/mycacheserver
sha256:d99ba180e875ff96fe0d95e1a101643238c34afabcac82a95392cbce6aa70971
```

> There is a reason I have used image name in format `[username]/[imagename]`, this makes publishing easy. In this case `vishwanathsrikanth` is the Docker Hub identifier or account name.

9. You should now see the Docker image we just created in the list of images on Docker host:

```
PS C:\Windows\system32> docker images
REPOSITORY                           TAG              IMAGE ID        CREATED          SIZE
vishwanathsrikanth/mycacheserver     latest           d99ba180e875    2 minutes ago    8.082 GB
microsoft/windowsservercore          10.0.14300.1030  02cb7f65d61b    3 months ago     7.764 GB
microsoft/windowsservercore          latest           02cb7f65d61b    3 months ago     7.764 GB
```

Yippee! But we still have a problem to solve, if you try to create a container using our custom image, this would not start the Redis server because we have not set the working directory and entry point arguments for our container. `docker commit` gives us an option to update or add the Dockerfile commands while creating an image from an existing container. The following are the set of commands that are allowed to be edited or added:

CMD, ENTRYPOINT, ENV, EXPOSE, LABEL, ONBUILD, USER, VOLUME, WORKDIR

Using the following command on our container will set the working directory, entry point, and configure ports:

```
docker commit --change='WORKDIR /redis' --change='CMD
powershell .\redis-server.exe' -c "EXPOSE 6379" 7542f093e262
vishwanathsrikanth/mycacheserver:v1
```

Now when you run the container using the following command, the Redis server starts instantly:

```
docker run -it vishwanathsrikanth/mycacheserver:v1
```

The preceding command gives the following output:

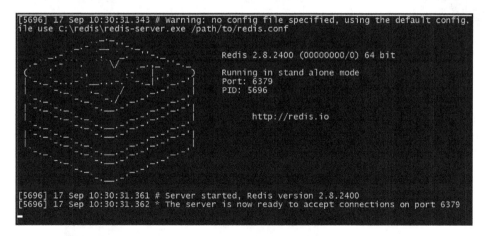

`docker commit` is very helpful when you want to create new versions of an existing image without using Dockerfile. In the next few sections, we will see more options to add features to a running container.

docker exec

Sometimes you might want to run commands on containers that are running in detached mode (in the background). `docker exec` provides an option to run commands in a running container either in detached mode by using the `-d` option or in interactive mode by using the `-it` flag. Before running `docker exec`, make sure the docker container is running and the container's primary process is running. For executing a command on the running container we would need the container ID or the container name.

Let's say we have created an instance of Redis server container in detached mode using the following command:

```
docker run -d vishwanathsrikanth/mycacheserver:v1
```

You can also see the container running using the following command:

```
docker ps
```

The preceding command gives the following output:

```
PS C:\Windows\system32> docker ps
CONTAINER ID      IMAGE                                  COMMAND                CREATED          STATUS
    PORTS              NAMES
5e24c14a2cc6      vishwanathsrikanth/mycacheserver:v1    "cmd /S /C 'powershel"  3 minutes ago    Up 3 minutes
    6379/tcp           naughty_yonath
```

The following command opens an interactive PowerShell session with the running container:

```
docker exec -it 5e24c14a2cc6 powershell
```

Now since we have Redis server running on this container you can connect to the Redis server using the Redis command-line client, which comes with the package we downloaded earlier to `c:\redis`. You can connect to the Redis server running locally, select the default database, and do some Redis stuff such as adding cache pairs as follows:

```
PS C:\redis> .\redis-cli.exe
127.0.0.1:6379> connect localhost 6379
localhost:6379> select 0
OK
localhost:6379> set welcomemessage 'hello windows'
OK
localhost:6379> get welcomemessage
"hello windows"
localhost:6379>
```

Run `exit` to exit from the interactive shell.

docker push

Applications or services can be packaged as containers, and can be shared across teams easily using publishing options provided by docker. Docker Hub is a public repository for all images irrespective of flavor of the base OS. Docker Hub holds containers made up of both Linux and Windows. Microsoft has an official repository for storing windows server images at `https://hub.docker.com/r/microsoft/aspnet/`. Docker command line provides commands to push images to public repositories such as Docker Hub, private repositories provided by Docker Hub (docker provides one private repository for free), or custom built Docker repositories. The following set of sections show you how to push or publish an image to public repository - Docker Hub. New users require an account on Docker Hub before publishing images. New accounts can be created by registering here at `https://hub.docker.com/register/`. The following registration page should be filled with Docker ID, which is a unique identifier for your account, user e-mail, and password:

Once you click **Sign Up** an activation email will be sent to the registered email address. Clicking on the link in the email will redirect you to the login page. Fill in the **Email Id** and **Password** fields selected during the registration and click on **Login**. You will be re-directed to the home page after successful login, as shown in the following screenshot:

Run the following command to create a new Windows Container image. You can also use any other images, but ensure that the image name is in the format `dockerid/imagename`, as follows:

```
docker commit --change='WORKDIR /redis' --change='CMD
powershell .\redis-server.exe' -c "EXPOSE 6379" 5e24c14a2cc6
learningwsc/mycacheserver:latest
```

Here I'm using a running **Redis Cache container** to create an image with the name `learningwsc/mycacheserver:latest`, where `learningwsc` is my Docker ID and `mycacheserver` is my new repository name. The tailing text `:latest` is used to tag the image as latest.

Docker assumes latest as the default tag, so in this case it is redundant just to show the usage.

Now in order to push the image to the Docker Hub we have to log in from the container host. Run the following command with the corresponding username (use Docker ID) and password as follows:

```
docker login --username learningwsc --password ********
```

The Docker daemon responds with a `Login Succeeded` message, as shown in the following screenshot:

```
PS C:\Windows\system32> docker login --username learningwsc --password
Login Succeeded
```

Use the following command to push the image we just created to Docker Hub. Docker identifies the first part of the image names as the Docker ID (`learningwsc` in this case) and the second part of the image as the repository name (`mycacheserver` in this case) and pushes the image to `docker.io/learningwsc/mycacheserver`. This is the reason why the following naming convention is recommended while creating images:

```
docker push learningwsc/mycacheserver
```

As you can see in the following screenshot, the Docker daemon intelligently pushes just the application layers to the repository, but not the base OS image, which makes our image size very small. The Docker daemon also prints out the `SHA256` digest and the image size at the end of the successful push:

```
PS C:\Windows\system32> docker push learningwsc/mycacheserver
The push refers to a repository [docker.io/learningwsc/mycacheserver]
e68f5f82afbe: Pushed
48136bbcc0cf: Pushed
72f30322e86c: Skipped foreign layer
latest: digest: sha256:93a01a08bcace9eb36795a21a653e3b305471c87b4621862434a7a91e9ef39a3 size: 1097
```

You should be able to see your image on Docker Hub as follows:

Clicking on the image name or details takes you to the image's home page, which can be used to add metadata to your image such as **Short Description**, **Full Description**, and so on including a sample command to pull your image using the docker command-line interface.

Apart from the metadata you will also find the **Tags** and **Webhooks** section, which are most important. The **Tags** section shows the different versions of your image. For example, you can create a new container using the latest image, run some updates, and then use the commit command again with a different tag. Use the docker push command to push to the same repository as follows:

```
docker run -it learningwsc/mycacheserver powershell
# Some updates to the container here...
docker commit e06a3982befa learningwsc/mycacheserver:v1
docker push learningwsc/mycacheserver:v1
```

The following screenshot shows the different tags or versions of the same image. Users can choose to pull images based on version or tag information available here:

When uploading the same image to Docker Hub with a different tag, the Docker daemon only pushes the differential layer to the repository instead of the complete image, as shown in the following screenshot:

```
PS C:\Windows\system32> docker push learningwsc/mycacheserver:v1
The push refers to a repository [docker.io/learningwsc/mycacheserver]
70fe36528891: Pushed
e68f5f82afbe: Layer already exists
48136bbcc0cf: Layer already exists
72f30322e86c: Skipped foreign layer
v1: digest: sha256:a54cf5baa9db9768b1b394a16c8acce1b911fbf2523f597773653165f9a450fc size: 1308
```

Webhooks are also helpful while working with continuous integration and deployment scenarios. Webhooks helps us configure an HTTP endpoint, which will be called whenever a new image is pushed to the repository.

Cleaning up containers or images

Obsolete containers or images occupy space, you might want to clean up images or containers from the host to clean up space or to install and run new ones. Docker provides the following options for cleanup:

- `docker stop`: `docker stop` can be used to stop a running container. A container cannot be removed unless it is in the stopped state. You can use the `-f` or `-force` option to force stop a container:

  ```
  docker stop [container id/name] -f
  docker stop $(docker ps -a -q) # stops all the containers
  ```

- `docker rm`: `docker rm` can be used to remove a stopped container. `docker rm` can be concatenated with other listing commands for a consolidated operation as follows:

  ```
  docker rm [container id/name] -force #removes
  container by id or name
  docker rm $(docker ps -a -q) #deletes all stopped
  containers
  ```

- `docker rmi`: `docker rmi` can be used to remove an image from the container host using the `image id`, `name`, `tag`, or `digest` value. If an image has multiple tags all the tagged images should be removed before removing the image from the host. You can use the `-f` or `-force` option to remove all the tagged images:

  ```
  docker rmi [image id/name] -force #removes
  ```

```
all the tagged images
docker rmi $(docker images -a -q) # removes
all the images from the container host.
```

Summary

The following topics are covered in this chapter:

- This chapter helps developers understand various commands and options available while building Windows Server Containers.
- Docker command line or PowerShell versions (yet to be released) communicate with a common API called Docker Remote API.
- Docker Hub is the public repository for storing Windows Server images (and Linux-based images too). Docker Hub provides one private repository for free. For better security users can also host their own private repositories.
- Users can start Windows Server Container development by using any existing image on Docker Hub as base image; a few examples are `microsoft/windowsservercore`, `microsoft/redis`, `microsoft/iis`, and so on.
- A Docker image is made up of layers. Each layer has a unique ID.
- `docker pull` can be used to download images from Docker Hub or any remote repository to Docker host. The Docker daemon does not download the layers that are already present on the host.
- A new Windows Server image can be built using Dockerfile and `docker build`. `docker build` creates the image using the build context as reference for files or directories and executes the instructions from the Dockerfile one by one.
- Windows Server images can be versioned using tags. An image can be published to the same repository using different tags.
- `docker commit` can be used to create an image using an existing container. The `commit` command is also used to update/add instructions to the Dockerfile.
- `docker push` command can be used to publish the image to the Docker Hub or any other remote repository. Users must create an account on Docker Hub before publishing an image.
- Docker provides commands `rm` and `rmi` to delete containers and images respectively. Users should stop the containers using the `docker stop` command before deleting the container.

4
Developing Container Applications

One of the major benefits of containers is that they are inherently decoupled with the application development process. Containers are hosting environments, which means the application development can run seamlessly while the operations team can work, in parallel, on configuring the host for deploying them as containers or even a farm of containers. This chapter teaches you how to convert an existing **ASP.NET Core** and ASP.NET 4.5 website into a Windows Server Container compatible application. ASP.NET Core is the next version of the ASP.NET web application development platform, which has been renamed as *Core* because of the changes that have been made from the ground up. ASP.NET Core is inherently an extensible application development platform. We are going to use Visual Studio 2015 and its extensible endpoints, which are provided by the ASP.NET Core web application template to plug into the Windows Server Container and automate build, run, clean, and publish steps.

The following topics will be discussed in this chapter:

- Setting up the development environment
- Understanding the underlying architecture of ASP.NET Core
- ASP.NET Core hosting options
- Introduction to the *Music Store* application
- Adding Windows Server Container features to the *Music Store* application
- Hosting *Music Store* on a Kestrel server running on the Windows Container
- Hosting ASP.NET 4.5 applications on IIS running on the Windows Container
- Working with container networking
- Troubleshooting Windows Server Container network issues

Setting up the development environment

Typically, developers work on traditional desktop OSes like Windows 7, Windows 8.1, or Windows 10. Though these OSes are still suitable to develop ASP.NET Core web applications or services, developing or debugging Windows Server Containers is not supported at this time. This is because Windows 10 OS with Anniversary update only runs Hyper-V Containers using `nanoserver` as a base OS image. In this chapter, we will be setting up the development environment on Windows Server 2016 for developing ASP.NET Core applications.

The following tools are necessary for developing ASP.NET Core applications:

- **Visual Studio 2015 Community or Enterprise**: Visual Studio 2015 Community is a full-featured, freely available IDE for developing modern web and mobile applications or services. Visual Studio 2015 Community can be downloaded from here, `https://www.visualstudio.com/vs/community/`.

- **.NET Core VS 2015 Tooling Preview**: This extension provides necessary runtimes, SDK, and project templates for working with .NET Core and ASP.NET Core applications. The latest setup can be downloaded from here, `https://go.microsoft.com/fwlink/?LinkId=827546`.

We can also work using **Visual Studio Code** with C# extension for ASP.NET Core and Windows Server Container development. Visual Studio Code is an open source, cross-platform IDE with traditional Visual Studio IDE features like Intellisense, debugging, and integration with source code repositories like **Git**, VSO, and so on. Visual Studio Code runs on Windows, Linux (Debian, Ubuntu, Red Hat, Fedora, and CentOS) and macOS. It also supports a variety of programming languages like Ruby, Java, PHP, Python, and so on. Visual Studio Code also supports Dockerfile syntax and Intellisense support.

Apart from the preceding tooling support, we will also need Windows PowerShell and Docker. Windows PowerShell comes out of the box with Windows Server 2016. As we are using Windows Server 2016 on Azure, Docker also comes out of the box. Refer to `Chapter 2`, *Deploying First Container* for setting up Windows Server 2016 on Azure or on-premise using hosted VM installation option.

After creating a Windows Server 2016 image on Azure, opening an instance of Microsoft Edge might throw an error which says, *Microsoft edge can't be opened using the built-in administrator account. Sign in with a different account and try again.*

This is just a security enhancement, perform the following steps and restart your machine to override this setting:

1. Use the search option in the taskbar, enter `secpol.msc` and press *Enter*.
2. Navigate to **Local Policies | Security Options**.
3. Double-click **User Account Control: Admin Approval Mode for the Built-in Administrator account**.
4. Set the policy to **Enabled** and click **Apply**.
5. Reboot the machine.
6. We can also use **Internet Explorer** by disabling the **Enhanced Security** setting from **Server Manager**.

Ensure tools are installed and configured correctly by opening Visual Studio 2015 Community as an administrator and navigating to **File | New Project**. We should be able to see the following .NET Core templates:

Understanding .NET Core and ASP.NET Core

.NET Core is the latest version of .NET from Microsoft which is a subset of .NET foundation. Microsoft has made .NET Core extremely flexible, the runtime can be packaged along with the application and run multiple versions of runtime in parallel on the same machine. Microsoft also made .NET Core open-source using MIT and an Apache 2 license which will be supported by both Microsoft and the GitHub community. The source code for .NET Core is available at `https://github.com/dotnet/core`.

.NET core has been built with the intention of removing the dependency on Windows OS libraries. It is backward compatible and cross-platform, supporting Windows, macOS, and Linux. It can be used on any device and even in the cloud. It comes with great tooling support which we will be looking at in the upcoming sections. Most operations can be performed using a single command-line tool called `dotnet`.

ASP.NET Core architecture

ASP.NET 5 is the latest version of the web application platform ASP.NET, renamed as ASP.NET Core. ASP.NET Core is a new cross-platform version of ASP.NET which can be used for building modern web applications or RESTful web services which are cloud-ready (and on-premises). ASP.NET Core runs on Windows, Linux, and Mac. It targets .NET Core by default, but you can also use the old .NET framework.

ASP.NET Core has gone through several architectural changes. It is no longer dependent on core OS libraries like `System.Web`. It is now more flexible, lean, and modular. It has a much smaller surface area than before which makes it a perfect fit for building microservices. The benefits of lesser app surface are tighter security, reduced servicing, improved performance, and decreased costs, as shown in the following image:

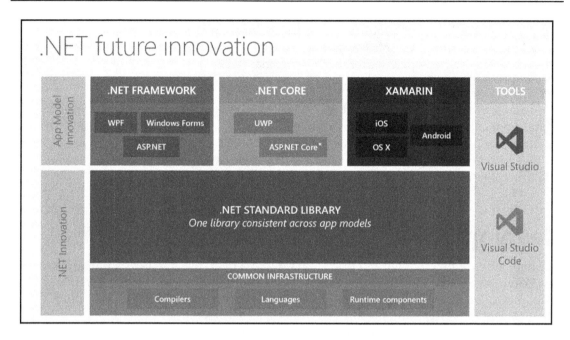

Hosting ASP.NET applications

ASP.NET Core applications obviously need a host to run, but the advantage here is ASP.NET Core is completely de-coupled from the hosting platform. Also, ASP.NET Core comes with a variety of hosting options, unlike the previous versions of ASP.NET like 4.5 and earlier versions. ASP.NET supports hosting in IIS, **IIS Express**, and can also be self-hosted using HTTP Servers like Kestrel, **WebListener**, and **NGINX**.

IIS is one of the most feature-rich web servers and is often preferred for production scenarios because of the management capabilities and access to other pluggable IIS modules. Technically, IIS simply acts as a reverse proxy in the case of ASP.NET Core, and the actual process receiving the requests would be Kestrel. Kestrel is a cross-platform web server based on **libuv**, a multi-platform asynchronous library. Kestrel is designed to run behind a proxy like IIS or NGINX, and should not be used to directly host ASP.NET Core or any other application in production environments. On a Windows-like platform including Windows Server Core, the ASP.NET Core module assists IIS in forwarding the requests to Kestrel for processing.

ASP.NET Core is also cross-platform and runs on Linux and macOS as well. If you are using Linux for hosting ASP.NET applications, NGINX can be used to act as the reverse proxy. NGINX is a free open-source, high performance HTTP server and reverse proxy, as well as an IMAP/POP3 proxy server.

Windows Server Containers can host ASP.NET Core in a variety of ways: you can run the application using just the **Kestrel server** or install IIS and ASP.NET Core module for IIS which acts as the reverse proxy for Kestrel server. We can also use NGINX in place of IIS. NGINX also works as load balancer, which can be configured to balance loads between multiple containers running identical applications.

Developing an ASP.NET Core application

The remainder of this chapter will teach you how to deploy the ASP.NET Core application as a Windows Server Container. The sample application that we will be using in this chapter is called *Music Store*. It teaches you how to convert an ASP.NET Core application into a Docker image by applying custom PowerShell scripts for building, publishing, and integrating them with Visual Studio so that application development and testing become seamless. In our example, we will be using a Kestrel server to host the application inside the container. The later chapters describe the steps for integration with code repositories like the **Visual Studio Team Services** (**VSTS**) system, which comes with great automation features like continuous integration and deployment. VSTS helps publish the image to Docker Hub and onto dev, test, or **user acceptance testing** (**UAT**) environments automatically as and when any modifications are made by the developer team to the central code repository.

 Microsoft has also released an extension to Visual Studio Tools for Docker which is used to build, run and deploy .NET Core applications as Docker containers on a Windows platform. At the time of writing this extension only supports Linux-based Docker images or containers. In the future we should be able to use the same tool to build any application and run it as a Linux/Windows Container based on the configuration.

The Music Store application

In this chapter, we will be building our sample using the ASP.NET Core sample application called *Music Store*. The *Music Store* is a website which can be used to buy music albums, users can sort or filter the albums, add them to the shopping card, and check out once done. Since Windows Server Container is an application hosting platform, the focus will be on converting the application to be hosted in a Windows Server Container (or even in a Hyper-V Container in the later chapters). Regardless of the applications features, the following steps can be replicated for any ASP.NET Core template to deploy as a Windows Server Container. The following image shows the **Music Store** home page:

Deploying ASP.NET Core application as Windows Server Container

The following steps describe how to add Docker/Windows Server Container features to the *Music Store* application so that it can deployed as a Windows Server Container. We are going to use ASP.NET Core extensibility features for building the image, creating a container, and publishing to Docker Hub by using the PowerShell scripts and Dockerfile:

1. From any desktop, login to the Windows Server 2016 Azure VM, `mstsc.exe`, we created in the earlier chapter using Remote Desktop, or create a new one as per the instructions provided in previous chapters.

2. Download the *Music Store* Visual Studio solution from GitHub at `https://github.com/vishwanathsrikanth/learningwsc`.

3. Click on **Clone** or **Download** on GitHub and then click on **Download Zip** to download a ZIP file by name `learningwsc-master.zip`.

4. Extract the downloaded ZIP file to `C:\`.

5. Copy the *Music Store* start template from `c:\learningwsc-master\chapter4\begin\aspnetcore` to `c:\samples\aspnetcore`.

6. Open VS 2015 Community or Enterprise Edition as administrator. Ensure the development environment is setup as per the instructions in the *Setting up the development environment* section on Windows Server 2016.

7. On Visual Studio, click on **File** | **Open** | **Project/Solution....**

8. Navigate to `C:\samples\aspnetcore` and select `MusicStore.sln` and then click **OK** to load the solution.

 Ignore any security warnings and press **OK**

9. Visual Studio will start restoring the packages as configured in `package.config` once the solution is opened. Wait for **Package Restore** to complete.

10. After package restore is completed, build the solution using *Ctrl + Shift + B* or by clicking on **Build** and then **Build Solution**.

11. Ensure the build is successful.

12. You can test the application by hitting *Ctrl + F5*, you should see the home page running on a random port as shown in the following screenshot:

Dockerizing the application

Now let's containerize our application by adding some additional files and modifying the ASP.NET Core build and publishing process:

1. As the first step, right-click on the `MusicStore` web project and navigate to **Add | New Folder**, name it `Docker`. This folder will hold all the artifacts which provide the necessary support for converting the application into a Windows Server Container.

2. Now add a new file called `Dockerfile` to the project. Right-click on the `Docker` folder we just created, navigate to **Add | New Item....**

 A Dockerfile is a special type of file with no extension, which only the Docker daemon can understand. Docker daemon looks for this file for instructions while building an image.

3. Select any file type as shown in the following image, and type the file name as
   `Dockerfile`:

4. Once the file has been added to the solution, select the file and then select the
   renaming option to remove the extension from the file. `Dockerfile` with no
   extension is shown in the following image:

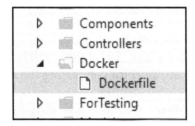

5. Copy and paste the following code in `Dockerfile`.

```
from microsoft/windowsservercore:latest
COPY ./Docker /Windows/Temp/Setups
RUN powershell -executionpolicy unrestricted
C:\Windows\Temp\Setups\Install-DotNetCore.ps1
WORKDIR /app
ENV ASPNETCORE_URLS http://*:80
EXPOSE 80
COPY ./publishoutput C:/app
```

Each step of `Dockerfile` is described after the code shown here and ordered by line numbers in ascending order:

1. Sets up the base OS image for the container. In this example, we will be using the Windows Server Core, tagged latest.
2. Copies the setup files from the `Docker` folder in the **VS studio solution** to the **Windows Server Container**.
3. Runs the custom PowerShell script which installs the .NET Core CLI and configures the **PATH** variables.
4. Sets up `c:/app` as the working directory.
5. Sets up an **Environmental Variable** for the Windows Server Container.
6. Exposes port `80` from the container.
7. Copies the binaries from ASP.NET Core publish path to `c:/app` on Windows Server Container.

6. Copy `Install-DotNetCore.ps1` from the extracted path `c:\learningwsc-master\chapter4\resources` to the `Docker` folder we just created from Visual Studio. Visual Studio will add the file to the solution automatically.

 As part of our `docker build` process `Install-DotNetCore.ps1` will be copied to the Docker container and invoked from within the container. The PowerShell script will then take care of installing the .NET Core runtime, CLI and SDK on to the new container.

7. The next step is to author the `DockerTask.ps1` script file which connects the ASP.NET Core code to the Windows Container building process. Right-click on the `Docker` folder and say **add new item**.
8. Name the file `DockerTask.ps1` and Click **Add**.

9. Add the following code at the top of the `DockerTask.ps1`. The following PowerShell parameters act as the switches to the common script which will be used for **Build**, **Clean** and **Run** (*F5*) actions from Visual Studio. There are also few parameters with default values which will be used in the image building process:

```
param
(
#This switch builds the Windows Container Image
[switch]$Build,
#This switch removes all the containers created if
any using the Windows Container Image created using
the build option 'MusicStore' in this case.
[switch]$Clean,
#This switch creates a container
[switch]$Run,
#This switch pushes the image to docker hub
[switch]$Publish,
[ValidateNotNullOrEmpty()]
#ProjectName will be used to create image name
[string]$ProjectName = "musicstore",
#Host Port which should be mapped to the container port
[ValidateNotNullOrEmpty()]
[String]$HostPort = 80,
#Container Port which maps to the Host Port
[ValidateNotNullOrEmpty()]
[String]$ContainerPort = 80,
[ValidateNotNullOrEmpty()]
#Project configuration Release/Debug
[String]$Configuration = "Debug" ,
[ValidateNotNullOrEmpty()]
#MusicStore image version
[String]$Version = "1.0.0" ,
[ValidateNotNullOrEmpty()]
#DockerHub Username
[String]$Username= "learningwsc",
[ValidateNotNullOrEmpty()]
#DockerHub Password
[String]$Password = "*************"
)
```

10. Add the following line to `DockerTask.ps1` to stop running the script in the case of errors.

    $ErrorActionPreference = "Stop"

11. Add the following function to the `DockerTask.ps1`. The following PowerShell function takes care of publishing the ASP.NET Core application and creates a Windows Server Container image using the published binaries and other resources like HTML, JS and CSS files. Intermediate containers are cached and reused so repeated builds will use the cached containers. This is only for a few Docker command; for example, `Docker COPY` command is never cached.

```
function Build(){
    #Publish music store to folder
    dotnet.exe publish --framework netcoreapp1.0
    --configuration $Configuration --output
    /samples/aspnetcore/musicstore/publishoutput
    --no-build
    #Build Docker Image
    docker build -t $ImageName&grave;:$Version
    -f ./Docker/Dockerfile .
}
```

12. Add the following PowerShell function to the `DockerTask.ps1`. This `helper` function creates a new container on hitting *Ctrl + F5* from Visual Studio. It also checks if there are any containers running on port `80` (we are using port `80` to host our application, but it can be any other port which is not blocked by the host's firewall). If there are any containers already using port `80` they should be stopped because the host's port cannot be shared across multiple containers.

    In this `helper` function, we will also be tagging our image using the `$Version` variable passed as part of the running the script. The default value will be `1.0.0` in our example:

```
function Run()
{
#Get Containers running on Port 80
$conflictingContainerIds = $(docker ps -a |
    select-string -pattern ":$HostPort|" | foreach
    { Write-Output $_.Line.split()[0] })

    #Stopping Containers running on Port 80
    if ($conflictingContainerIds) {
        $conflictingContainerIds = $conflictingContainerIds
        -Join ' '
```

```
Write-Host "Stopping conflicting containers using
port $HostPort"
docker stop $conflictingContainerIds
}

#Creates a Music Store Container
docker run -p $HostPort&grave;:$ContainerPort
$ImageName&grave;
:$Version dotnet musicstore.dll
}
```

13. Docker smartly updates the image if it finds one with the same name while building and image, but cleaning images is always a good practice. If you want to clean all the existing images before creating a new one on every build, the following `helper` function can be used. In this function, we will be using PowerShell regular expression features to identify and remove all the images that match the regular expression created using the image name. This helps in removing all the versions of the images. Copy the following function to `DockerTask.ps1`:

```
function Clean(){
#Regex for image name
$ImageNameRegEx = "\b$ImageName\b"
    #Removes all images with name matching the
    ImageNameRegEx, Ex: musicstore
    docker images | select-string -pattern $ImageNameRegEx |
    foreach {
        $imageName = $_.Line.split(" ",
        [System.StringSplitOptions]::RemoveEmptyEntries)[0];
        $tag = $_.Line.split(" ",
        [System.StringSplitOptions]::RemoveEmptyEntries)[1];
        Write-Host "Removing image ${imageName}:$tag";
        docker rmi ${imageName}:$tag --force
    }
}
```

14. Once we are done developing and testing the application we want to publish to the Docker Hub. The following `helper` function helps the login to the Docker Hub and publish the image using the `$version` variable we passed as an argument. Copy the following helper function to `DockerTask.ps1`:

```
function Publish(){

#Login to Docker Hub
docker login --username $username --password $password
#Push the image to docker hub
docker push $ImageName&grave;:$Version
}
```

15. To use the dotnet CLI and Docker commands on the Windows Container we need to set up a few environmental variables. The following script will set the required environmental variables for the `PATH` variable inside the container. Add the following script below the helper functions:

```
$env:Path = ".\node_modules.\bin;%PATH%;C:\Program
Files\dotnet;"
```

16. The following script initializes the image name in `dockerid/imagename` format. This format is necessary while publishing the image to the Docker Hub. Add the following script to `DockerTask.ps1` file:

```
$ImageName = "learningwsc/${ProjectName}".ToLowerInvariant()
```

17. Finally add the following script which will invoke the `helper` function based on the flag passed:

```
if($Build) {
    Build
}
if($Run){
    Run
}
if($Clean){
    Clean
}
if($Publish){
    Publish
}
```

Connecting the dots

Up to this point we have created three individual files called `Dockerfile`,
`DockerTask.ps1,` and `Install-DotNetCore.ps1`. The following steps connect these files
with the Visual Studio build and publish process:

1. Open `project.json` from the `MusicStore` project and add the following line
   under the scripts section. This line invokes the `DockerTask.ps1` with a build
   flag after successful compilation. It extends the Visual Studio build step to create
   a Docker image using the Windows Server Core base OS image every time the
   project is successfully compiled:

   ```
   "postcompile": [ "powershell ./Docker/DockerTask.ps1
   -Build -ProjectName '%project:Name%' -Configuration
   '%compile:Configuration%' -Version '1.0.0'" ]
   ```

    This could be a time-consuming process: even though the Docker daemon
   caches only a few containers, it must run a few steps from the Dockerfile
   every time the solution is built. Since this is just a configuration you can
   unplug this while the application is in development and plug it back in
   once you are ready to build the image.

2. Remove the following line from `project.json`, we will not be using the default
   publishing process in this example.

   ```
   "postpublish": [ "dotnet publish-iis --publish-folder
   %publish:OutputPath% --framework %publish:
   FullTargetFramework%" ]
   ```

3. The next step is to configure Visual Studio debug so that Docker daemon creates
   a container using the `MusicStore` image. Perform the following set of steps to
   configure **Debug** and **Run**:
   1. Right-click the `MusicStore` project and click on **Properties**.
   2. Click on the **Debug** option.
   3. Click **New Profile**.
   4. Enter `Docker` as name in **Profile** and Click **OK**.
   5. Ensure **Executable** is selected as the launch option.
   6. Copy the path of the PowerShell command line in the executable
      section as shown in the following code:

   ```
   C:\Windows\System32\WindowsPowerShell\v1.0\powershell.exe
   ```

4. Copy the following code to the **Application Arguments** section:

```
-ExecutionPolicy Unrestricted  ./Docker/DockerTask.ps1 -Run
```

The arguments invoke the `DockerTask PowerShell` script with a `Run` flag every time the application is run:

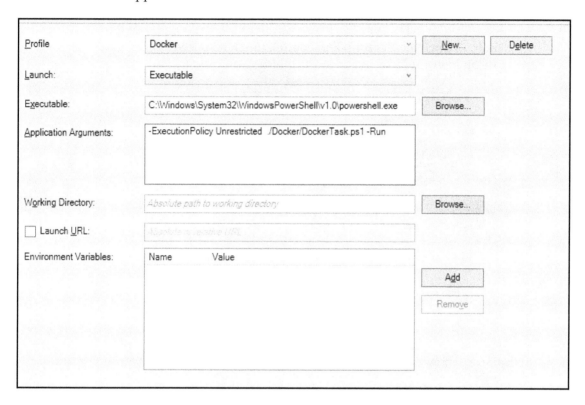

Test and run on a developer machine

With the preceding settings, we have configured the application to build and run as Windows Server Container. Let us start testing the application from Visual Studio using the following steps:

1. **Building image**: Press *Ctrl + Shift + B* or click on **Build | Build Solution** from Visual Studio to build the solution. Observer the build log from the build output window. Once the clean-up and compilation has successfully completed, the post-build event kicks in and starts building our image:

```
Step 1 : FROM microsoft/windowsservercore:TP5
 ---> 02cb7f65d61b
Step 2 : COPY ./Docker /Windows/Temp/Setups
 ---> debb938e7e21
Removing intermediate container ebe51418a7f8
Step 3 : RUN powershell -executionpolicy unrestricted C:\Windows\Temp\Setups\Install-DotNetCore.ps1
 ---> Running in 2c4c427d6f64
dotnet-install: Downloading https://dotnetcli.azureedge.net/dotnet/Sdk/1.0.0-preview3-003786/dotnet-dev-win-x64.1.0.0-preview3-003786.zip
dotnet-install: Extracting zip from https://dotnetcli.azureedge.net/dotnet/Sdk/1.0.0-preview3-003786/dotnet-dev-win-x64.1.0.0-preview3-003786.zip
dotnet-install: Adding to current process PATH: "C:\Users\ContainerAdministrator\AppData\Local\Microsoft\dotnet\". Note: This change will not be v:
dotnet-install: Installation finished
 ---> 6c33b0fcf2e7
Removing intermediate container 2c4c427d6f64
Step 4 : WORKDIR /app
 ---> Running in bef37f5f5266
 ---> eaf528c5bea4
Removing intermediate container bef37f5f5266
Step 5 : ENV ASPNETCORE_URLS http://*:80
 ---> Running in 04401140c7e7
 ---> 61bc0fbd9963
Removing intermediate container 04401140c7e7
Step 6 : EXPOSE 80
 ---> Running in 5d8332233b37
 ---> 6eab0d9bb759
Removing intermediate container 5d8332233b37
Step 7 : COPY ./publishoutput C:/app
 ---> c54f3cea4fff
Removing intermediate container 6e04eae6dce8
Successfully built c54f3cea4fff
:\samples\aspnetcore\musicstore\Controllers\ManageController.cs(129,42): warning CS1998: This async method lacks 'await' operators and will run syn
Compilation succeeded.
    1 Warning(s)
    0 Error(s)
```

Ensure the image is built successfully. Check that the `MusicStore` Docker image is successfully built by running Docker images command as shown in the following screenshot:

```
PS C:\Windows\system32> docker images
REPOSITORY                    TAG              IMAGE ID
learningwsc/musicstore        1.0.0            c54f3cea4fff
```

2. **Create container**: Ensure `Docker` profile is selected in the **Run** option as shown in the following screenshot:

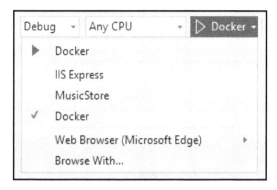

Press *Ctrl* + *F5*:

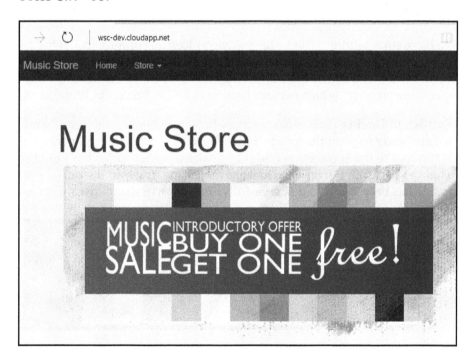

Ensure port 80 is accessible on the container host. Since I was using an Azure VM in this exercise, I added an endpoint on the VM.

Finally, you should see that a PowerShell window opens with the following log asserting the application is up and running on port 80. The portal should be accessible on port 80, `wsc-dev.cloudapp.net` in my case:

```
Administrator: C:\Windows\System32\WindowsPowerShell\v1.0\powershell.exe
Hosting environment: Production
Content root path: C:\app
Now listening on: http://*:80
Application started. Press Ctrl+C to shut down.
```

We have successfully hosted *Music Store* on Kestrel running in a Windows Server Container. Remember, we haven't add any persistent storage or database capabilities to our *Music Store* application. We'll extend the features in the upcoming chapters which explain how to run SQL Server on Windows Container.

3. **Publish to Docker Hub**: Since we now have a Docker image tested and verified, we are ready to push the image to the Docker Hub. Use the following command at the root of the application folder to push the image to the Docker Hub account. This can be verified from the Docker Hub by logging into the portal once the image has been published successfully, as shown in the following screenshot:

```
PS C:\samples\aspnetcore\musicstore> .\Docker\DockerTask.ps1 -Publish
Login Succeeded
The push refers to a repository [docker.io/learningwsc/musicstore]
f5da4334e939: Pushed
32bd2b5a4763: Pushed
43436561ec91: Pushed
8650a42f91e2: Pushed
ac80bc6eb0f5: Pushed
3f6e77b42e20: Pushed
72f30322e86c: Skipped foreign layer
1.0.0: digest: sha256:418a2a1000aae34ba04e2c224f932484a49c0633b841c97e018cb3966222b12b size: 1927
```

The completed version of this sample can be downloaded from here: `https://github.com` `/vishwanathsrikanth/learningwsc/tree/master/chapter4/completed/aspnetcore.`

Hosting ASP.NET Core on IIS in Windows Server Container

Traditionally, web applications are always hosted on fully fledged web servers like IIS. Though we could launch *Music Store* using self-hosting and Kestrel web server, this would not be an ideal scenario in production environments. IIS is a full-blown web-server which comes with many additional features like PowerShell support, web module plugins, custom handlers, a certificate manager, and so on. Since Windows Server core is a non-GUI OS, a strong PowerShell skillset is also necessary for performing operations like creating application pools, applying access restrictions, monitoring, restarting app pools or web applications, and so on.

The following brief steps should be used for hosting an ASP.NET Core website on IIS:

1. Install IIS web server.
2. Install the ASP.NET Core web Server hosting.
3. Configure ASP.NET Core to use IIS.
4. Configure .NET Core CLI and class paths for IIS to invoke the process.

Technically IIS acts as a reverse-proxy between the application and Kestrel server. When a request comes for an application to IIS, IIS just forwards the request to a Kestrel process which is hosting the application. This is taken care of by the new module called ASP.NET Core module which is present in the `web.config`, and therefore it is always necessary to place `web.config` with the following instructions at the root path of the application when hosted on IIS:

```
<configuration>
  <system.webServer>
    <handlers>
      <add name="aspNetCore" path="*" verb="*"
      modules="AspNetCoreModule" resourceType="Unspecified" />
    </handlers>
    <aspNetCore processPath="dotnet" arguments=".\musicstore.dlls"
    stdoutLogEnabled="false" stdoutLogFile=".\logs\stdout"
    forwardWindowsAuthToken="false" />
  </system.webServer>
</configuration>
```

The following Dockerfile contents help run the `MusicStore` application on IIS running inside a Windows Server Container. Now try to integrate this into the existing *Music Store* solution (as we did for the Kestrel server) to clean, build and run the application from Visual Studio:

```
FROM microsoft/windowsservercore:TP5

COPY ./Docker/Setups /Windows/Temp/Setups

COPY ./publishoutput C:/inetpub/wwwroot

ENV ASPNETCORE_URLS http://*:80

EXPOSE 80s

RUN powershell -Command Add-WindowsFeature Web-Server

RUN powershell -executionpolicy unrestricted
C:\Windows\Temp\Setups\Install-DotNetCore.ps1

RUN powershell -Command C:\Windows\Temp\Setups\DotNetCore.1.0.0
-WindowsHosting.exe -quiet
RUN powershell -Command C:\Windows\Temp\Setups\vc_redist.x64.exe
-quiet

RUN powershell -executionpolicy unrestricted
C:\Windows\Temp\Setups\Configure-IIS.ps1

WORKDIR /inetpub/wwwroot
```

Developing ASP.NET 4.5 applications as Windows Server Containers

In the earlier section, we learned how to run an ASP.NET Core application on Kestrel, packaged and deployed as a Windows Server Container image. In this section, we will be converting an existing ASP.NET 4.5 application as a Windows Server Container package which runs on IIS within the windows server core:

1. Let us start with creating a basic ASP.NET 4.5 MVC application on Visual Studio 2015. Click on **File** | **New** | **Project** or *Ctrl + Shift + N* from keyboard to create a new project.

2. Select ASP.NET Web Application (.NET Framework) template. Ensure **.NET Framework 4.5.2** is selected on the framework section on top. Click **OK**.

3. Select `c:\samples\aspnet4.5\` as the location for storing the project artifacts. Let us also name the project as `WindowsContainerSample`:

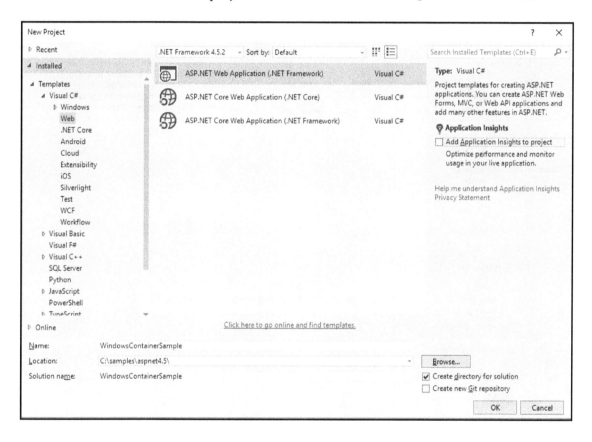

4. Select **MVC** template from **ASP.NET 4.5.2 Templates**. Click on **Change Authentication** and select **No Authentication.** Click **OK** on the **Change Authentication** window and then click **OK** on the template selection window:

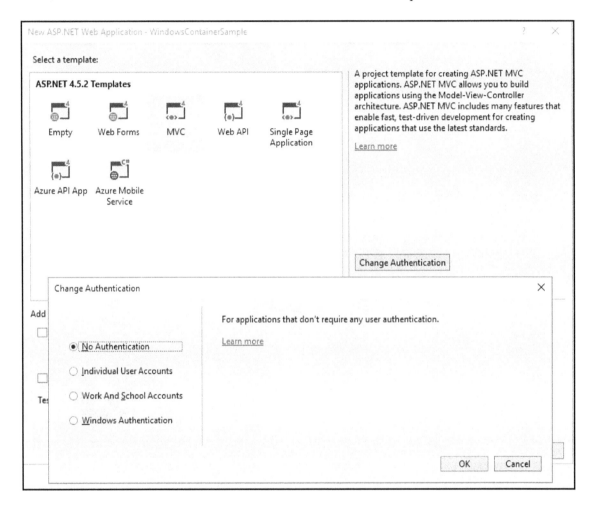

5. Ensure the application builds successfully by pressing *Ctrl + Shift + B*.
6. Ensure the application runs successfully on IIS Express by pressing *Ctrl + F5*.

Dockerizing ASP.NET 4.5 Web Application

Now let us now add Docker features to the application to run it on a Windows Server Container:

1. First, publish the application to file system. Right-click on the **Project** and click **Publish**.
2. Name the **Profile** field as `publish-iis` and then click **OK**.
3. Select the **Publish method** as **File System** and **Target location** as shown in the following image. We will be using the published binaries to build our Windows Container image:

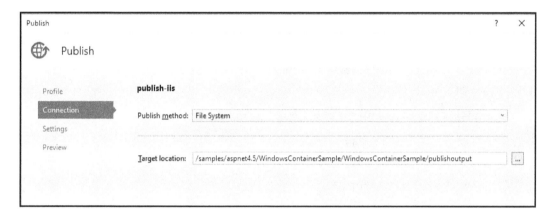

4. In the next window select **Release** in **Configuration:** and click **Publish**. Check that publish is successful.
5. Right-click on the project and add a new folder called `Docker`.
6. Let us add a new file to the `Docker` folder and call it `Dockerfile`.
7. Copy the following contents on to the `Dockferfile`. Since our intention is to deploy the ASP.NET application on IIS, we will be using `Microsoft/iis latest` as the base OS version which comes with IIS pre-installed:

```
FROM microsoft/iis:latest
SHELL ["powershell"]
RUN Install-WindowsFeature NET-Framework-45-ASPNET
RUN Install-WindowsFeature Web-Asp-Net45
COPY ./publishoutput c:/inetpub/wwwroot
EXPOSE 80
CMD Write-Host IIS Started....; \
    While ($true) { Start-Sleep -Seconds 3600 }
```

8. Add another new file to the Docker folder and name it `DockerTask.ps1`. The structure of the application should look like the following. Copy the following contents to the `DockerTask.ps1`. The code contains helper functions for cleaning, building and running the Windows Container image:

```
param
(
#This switch builds the Windows Container Image
[switch]$Build,
#This switch removes all the containers created if any
using the Windows Container Image created using the build option
'MusicStore' in this case.
[switch]$Clean,

#This switch creates a container
[switch]$Run,

#This switch publishes the image to docker hub
[switch]$Publish,

[ValidateNotNullOrEmpty()]
#ProjectName will be used to create image name
[string]$ProjectName = "aspnet45_windowscontainer",

#Host Port which should be mapped to the container port
[ValidateNotNullOrEmpty()]
[String]$HostPort = 80,

#Container Port which maps to the Host Port
[ValidateNotNullOrEmpty()]
[String]$ContainerPort = 80,

[ValidateNotNullOrEmpty()]
#MusicStore image version
[String]$Version = "1.0.0" ,

[ValidateNotNullOrEmpty()]
#DockerHub Username
[String]$Username= "learningwsc",

[ValidateNotNullOrEmpty()]
#DockerHub Password
[String]$Password = "Password@123"
)

$ErrorActionPreference = "Stop"
```

```
function Build(){
    #Build Docker Image
    docker build -t $ImageName&grave;:$Version -f
    ./Docker/Dockerfile .
}

function Run()
{
    #Get Containers running on Port 80
    $conflictingContainerIds = $(docker ps -a |
    select-string -pattern ":$HostPort|" | foreach
    { Write-Output $_.Line.split()[0] })

    #Stopping Containers running on Port 80
    if ($conflictingContainerIds) {
        $conflictingContainerIds = $conflictingContainerIds
        -Join ' '
        Write-Host "Stopping conflicting containers using
        port $HostPort" docker stop $conflictingContainerIds
    }

    #Creates a Music Store Container
    docker run -p $HostPort&grave;:$ContainerPort
    $ImageName&grave;:$Version
}

function Clean(){
    #Regex for image name
    $ImageNameRegEx = "\b$ImageName\b"

    #Removes all images with name matching the ImageNameRegEx,
    Ex: musicstore
    docker images | select-string -pattern $ImageNameRegEx |
    foreach {
        $imageName = $_.Line.split(" ",
        [System.StringSplitOptions]::RemoveEmptyEntries)[0];
        $tag = $_.Line.split(" ",
        [System.StringSplitOptions]::RemoveEmptyEntries)[1];
        Write-Host "Removing image ${imageName}:$tag";
        docker rmi ${imageName}:$tag --force
    }
}

function Publish(){
    #Login to Docker Hub
    docker login --username $username --password $password
    #Push the image to docker hub
    docker push $ImageName&grave;:$Version
```

```
}

$ImageName = "learningwsc/${ProjectName}".ToLowerInvariant()

if($Build) {
    Build
}
if($Run){
    Run
}
if($Clean){
    Clean
}
if($Publish){
    Publish
}
```

Connecting the dots

Now you can plug in the clean, build and run steps of the ASP.NET 4.5 application to Visual Studio's build process as we did earlier for ASP.NET Core; or you can also call the script directly from PowerShell as shown in the following steps:

1. **Building the image**: Run the following command at the application root to build a Windows Container image which can host ASP.NET 4.5 application:

   ```
   .\Docker\DockerTask.ps1 –Build
   ```

The output should be as shown in the following screenshot:

```
PS C:\samples\aspnet4.5\WindowsContainerSample\WindowsContainerSample> .\Docker\DockerTask.ps1 -Build
Sending build context to Docker daemon  16.7 MB
Step 1 : FROM microsoft/iis:TP5
TP5: Pulling from microsoft/iis

1239394e5a8a: Already exists
847199668046: Pull complete
4b1361d2706f: Pull complete
Digest: sha256:1d64cc22fbc56abc96e4b7df1b51e6f91b0da1941aa155f545f14dd76ac522fc
Status: Downloaded newer image for microsoft/iis:TP5
 ---> accd044753c1
Step 2 : SHELL powershell
 ---> Running in 17a50d506c76
 ---> d2a87685abcb
Removing intermediate container 17a50d506c76
Step 3 : RUN Install-WindowsFeature NET-Framework-45-ASPNET
 ---> Running in 9dfeb54c47cd

Success Restart Needed Exit Code    Feature Result
------- -------------- ---------    --------------
True    No             Success      {ASP.NET 4.6}


 ---> 33aa62f9d7bd
Removing intermediate container 9dfeb54c47cd
Step 4 : RUN Install-WindowsFeature Web-Asp-Net45
 ---> Running in 48db28a9153e

Success Restart Needed Exit Code    Feature Result
------- -------------- ---------    --------------
True    No             Success      {Application Development, ASP.NET 4.6,...


 ---> aa071c3a19fb
Removing intermediate container 48db28a9153e
Step 5 : COPY ./publishoutput c:/inetpub/wwwroot
 ---> f0b38ac030aa
Removing intermediate container 4b46a3026fdc
Step 6 : EXPOSE 80
 ---> Running in 3ace50f17e4e
 ---> 09a220c65187
```

Ensure the application image is built by running command `docker images`:

```
PS C:\samples\aspnet4.5\WindowsContainerSample\WindowsContainerSample> docker
REPOSITORY                              TAG        IMAGE ID
learningwsc/aspnet45_windowscontainer   1.0.0      0cabe60c8257
learningwsc/musicstore                  1.0.0      c54f3cea4fff
microsoft/iis                           TP5        accd044753c1
microsoft/windowsservercore             TP5        02cb7f65d61b
```

2. **Creating a container**: Run the following command at the application root to create a container:

```
.\Docker\DockerTask.ps1 -Run
```

The output should be as shown in the following screenshot:

```
PS C:\samples\aspnet4.5\WindowsContainerSample\WindowsContainerSample> .\Docker\DockerTask.ps1 -Run
IIS Started....
```

We can now browse the application using the DNS of the computer host on port
80:

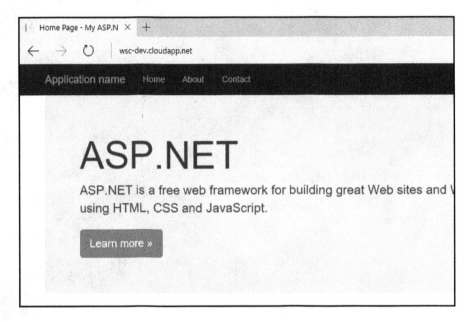

3. **Publishing to Docker Hub**: Now that we have our application running
   successfully, we can publish our image to the Docker Hub for distribution by
   running the following command:

   ```
   .\Docker\DockerTask.ps1 -Publish
   ```

The output should be as shown in the following screenshot:

```
PS C:\samples\aspnet4.5\WindowsContainerSample\WindowsContainerSample> .\Docker\DockerTask.ps1 -Publish
Login Succeeded
The push refers to a repository [docker.io/learningwsc/aspnet45_windowscontainer]
6df6eb65c1e4: Pushed
0ef837921e42: Pushed
b77f38540b81: Pushed
9f9d16165748: Pushed
b07214180e40: Pushed
6f6d305efeaa: Pushed
fbb9343bb390: Layer already exists
23adcc284270: Layer already exists
72f30322e86c: Skipped foreign layer
1.0.0: digest: sha256:9ce6da7dd563f3c1686b0f221ce4e6aacf9a30d1303fdabb2930a909b24d2ed3 size: 2351
```

We can also see our application tagged as version 1.0.0 on the Docker Hub ready for distribution as shown in the following screenshot:

4. **Cleaning up the images**: Finally, when you want to clean all the existing images from the container host, run the command as shown in the following screenshot:

```
PS C:\samples\aspnet4.5\WindowsContainerSample\WindowsContainerSample> .\Docker\DockerTask.ps1 -Clean
Removing image learningwsc/aspnet45_windowscontainer:1.0.0
Untagged: learningwsc/aspnet45_windowscontainer:1.0.0
Untagged: learningwsc/aspnet45_windowscontainer@sha256:9ce6da7dd563f3c1686b0f221ce4e6aacf9a30d1303fdabb2930a909b24d2ed3
Deleted: sha256:0cabe60c825785ade717158b5dcdf4a740eeca3ce18268cb1e3e677fdbf776fc
Deleted: sha256:09a220c65187c3855804e35a4eb750d6ee231aee3aec811396c8111f53dc58b3
Deleted: sha256:f0b38ac030aaf9f1bb703843c2f21d2348382aaad5e9a4012b454c13e8e17eb1
Deleted: sha256:aa071c3a19fbf129a452a1990164945c069b1500aa1cb2bb84653a79f4a63790
Deleted: sha256:33aa62f9d7bd50190d2ea9775408082e9309a6763ab4995311e4886a8b99b91c
Deleted: sha256:d2a87685abcb7132d232e3f571f3b57aba1d56800f5ecffdcdedf4e3c61ccebb
```

The output should be as shown in the following screenshot:

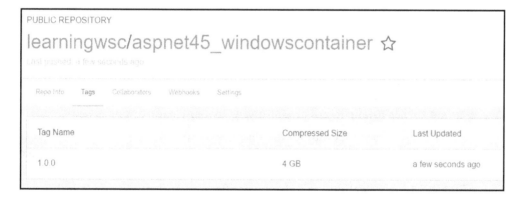

The completed version of this sample can be obtained from here: https://github.com/vis hwanathsrikanth/learningwsc/tree/master/chapter4/completed/aspnet4.5/Windows ContainerSample.

Windows Server Container networking

When we enabled containers and Docker features on Windows Server 2016, a default network is created which is called `nat` with IP prefix `172.16.0.0/12`. All the containers created inside the container host are created using this virtual network. Each of them have an adapter which is connected to a virtual switch over which inbound and outbound traffic is forwarded. Windows Server 2016, which comes with Docker daemon, might block you from creating new containers on a host and port even though there are no containers using the host's port. You might see an error similar to this:

```
C:\Program Files\Docker\docker.exe: Error response
from daemon: failed to create endpoint
condescending_albattani on net
work nat: HNS failed with error : Failed to create endpoint.
```

In such cases run the following script on the container host which resets the Docker's container network. We'll be discussing Windows Containers networking more in later chapters:

```
Stop-Service docker
Get-ContainerNetwork | Remove-ContainerNetwork -Force
Get-NetNat | Remove-NetNat
Get-VMSwitch | Remove-VMSwitch
Start-Service docker
```

Summary

We covered the following topics in this chapter:

- ASP.NET Core is a new version of the ASP.NET web application platform which is flexible, lean, open-sourced and cross-platform
- ASP.NET Core can be hosted using IIS, Kestrel or any HTTP Server
- The Windows Server Container development environment can only be set up on Windows Server 2016 because traditionally desktop OSes like Windows 10 do not support Windows Server Containers
- ASP.NET 4.5 applications can also be configured and run inside Windows Server Containers using IIS
- The container host's ports cannot be shared across multiple containers

- Visual Studio's ASP.NET Core template provides extensibility features for developers to plug in custom build and publish options which we can use to clean, build, and run Docker/Windows Container images
- All the containers created inside the container host are created using a virtual network called `nat`, and each container has an adapter which is connected to a virtual switch, over which inbound and outbound traffic is forwarded

5
Deploying Container Applications

In this chapter, we will learn to deploy containerized applications to Azure and on-premise environments remotely. The scripts authored in this chapter will be used to configure continuous integration and delivery pipelines in the next chapters. Windows-based container images have an additional privilege of being deployed as Windows Containers or Hyper-V Containers, and this is irrespective of how the container is built and published. This provides the great advantage of selecting the isolation level during deployment, and this chapter focuses on the process versus user isolation types, which are two different types of container deployments. As in the previous chapter, we will be using Microsoft Azure to provision Azure resources required for container deployment. Apart from the container deployment you will also learn to manage a container host from any client machine remotely, to secure the connection, and to automate the process of creating Azure resources.

The following topics will be discussed in this chapter:

- Deploying Windows Server 2016 VMs on Azure using ARM templates
- Configure remote management
- Enable remote connectivity for the Docker host
- Deploy the *Music Store* application remotely
- Configure the load balancer
- Deploy *Music Store* as Hyper-V Containers
- Manage dangling images

Deploy Azure VMs using ARM

For any organization to deliver software at a faster pace, infrastructure automation must be part of their delivery chain. Infrastructure automation provides the ability to create and configure the infrastructure required for deploying applications in a completely scripted manner. Azure provides abundant options to create and configure infrastructure for Windows and non-Windows platforms. **Azure Resource Manager** (**ARM**) is one such feature. ARM allows you to script the infrastructure and its configuration using the easily editable JSON schema. Using ARM, you can combine your infrastructure, which might consist of VM, storage, network resources and static/dynamic IP configuration, into a single entity. You can manage, tag, monitor and re-create the same environment anytime using ARM and Azure resource groups. For non-Windows users ARM-based deployments can be performed using Azure CLI. Azure CLI is a cross-platform command-line tool, and users can benefit from using the same commands from a Mac or Windows-based OS.

 Resources created using ARM templates will be visible only on the new Azure portal (`https://poral.azure.com`). The old portal (`https://manage.azure.com`) shows only non-ARM/classic resources.

The following sections explain how to create an Azure environment using ARM and Azure PowerShell for hosting our *Music Store* application:

1. To log in to Azure from client machines and to deploy using ARM templates, we need Azure PowerShell SDK. Download and install the latest Azure PowerShell SDK by navigating to the Azure downloads page at `https://azure.microsoft.com/en-in/downloads/` and click on **Windows Install** under the **Command-Lines** | **PowerShell** section.

2. Open **Windows Azure PowerShell client** as **Administrator** and ensure the Azure PowerShell is installed successfully by running the following command:

   ```
   Get-Module -ListAvailable
   ```

3. You should see the AzureRM module listed as shown in the following screenshot:

```
PS C:\WINDOWS\system32> Get-Module -ListAvailable


    Directory: C:\Program Files\WindowsPowerShell\Modules


ModuleType Version     Name
---------- -------     ----
Script     3.0.0       AzureRM
```

4. We need to login to Azure using our live/organization account which is associated with an Azure subscription. Once logged in we can perform all the actions against our subscription using Azure PowerShell.

   Login-AzureRMAccount

 The actions that can be performed on a subscription can be limited if the user is not an administrator on the subscription. Azure offers role-based access control, so ensure you have right permissions to create and manage resources.

5. Run the following command from Azure PowerShell CLI in administrator mode. This opens a browser based login window, login with your Azure account. You can download sample ARM template and PowerShell scripts from: `https://github.com/vishwanathsrikanth/learningwsc/tree/master/chapter5/resources/template`. To download you can either clone or download the complete repository from: `https://github.com/vishwanathsrikanth/learningwsc`.

6. Copy the templates folder to the `C:\learningwsc\chapter5\template` folder on your development machine.

7. Open the template using JSON editor like Visual Studio and notice the key configurations, which we've listed here:

   - The `template.json` file contains the following elements:
     - **Parameters**: The parameters section describes the datatype of each parameter which will be passed to the script as a separate file
     - **Variables**: This section holds the derived values
     - **Resources**: This section contains configuration for different types of resources created on Azure, and can be used for configuring VM properties, configuring network, endpoints, and storage accounts

- **Output**: Contains the values that will be flushed to the screen after successful run of the script

- The `parameters.json` file contains the values for all the parameters defined in the `template.json` file's parameters section

 Azure requires few resource values to be universally unique and adhere to the naming conventions or rules. The script can fail if the rules are violated or if the names are already taken. Users can check for availability of any resource name by checking the availability from the Azure Portal or by using `Test-*` PowerShell commands. For more information on commands, visit `https://msdn.microsoft.com/en-us/library/dn 757692.aspx`.

- The last file which is important here is `Deploy.ps1` which contains the PowerShell script for deploying the environment

8. Now that you know what each file is doing, run the following command to provision a Windows Server 2016 VM and other related Azure Resources. Before you run the following command ensure you are logged in to Azure by running the command shown in point 3:

    1. Open PowerShell Window as administrator.
    2. Navigate to `c:\learningwsc\chapter5\template`.
    3. Copy the following command onto the PowerShell window:

        ```
        .\deploy.ps1 -subscriptionId "<SubscriptionId>"
        -resourceGroupName "wschost-staging-rg"
        -resourceGroupLocation "southeastasia"
        -deploymentName "wschoststaging"
        -templateFilePath "C:\learningwsc\chapter5\
        template\template.json"
        -parametersFilePath "C:\learningwsc\chapter5\template\
        parameters.json"
        ```

    4. Replace the `<SubscriptionId>`.
    5. Optionally you can also update the values in `parameters.json`, which will be used as resource names in `template.json`.
    6. Hit *F5* or *Enter*.

9. Ensure the deployment is successful, by checking the output window or by logging into the Azure portal. To search from the Azure portal, login to `https://portal.azure.com` and search with the value passed in as a parameter for `resourceGroupName` passed.

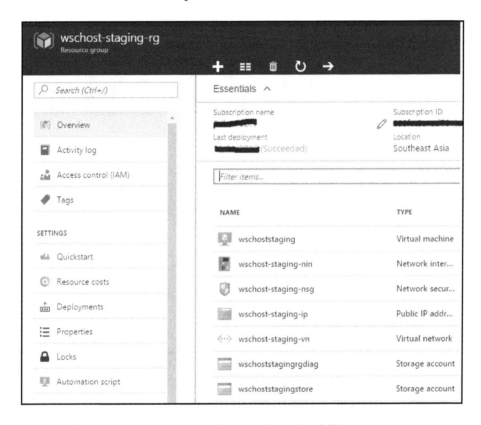

10. Ensure the deployment is intact by checking for following resources:

   - Azure VM with Windows Server 2016 as image
   - Network interface
   - Network security group
   - Public IP
   - Virtual network
   - Two storage accounts (one for diagnostics and the other for storing disks)

11. Click on the **Virtual Machine** row, this should open a new blade with VM details.

12. Notice the value for **Public IP address/DNS name label** as shown in the following screenshot. The value shows a public IP address, which by default is not static; a new IP will be assigned every time the machine is restarted. We can use the IP address mentioned here or else assign a DNS name which is a better practice. Click on the value to assign a DNS name:

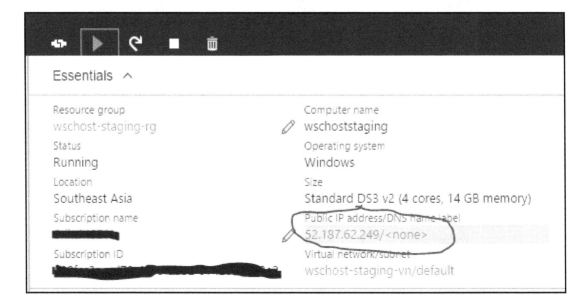

13. A new blade for **Public IP address** opens, click on **Configuration** option on the new blade and choose a DNS name as shown in the following screenshot:

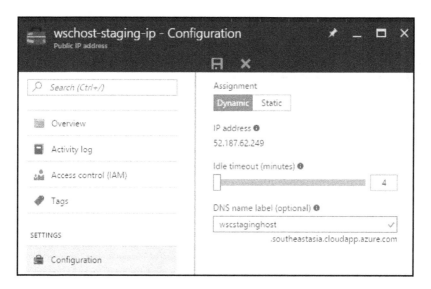

14. Click on **Save**.
15. (Optional) You can also assign a static IP to the machine (which comes at an additional cost) by clicking on the **Static** tab under the **Assignment** section.
16. Close the **Public IP address** blade.
17. Click on **Network Interface** on the **VM Settings** section and then click on the first row. This opens a new **Network Interface** blade. Ensure the following rules are configured by clicking on the **Effective security rules** section. These rules expose the containers and the Docker host running inside the host over a publicly reachable IP address or the DNS name that we've just configured:

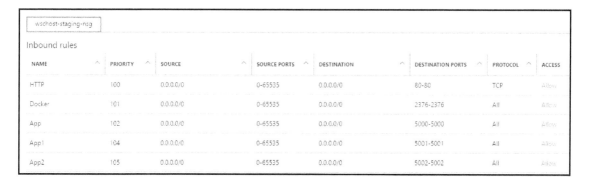

Inbound rules

NAME	PRIORITY	SOURCE	SOURCE PORTS	DESTINATION	DESTINATION PORTS	PROTOCOL	ACCESS
HTTP	100	0.0.0.0/0	0-65535	0.0.0.0/0	80-80	TCP	Allow
Docker	101	0.0.0.0/0	0-65535	0.0.0.0/0	2376-2376	All	Allow
App	102	0.0.0.0/0	0-65535	0.0.0.0/0	5000-5000	All	Allow
App1	104	0.0.0.0/0	0-65535	0.0.0.0/0	5001-5001	All	Allow
App2	105	0.0.0.0/0	0-65535	0.0.0.0/0	5002-5002	All	Allow

If the rules and configurations are as expected, we have successfully created our staging environment on Azure for hosting the *Music Store* application using ARM templates.

Configure VM for remote connectivity

The essence of a successful product delivery lies in automation; the amount of work that can be completely automated decides how much faster we can deliver. As part of automation we should certainly include configuration of resources, which include dependency installations, firewall or network port configuration, storage allocation, and so on. These factors shorten the time for delivery and ensure error-free code if tried and tested rigorously. Therefore, infrastructure automation is the epitome of success for any product delivery chain. With the above section, we have achieved some automation by being able to automatically create the required resources for our deployment. In this section, we will see how to remotely connect to those Azure VMs and enable remote PowerShell so that we can deploy *Music Store* onto a remote Docker host without establishing a remote desktop session which is a manual step.

Enabling remote PowerShell on Azure ARM VM is a multi-step process; it requires changes to the firewall and a self-signed certificate to be installed with the DNS name of the client from where we intend to connect. The following process uses the Azure custom VM extension process to upload a PowerShell script to an existing VM and run from inside the machine to enable remote PowerShell.

 Azure has two flavors of VMs called classic and ARM. Classic VM is an old-fashioned way of creating VMs using classic portal/PowerShell whilst using the ASM API for creating/updating resources. *Azure ARM* machines are resource group centric, each deployment is considered as a set of closely coupled resources. For more information on the difference visit (https://azure.microsoft.com/en-in/documentation/articles/resource-manager-deployment-model/).

The following set of steps enables remote PowerShell on ARM VM using Azure PowerShell:

1. Open PowerShell ISE as administrator.
2. Navigate to `c:\learningwsc\chapter5\template`.

3. Ensure you are logged-in to the subscription we used in the section above by running `Login-AzureRmAccount`.

4. Run the `Configure-RemotePS.ps1` by passing three arguments as described here:

   - `VMName`: Name of the VM we created above, and ensure the VM is in a running state.
   - `ResourceGroupName`: Name of resource group which includes the VM.
   - `StorageAccountName`: Azure storage account name which is co-located with VM. This account will be used to upload a PowerShell script which will eventually be run on the VM specified above. Ensure the storage account used here is a standard account, which allows block blob storage.

Next, let's look at a sample run. The following statements create a folder called *scripts* in the Azure storage account, passed in as parameter, and upload a PowerShell script named `ConfigureWinRM_HTTPS.ps1` which is in the same folder:

```
.\Configure-RemotePS.ps1 -VMName "wschoststaging"
-ResourceGroupName
"wschost-staging-rg" -StorageAccountName
"wschoststagingrgdiag"
```

`ConfigureWinRM_HTTPS` is then installed on the target machine using an Azure PowerShell command `Set-AzureRmVMCustomScriptExtension` with the client machine's host name as the DNS Name. Additionally, the script also creates a new endpoint on the Azure VM to allow traffic on the default remote PowerShell port `5986`. At the end of a successful run, the following message will be written to the console:

```
Enter-PSSession -ComputerName <IP-Address> -Credential
<admin_username> -UseSSL -SessionOption (New-PsSessionOption
-SkipCACheck - SkipCNCheck)
```

1. Copy the preceding command, click on **File** | **New** on the PowerShell ISE editor and paste the command onto the new window.
2. Replace the `<IP-Address>` with the public IP of your VM.
3. Press *F5* or Click **Run**.

4. You will see a Windows prompt, fill the username and password of the VM given while provisioning the VM (you can also check for username and password in `parameters.json` file) and Click **OK**.

You should now be able to run PowerShell scripts on a remote Azure VM without even establishing a remote desktop session. The PowerShell console window is now connected to a remote machine (`104.43.14.235` in my case) as shown in the following screenshot:

```
PS C:\WINDOWS\system32> Enter-PSSession -ComputerName 104.43.14.235 -Credential wscadmin -UseSSL -SessionOption (New-P
sSessionOption -SkipCACheck -SkipCNCheck)
[104.43.14.235]: PS C:\Users\wscadmin\Documents>
```

Configuring VM for remote connectivity is a onetime activity; you can connect to the machine anytime using the preceding command.

 Azure VM's IP changes every time the host is rebooted (if static IP is not configured), so ensure to use the latest IP while you are trying to connect using `Enter-PSSession`.

Configuring remote Docker host

In the previous chapters, we ran Docker commands by logging into the machine and by using docker daemon running on the local host. Docker daemon can also be configured to listen for remote clients. The client can be running on Windows or Linux machines. In a Windows environment , the Docker daemon process or runtime named `dockerd.exe` is installed by default at `C:\Program Files\docker\dockerd.exe`. Docker daemon can listen over TCP using secure and unsecured connections. The default port used by Docker daemon to listen over TCP is `2375`.

Running the following command on a remote PowerShell session connected to Azure VM will configure Docker daemon to listen on port `2375`:

```
dockerd.exe -H 0.0.0.0:2375
```

docker.pid

The `docker.pid` file stores the Windows process ID of the Docker daemon. When you try to host Docker daemon on port `2375` you might see an error as shown in the following screenshot:

As the error explains, `docker.pid` already exists which means `dockerd.exe` is already running on the host machine. To run the Docker daemon on a different port, the existing process should be killed or `docker.pid` file should be deleted. The following command deletes the `docker.pid` file from the default path:

```
Remove-Item C:\ProgramData\docker.pid -Force
```

We should also stop the `dockerd` process which is already running on a random port. Use the following command to find and stop the process forcibly:

```
Get-Process dockerd | Stop-Process -Force
```

Now the Docker daemon can be configured to listen on port 2375 by running the preceding command. The following log shows that dockerd is running on port 2375 and open for connections from remote clients. To stop the process from a Windows machine, press *Ctrl + C*:

```
[104.43.14.235]: PS C:\Users\wscadmin\Documents> dockerd.exe -H 0.0.0.0:2375
dockerd.exe : time="2016-11-03T06:43:46.4498863002" level=warning msg="[!] DON'T BIND ON ANY IP ADDRESS WITHOUT setting
-tlsverify
IF YOU DON'T KNOW WHAT YOU'RE DOING [!]"
    + CategoryInfo          : NotSpecified: (time="2016-11-0...'RE DOING [!]":String) [], RemoteException
    + FullyQualifiedErrorId : NativeCommandError
time="2016-11-03T06:43:46.4808872002" level=info msg="Windows default isolation mode: process"
time="2016-11-03T06:43:46.4808872002" level=info msg="[graphdriver] using prior storage driver: windowsfilter"
time="2016-11-03T06:43:46.5546002002" level=info msg="Graph migration to content addressability took 0.00 seconds"
time="2016-11-03T06:43:46.5546002002" level=info msg="Loading containers: start."
time="2016-11-03T06:43:46.5846004002" level=error msg="Resolver Setup/Start failed for container none, \"json: cannot u
nmarshal
array into Go value of type hcsshim.HNSNetwork\""
time="2016-11-03T06:43:46.7047882002" level=info msg="Loading containers: done."
time="2016-11-03T06:43:46.7047882002" level=info msg="Daemon has completed initialization"
time="2016-11-03T06:43:46.7047882002" level=info msg="Docker daemon" commit=050b611 graphdriver=windowsfilter
version=1.12.2-cs2-ws-beta
time="2016-11-03T06:43:46.7097850002" level=info msg="API listen on [::]:2375"
```

dockerd configuration options

dockerd runtime comes with configuration options which give you more control over the runtime and allows users to host it in different ways. A few options are described in this section. To apply the configuration options to dockerd, appended the option to command while invoking the process.

Debug

-D should be used along with dockerd command to enable debug mode. In debug mode, detailed host information is flushed to the default stream (console in our case) and daemon configuration values like max-concurrent-downloads, max-concurrent-uploads, DefaultNetwork, DefaultDriver, and so on are printed while the daemon is running and waiting for connections.

Usage: dockerd.exe -D

max-concurrent-downloads

Docker daemon is one runtime which acts as both client and server. `max-concurrent-downloads` restricts the number of downloads for each pull.

Usage: `dockerd.exe -max-concurrent-downloads=3`

max-concurrent-uploads

Like `max-concurrent-downloads`, `max-concurrent-uploads` restrict the number of concurrent uploads for each push. Configuring `max-concurrent-downloads` or `max-concurrent-downloads` to a lower number might create a bottle neck in large teams so the number should be chosen wisely.

Usage: `dockerd.exe -max-concurrent-uploads=5`

Host

`-H` or `-host` option is used to specify where the daemon will listen for connections. This option can be used to make the host Docker daemon listen on multiple ports as shown here:

Usage: `dockerd.exe -H 0.0.0.0:2375 -H 0.0.0.0:2376`

Security

The above-mentioned configuration options host the Docker daemon on an unsecured connection, any client with IP and credentials can connect to the host, but this is not a recommended option in production environments. The recommended approach for connecting to remote Docker hosts is using a secured connection using certificate-based authentication. Docker provides the following options for securing the connection using TLS. **Transport layer security** (**TLS**) can be used to secure remote connections to the container host. Docker provides an important flag called `tlsverify`. When this is set to `true` the daemon searches for a certificate in a default location. The default location of the certificates can also be managed by using option `tlscacert`. You can also use self-signed certificates if CA is not available. You can enable TLS by specifying `tlsverify` flag and pointing Docker's `tlscacert` flag to a trusted CA certificate (or self-signed certificate for test environments).

If `tlsverify` is set to `true`, the Docker daemon allows connections only from a client which contain the certificates signed by same CA (or same self-signed certificates installed on the host machine). If `tlsverify` is set to `true` on the client while connecting to a remote container host, the client can only connect to a container host which contains certificates signed by the same CA.

If Docker is started in daemon mode inside a container host, it accepts connections only from authorized clients, the authentication in this case happens using a certificate signed by same CA. In the client mode, the Docker client can only connect to the container hosts which contain the certificate issued by the same CA.

 Configuring Docker hosts using the TLS is an advanced topic and requires expert knowledge on OpenSSL, X.509 and TLS before using in a production environment. Microsoft has provided scripts that utilize OpenSSL to create self-signed keys and certificates for Docker on Windows. The scripts and the instructions are available at: `https://githu b.com/Microsoft/Virtualization-Documentation/blob/master/windo ws-server-container-tools/DockerTLS/readme.md`.

Deploying containers remotely

In the previous section, we learned to connect to a remote Azure machine and configured Docker to listen on a remote port. In this section, we will learn to deploy the *Music Store* application remotely and configure load balancing using a software based load balancer called NGINX by downloading the image from the Docker Hub.

Before we proceed, a `musicstore` Windows Container image needs to be published to the Docker Hub. The source code for this updated image is available under `chapter5/musicstore`. This sample contains a special feature which will be used to test the load balancer configuration. Open the solution using Visual Studio and build and publish to the Docker Hub. (Refer to `Chapter 4`, *Developing Container Applications*, on instructions to build and publish to the Docker Hub).

The following set of steps explain the process of deploying *Music Store* on a remote Docker host:

1. Create a new remote PowerShell session with remote Docker host by running the following command. Enter the host's password when prompted and press OK:

   ```
   Enter-PSSession -ComputerName 52.163.227.162 -Credential
   wscadmin -UseSSL -SessionOption (New-PsSessionOption
   -SkipCACheck -SkipCNCheck)
   ```

2. Once we are connected to the host, we must open a firewall port on the host machine so that the client's connections to port 2375 are blocked. Run the following command to unblock port 2375 on the host:

   ```
   New-NetFirewallRule -Name "Docker" -DisplayName "Docker"
   -Enabled True -Profile Any -Action Allow -Direction Inbound
   -LocalPort 2375 -Protocol TCP
   ```

3. Ensure the remote Docker host is in debug mode by running the following command on the host using remote PowerShell. Do not close this window:

   ```
   dockerd.exe -H 0.0.0.0:2375 -D
   ```

4. Open a new PowerShell window from your desktop machine and run the following command to get the installed images from the remote Docker host, which we configured in the preceding steps. Here we used the

   -H option to specify the remote IP and port details, while images is the actual command we wanted to run on the host:

```
PS C:\WINDOWS\system32> docker -H tcp://52.163.227.162:2375 images
REPOSITORY                      TAG              IMAGE ID        CREATED        SIZE
microsoft/windowsservercore     10.0.14393.321   93a9c37b36d0    6 weeks ago    8.675 GB
microsoft/windowsservercore     latest           93a9c37b36d0    6 weeks ago    8.675 GB
microsoft/nanoserver            10.0.14393.321   e14bc0ecea12    6 weeks ago    810.3 MB
microsoft/nanoserver            latest           e14bc0ecea12    6 weeks ago    810.3 MB
```

5. Specifying -H is not necessary every time we want to run commands on the remote host. We can configure the IP address of the remote host once and for all using the environmental variables. Run the following command to configure the remote host Docker should connect to. Remember, once the environment variable is set we will not be able to connect to the local Docker runtime:

```
$env:DOCKER_HOST = "tcp://52.163.227.162:2375"
Or
set DOCKER_HOST=tcp://52.163.227.162:2375
```

6. Now we can run Docker commands from client machine without using the -H option as shown in the following screenshot:

```
PS C:\WINDOWS\system32> docker info
Containers: 0
 Running: 0
 Paused: 0
 Stopped: 0
Images: 2
Server Version: 1.12.2-cs2-ws-beta
Storage Driver: windowsfilter
 Windows:
Logging Driver: json-file
Plugins:
 Volume: local
 Network: nat null overlay
Swarm: inactive
Security Options:
Kernel Version: 10.0 14393 (14393.321.amd64fre.rs1_
Operating System: Windows Server 2016 Datacenter
OSType: windows
Architecture: x86_64
CPUs: 4
Total Memory: 14 GiB
```

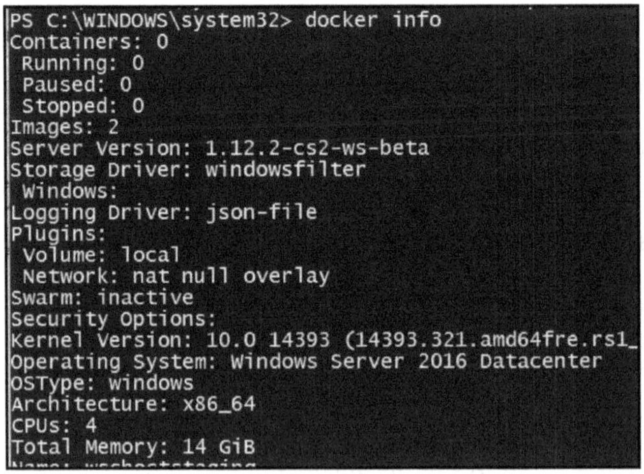

7. Run the following command to pull the musicstore container image onto the remote host:

```
docker pull learningwsc/musicstore:1.0.0
```

8. Run the following command to create a new container using the musicstore image inside the remote Docker host:

```
docker run --name musicstore -d -p 80:80
learningwsc/musicstore:1.0.0 dotnet musicstore.dll
```

9. We should be able to see the home page of the *Music Store* application by browsing the site by IP or DNS name as shown in the following screenshot:

Configuring load balancer

Running a single instance of an application does not guarantee availability. To maximize availability and provide best performance to our users we should be able to easily scale our applications. In this section, we will use an NGINX server to configure load balancing among multiple *Music Store* containers:

1. On the Azure Portal, click on the IP address to assign a custom DNS name to the remote host. We will use this DNS name to configure load balancer endpoints.

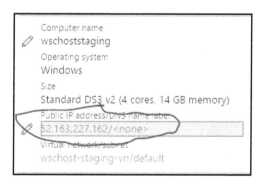

2. Click on **Configuration** on the **Public IP address** section.

3. Assign your favorite name in the **DNS name label (optional)** section and click on **Save** as shown in the following screenshot:

4. Let us create a new NGINX Windows Container image from the development environment and publish it to Docker Hub. The resources for creating NGINX images are available under `chapter5/resources/musicstore-nginx-azure`. There are two files that we will be using here: Dockerfile contains the instructions to install NGINX on a windows server core-based image; and the `nginx.conf` file contains the configuration options for the NGINX server.

5. Open the `nginx.conf` file and replace the string `<dnsnamehere>` with the DNS name chosen above. The resulting file should look like following:

```
events {
  worker_connections 1024;
}

http {
    upstream myapp1 {
        least_conn;
        server wsc-hosting.southeastasia.cloudapp.
        azure.com:5000;
        server wsc-hosting.southeastasia.cloudapp.
        azure.com:5001;
        server wsc-hosting.southeastasia.cloudapp.
        azure.com:5002;
    }
```

```
server {
    listen 80;
    server_name wsc-hosting.southeastasia.cloudapp.
    azure.com;
    location / {
      proxy_pass http://myapp1;
    }
  }
}
```

6. On the developer machine open a new **PowerShell** window, navigate to chapter5/resources and run the following command to create an NGINX image:

```
docker build -t learningwsc/nginx:1.0.0 .
```

7. Let us now push the image to the Docker Hub with the following command so that we can use it in our staging environment:

```
docker login --username learningwsc --password ******
docker push learningwsc/nginx:1.0.0
```

8. Before configuring the NGINX container on the staging environment, we create three containers of musicstore on ports 5000, 5001, and 5002. The endpoints for the above-mentioned ports are created on the staging environment as part of the ARM template. Run the following commands one-by-one to create three containers of musicstore each hosted on a different port:

```
docker run --name musicstore-1 -d -p 5000:80
learningwsc/musicstore:1.0.0 dotnet musicstore.dll
docker run --name musicstore-2 -d -p 5001:80
learningwsc/musicstore:1.0.0 dotnet musicstore.dll
docker run --name musicstore-3 -d -p 5002:80
learningwsc/musicstore:1.0.0 dotnet musicstore.dll
```

9. Ensure the containers are running by running the following command:

```
docker ps
```

The preceding command gives the following output:

```
PS C:\WINDOWS\system32> docker ps
CONTAINER ID        IMAGE                                       COMMAND
                        NAMES
fdd74c8ffa4a            learningwsc/musicstore:1.0.0    "dotnet musicstore.dl"
0.0.0.0:5002->5002/tcp    musicstore-3
df46f0e59961            learningwsc/musicstore:1.0.0    "dotnet musicstore.dl"
0.0.0.0:5001->5001/tcp    musicstore-2
9bf65ce20676            learningwsc/musicstore:1.0.0    "dotnet musicstore.dl"
0.0.0.0:5000->5000/tcp    musicstore-1
```

10. Run the following commands to open ports `5000`, `5001`, and `5002` on the staging environment's firewall:

    ```
    New-NetFirewallRule -Name "App" -DisplayName "App"
    -Enabled True -Profile Any -Action Allow -Direction Inbound
    -LocalPort 5000 -Protocol TCP
    New-NetFirewallRule -Name "App1" -DisplayName "App1" -Enabled
    True -Profile Any -Action Allow -Direction Inbound -LocalPort
    5001 -Protocol TCP
    New-NetFirewallRule -Name "App2" -DisplayName "App2" -Enabled
    True -Profile Any -Action Allow -Direction Inbound -LocalPort
    5002 -Protocol TCP
    ```

11. To create a container using the NGINX image we built, let us pull the image on the staging environment using the following command:

    ```
    docker pull learningwsc/nginx:1.0.0
    ```

12. Run the following command to create a container using image `learningwsc/nginx`. We will be using port `80` for the load balancer and balance the incoming requests across ports `5000–5002` using a *least connection* algorithm as configured in the `nginx.config`:

    ```
    docker run -d -p 80:80 learningwsc/nginx:1.0.0
    ```

13. Now we should be able to browse the site using the DNS name as shown in the following image:

14. There is a special page called **Counter** which increases the counter by one every time you refresh the page. To test the load balancer configuration, the counter variable is made static. Now, if we open the following URL using different *Incognito* browser windows, they should be showing different counter values. This proves that they are indeed coming from three different instances:

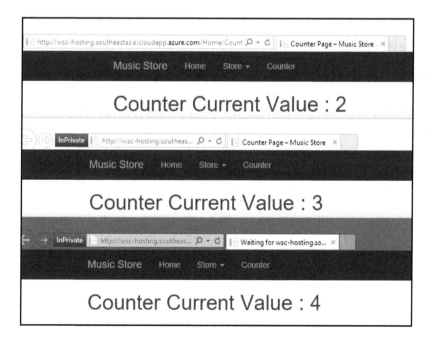

Deploy Hyper-V Containers

Business or IT administrators need a highly available and quickly creatable environment with the highest security. Though Windows Server Containers are easily to spin up and can guarantee high-availability, they cannot be used to host mission critical or highly secure environments. Because they all share the same kernel shell, any malware attacks on the OS easily pass through the container and will impact the applications as well. So Microsoft built another variation of the container technology called Hyper-V Containers (Linux containers have only one type of isolation). Unlike Windows Server Containers, Hyper-V have their own OS, and nothing is shared across co-existing containers, so therefore they are more secure than the shared containers. Microsoft also added a great benefit by partnering with Docker: the same Docker commands can be used to build, run or test any Windows Container images.

Also, note that, while Hyper-V is the runtime technology powering Hyper-V, isolated containers are not Hyper-V VMs and cannot be managed with classic Hyper-V tools. With Hyper-V Containers, it is up to the user to decide which isolation technology to use to by using a flag at the time of container creation. Azure does not support Hyper-V Containers at this point, so in this chapter we will learn to create and run *Music Store* using Hyper-V Containers in an on-premise environment.

Pre-requisites

The following are some of the pre-requisites for deploying Hyper-V Containers:

- A Windows machine with Hyper-V enabled for hosting the Windows Server 2016 VM
- 8 GB memory (a minimum of 2 GB should be allocated to the VM)
- Minimum 20 GB storage space for storing the VHD files
- Hyper-V feature on Windows 10

Steps to run Music Store as a Hyper-V Container

The following steps explain the process of running Hyper-V Containers in an on-premise environment simulated on a Windows 10 machine with anniversary update:

1. Ensure Hyper-V feature is enabled on the Windows 10 machine.
2. Download the latest **Windows Server 2016 ISO** from
   `https://www.microsoft.com/en-in/evalcenter/evaluate-windows-server-tec`
   `hnical-preview`:
3. Create a new machine using Hyper-V Manager.
4. Ensure the network adapter is configured for the VM and that VMs have access to the Internet for performing push/pull operations from the Docker Hub.
5. Install **Windows Server** using the ISO downloaded previously.
6. Ensure the base images are installed as shown in the following screenshot:

```
PS C:\Users\Administrator> docker images
REPOSITORY                    TAG           IMAGE ID
microsoft/windowsservercore   latest        93a9c37b36d0
microsoft/nanoserver          latest        e14bc0ecea12
```

7. Run the following command to download the latest `musicstore` image onto the on-premise machine:

```
PS C:\Users\Administrator> docker pull learningwsc/musicstore:1.0.0
1.0.0: Pulling from learningwsc/musicstore

9c7f9c7d9bc2: Already exists
de5064718b3f: Already exists
4b99fabcdc26: Pull complete
cf526c50c801: Pull complete
1a02c54bd2ae: Pull complete
6dc56f5d507c: Pull complete
aa7b5de3b4d7: Pull complete
0ba9eb88eebc: Pull complete
Digest: sha256:e36586cbd59c17075592cb0c17b938612388586a0055c46e7cc77cf3429618e2
Status: Downloaded newer image for learningwsc/musicstore:1.0.0
```

8. Run the following set of commands to install/create three instances of the *Music Store* application as Hyper-V Containers. Notice the `isolation` flag provided for each command; this is a special flag which is valid only for windows machines:

```
docker run --isolation=hyperv -d -p 5000:80
learningwsc/musicstore:1.0.0 dotnet musicstore.dll
docker run --isolation=hyperv -d -p 5001:80
learningwsc/musicstore:1.0.0 dotnet musicstore.dll
docker run --isolation=hyperv -d -p 5002:80
learningwsc/musicstore:1.0.0 dotnet musicstore.dll
```

9. Copy the contents from `learningwsc/chapter5/resources/musicstore-nginx-hyperv` to the on-premise machine.

10. Open `nginx.conf` and replace `$hostIP` with the IP address of the VM. Save the contents of the file and close.

11. Run the following command to build an NGINX image using the configuration file updated previously:

```
docker build -t nginx .
```

12. Run the following command to create Hyper-V NGINX Container:

```
docker run --isolation=hyperv -d -p 80:80 nginx:latest
```

13. Open any browser and access the portal using `http://$hostIP`, where `$hostIP` is the IP address of the machine as shown in the networking section of the VM.

Dangling images

Docker creates few images with no name and version called **dangling images**, these images can be observed while using the command `docker images -a` as shown in the following screenshot:

```
PS C:\musicstore-nginx-hyperv> docker images -a
REPOSITORY                      TAG        IMAGE ID
nginx                           latest     d2b969ece4dc
<none>                          <none>     f205d7cb6a99
<none>                          <none>     ba38c317660c
<none>                          <none>     0ccc767b33f8
<none>                          <none>     b341ab61cb28
learningwsc/musicstore          1.0.0      a2ce5bcf5740
microsoft/windowsservercore     latest     93a9c37b36d0
microsoft/nanoserver            latest     e14bc0ecea12
```

To understand more about dangling images, let us understand first how Windows operating systems store downloaded container images. By default, the images are stored at the Docker root directory which is `C:\ProgramData\docker` (`ProgramData` is a hidden folder). To find out what the Docker root is on your machine you can run the following command:

```
PS C:\Users\Administrator> docker info
Containers: 11
 Running: 0
 Paused: 0
 Stopped: 11
Images: 2
Server Version: 1.12.2-cs2-ws-beta
Storage Driver: windowsfilter
 Windows:
Logging Driver: json-file
Plugins:
 Volume: local
 Network: nat null overlay
Swarm: inactive
Default Isolation: process
Kernel Version: 10.0 14393 (14393.321.amd64fre.rs1_release_inmarket.161004-2338)
Operating System: Windows Server 2016 Standard Evaluation
OSType: windows
Architecture: x86_64
CPUs: 2
Total Memory: 2 GiB
Name: WIN-17SA4TTL63Q
ID: SYEQ:PRTR:QSQK:5PN3:HH7E:SOAV:UREU:Z3FP:PVRL:PEC6:4QR2:35D7
Docker Root Dir: C:\ProgramData\docker
Debug Mode (client): false
Debug Mode (server): false
```

As we know Docker on Windows follows a layered storage system, and each layer is connected via a parent-child relationship with another layer. When we try to pull an image from the hub, Docker pulls one layer at a time and stores the intermediate layers at the Docker root directory. These intermediate layers are named as <none>:<none> these are good unnamed images. You can see the list of intermediate images and corresponding Identifier information using the -a with docker images command. Docker stacks the layers which together constitute an image. A thin writable layer is created on an image when we create a container. The overall structure of an image, which includes read-only and writable layers, are shown in the following image:

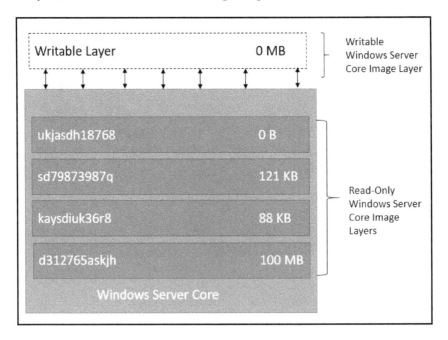

Each layer is identified with a unique identifier, and images are identified by name or SHA256 values. The SHA256 value of each image can be found by default in the C:\ProgramData\docker\image\windowsfilter\repository.json file.

Now, what are dangling images and why are they bad? Docker does not have any automated memory clean-up route which continuously cleans up unused layers; thus any layers which are broken from parent-child relationship consume space and lie forever on the host's disk space. These image layers are bad images called dangling images. Unlike good images, bad layers are visible even without the −a option. These images are created when the `docker build` or `pull` command is used. Fortunately, Docker can identify the dangling images and tag them. Docker sets a flag on the dangling images which can be used to clean up as shown in the following command:

```
docker rmi $(docker images -f "dangling=true" -q)
```

The preceding command can be used to remove any unused image layers, this serves the purpose of a garbage collector.

A Docker image is composed of layers and each layer is participant of parent-child hierarchy. When you list all the docker images you will find few images with name `<none>:<none>` and the number of such images increases with the number of pulls from Docker Hub or any remote repository. This is because, when we try to pull an image, Docker pulls them one layer at a time. First the downloaded layer is unnamed or named as `<none>:<none>`. Since this layer is an intermediate layer, Docker marks it as an intermediate image and hence it is only visible when used with −a option.

There are two types of dangling images: the *good* ones and the *bad* ones. The good ones do not create any disk space problems, but the bad ones occupy a lot of space. The bad ones are the dangling images which are visible even without using the −a option, these types of images occupy space and are not referred by any images so the memory cannot be re-collected. These are the images which need to be cleaned. These dangling images are produced because of `docker build` or `pull command`.

Summary

In this chapter, we have learned to create container host environments on Azure using automation and to configure it to be used as a remote container host. The following is a summary of what we have learned in this chapter:

- Azure ARM provides a fool-proof way of creating Windows Container hosts using configuration driven automation
- Windows Container hosts can be configured for remote connectivity using secure/non-secure connection types
- For configuring a secured connection we need OpenSSL and CA server
- Docker provides multiple isolation options called Windows Containers (default) and Hyper-v Containers using the same client and server process
- Specifying the isolation type is a runtime decision
- Hyper-V Containers provide greater isolation and have high boot times
- Hyper-V Containers are not VMs, so they cannot be managed using traditional Hyper-V tools
- There are good and bad intermediate/dangling images, bad images occupy space on the container host and hence should be deleted manually on a periodic basis

6
Storage Volumes

So far, we have built applications which are not persistent. Traditional applications store data which can be in any form, such as text, images, media, and so on, or relational data, which is stored using well-known relational database management systems such as MySQL, SQL Server, or Oracle. With storage devices or storage space being available at cheaper rates, modern web applications are built to make the most out of this by building cost-effective and scalable storage designs. Also, when storage gets accumulated over a period of years, availability and accessibility of storage is also very important for further usage analysis and deep learning to provide a richer user experience. In this chapter, we will learn the options provided by Windows Server 2016 Containers features to add and manage the container' storage using storage volumes and shared storage across containers and making the storage accessible and available all times. No enterprise application can survive without relation stores and containerized applications are no exception. In this chapter, we also impart learning to build web applications which can use storage volumes to store non-relational or binary data. We will also learn building applications using traditional RDMS systems like SQL Server for building containerized web applications.

The following topics will be discussed in this chapter:

- Storage volumes, mapping volumes to containers
- Sharing data across containers
- Building applications using shared container storage
- Building Microsoft SQL Server container image
- Developing persistent applications using SQL Server containers
- Managing SQL Server using familiar tools

Storage volumes

Docker on Windows Server is responsible for managing images and container storage on the container host. Docker manages this using a separate storage driver and using the *copy-on-write* mechanism. To serve at a faster pace, Docker stores data in a layered manner; a container is made up of multiple layers. A container's view of a single filesystem is a union of filesystems on each read-only layer which make up the container. The container uses its filesystem to store data but in general the filesystem of the container is an illusion created by the Docker daemon. When a new write happens to any file in the container, Docker creates a copy of the read-only file and places a read-write on the top layer, whilst the underlying read-only copy of the file is never deleted. If the container is deleted, all the changes made to the writable layer are gone forever. If a new container is created using the old image, a new read-only copy of the image is created with a writable layer on it. This mechanism of managing storage using read-only and writable layers is called **union file system**. Docker also uploads the layers in an optimum manner so that only the bare minimum is uploaded using the same layered storage mechanism. When we create a new container Docker Engine on a Windows Server it provides a C drive with around 20 GB of storage. This storage contains the OS files and software or the application files which are copied as part of the image build process (using `Docker COPY` command). Like many traditional storage scenarios, the application requires separate storage to store application specific files so that they can be independently managed, backed up or archived periodically. This option is provided by storage volumes in Windows Server Containers.

Storage volumes is not a new concept, in fact all the virtualized infra-providers or hosted virtualization vendors (such as virtual PC, Hyper-V Manager, and VMware) use the same approach to provide storage capacity to VMs running on the host. The same idea is adapted by Windows Server 2016 Containers using storage volumes. A storage volume is a section of storage space on the container's host which is shared with the container so that applications, services or any software running on the container can store any type of data. Docker provides a -v flag to create a data volume while creating a container.

The following command line creates a container and shares the folder c:\temp, which is located on the host:

```
docker run -it -v c:\temp --name mycontainerstorage
microsoft/windowsservercore:latest
```

The $-it$ flag is used to open an interactive window to the running container, the only important option above is $-v$ c:\temp. The following screenshot shows the list of folders created inside the container:

```
c:\>dir
 Volume in drive C has no label.
 Volume Serial Number is 961B-B7B6

 Directory of C:\

10/10/2016  06:20 AM             1,894 License.txt
07/16/2016  01:18 PM    <DIR>          PerfLogs
11/18/2016  06:12 PM    <DIR>          Program Files
07/16/2016  01:18 PM    <DIR>          Program Files (x86)
11/18/2016  06:11 PM    <SYMLINKD>     temp [\\?\ContainerMappedDirectories\A035C152-3974-40F2-B56B-2381B818F1CC]
11/18/2016  06:12 PM    <DIR>          Users
11/18/2016  06:14 PM    <DIR>          Windows
               1 File(s)          1,894 bytes
               6 Dir(s)  21,174,292,480 bytes free
```

Notice that temp folder is listed inside the container and it also shows that it is symbolically linked (SYMLINKD) to a target folder temp[\\?\ContainerMappedDirectories\A035C152-3974-40F2-B56B-2381B818F1CC] on the host. Here A035C152-3974-40F2-B56B-2381B818F1CC is the identifier of the volume.

Now, let's try to add a new file in the temp shared folder. Run the following command to create a new text file in the temp folder:

```
New-Item -path . -Name 'sample.txt' -Value 'This is a sample
text' -ItemType file
```

The preceding command gives the following output:

```
C:\temp>powershell
Windows PowerShell
Copyright (C) 2016 Microsoft Corporation. All rights reserved.

PS C:\temp> New-Item -path . -Name 'sample.txt' -Value 'This is a sample text' -ItemType file


    Directory: C:\temp


Mode                LastWriteTime         Length Name
----                -------------         ------ ----
-a----        11/18/2016     6:41 PM           21 sample.txt
```

The file named `sample.txt` is created in the container on a writable layer, while the actual file is stored on the container host. But where is it stored on the host? It is not on `c:\temp` on the host. Docker stores all volumes under `c:\programdata\docker\volumes` by default. If we navigate to the `volumes` folder on the container host, we'll see many folders with long names, which are volume identifiers as shown in the following screenshot:

These are all the volumes linked to the containers running on the host. How do we know which volume is mapped to our container named `mycontainerstorage`? There is a `docker` command which shows all the metadata information of any container - `docker inspect`. Run the following command to get the metadata of the container we just created:

```
docker inspect mycontainersstorage
```

Notice the `Mounts` section as shown in the following screenshot. The name section also works as the identifier for a folder. A folder with same name would exist under `c:\programdata\docker\volumes`, however the `Source` folder shows the completed path to the volume:

```
"Mounts": [
    {
        "Type": "volume",
        "Name": "677dcc6a338aee4ce60bbf47eff6460c7f324300b057cf2d61d46f6c1a56a50a",
        "Source": "C:\\ProgramData\\docker\\volumes\\677dcc6a338aee4ce60bbf47eff6460c7f324300b
        "Destination": "c:\\temp",
        "Driver": "local",
        "Mode": "",
        "RW": true,
        "Propagation": ""
    }
}
```

The file we created from the `sample.txt` container should exist under the path in the preceding image under a special subfolder called `_data`. Any updates we do to the text file from the host will be reflected in the running container too:

```
PS C:\temp> Get-Content sample.txt
This is a sample text, updated from host !!
PS C:\temp>
```

Docker volumes

Docker volumes are outside the union filesystem and exist as normal directories on the host filesystem. We can also share an existing folder with a container; all the files available in the folder will be available on the container. This enables a great way of sharing large quantities of data between host and container. Let us say we want to install software on a container, such as SQL Server or MySQL. We do not have to copy the huge file. Instead we can mount the folder to the container and use the relative path within the container to complete the installation. This section explains the options available to create and manage Docker volumes.

Docker provides an option to list volumes which are available on a container host. It also provides a pre-create option which can be attached to container(s) later. We can use the `docker volume` command to manage volumes. The following command shows the options available with `docker volume`:

```
PS C:\> docker volume

Usage:  docker volume COMMAND

Manage volumes

Options:
      --help    Print usage

Commands:
  create     Create a volume
  inspect    Display detailed information on one or more volumes
  ls         List volumes
  rm         Remove one or more volumes
```

To list all the volumes available on the container, run the following command:

```
docker volume ls
```

The preceding command gives the following output:

```
PS C:\> docker volume ls
DRIVER                 NAME
local                  24ca491bf05512145f1835581773532239f3f07c6dd1bb46ce90f0a58f45470c
local                  62aa1c66b201701e6f59e43575ed2733318b7e9d491fff3cc33ee81fd0c4676f
local                  677dcc6a338aee4ce60bbf47eff6460c7f324300b057cf2d61d46f6c1a56a50a
local                  84f863e1941c733eee513a1560e45a7995bdd08296e0df180ad68644415f5373
local                  ae188c101d5a6f132cecb765fc0853604ae1ab774460fe4198c9796c91a1d73e
local                  b0f4e92a9ed1422e537fce2f6267082d9ae1a5c336b0f118f465297f65c1ed3b
local                  c917a4c4e6c2a53369d77e68af747e0639ee87af7e0991115b19635682866640
local                  e5ccbb4bd609002fc92fea117a4bd109bf16e5814cc47e668a31704cc2569101
local                  f62015c991f92a407a91df4506dd7f2c01d93f8d0c416742255e498aa7d3e85b
```

If we want to know where the container is stored, the following command can be used:

```
docker inspect volume [volumeidentifier]
```

The preceding command gives the following output:

```
PS C:\> docker volume inspect 677dcc6a338aee4ce60bbf47eff6460c7f324300b057cf2d61d46f6c1a56a50a
[
    {
        "Name": "677dcc6a338aee4ce60bbf47eff6460c7f324300b057cf2d61d46f6c1a56a50a",
        "Driver": "local",
        "Mountpoint": "C:\\ProgramData\\docker\\volumes\\677dcc6a338aee4ce60bbf47eff6460c7f324300b
        "Labels": null,
        "Scope": "local"
    }
]
```

Docker volume identifiers are insanely large and difficult to read. To overcome this option Docker provides an option to create name volumes using the following `docker volume create` command:

```
docker volume create --label desc='stores data for
my container' mycontainervolume
```

With `docker volume create` option we can use `--label` to add more metadata to the volume which will be shown to anyone inspecting the volume as shown in the following screenshot:

```
PS C:\> docker volume inspect mycontainervolume
[
    {
        "Name": "mycontainervolume",
        "Driver": "local",
        "Mountpoint": "C:\\ProgramData\\docker\\volumes\\mycontainervolume\\_data",
        "Labels": {
            "desc": "stores data for my container"
        },
        "Scope": "local"
    }
]
```

Now, we can use the named volume to attach to a container using the following command:

```
docker run -it -v c:\programdata\docker\volumes\mycontainervolume:
c:\storagevolume --name mycontainer
microsoft/windowsservercore:latest
```

Once the container is created, the named volume will be available under `c:\storagevolume` as mentioned in the command. We can also share multiple volumes or physical paths on the container host with the container each specified with `-v` as shown in the following command:

```
docker run -it -v c:\programdata\docker\volumes\
mycontainervolume1:c:\storagevolume1 -v
c:\programdata\docker\volumes\mycontainervolume2:
c:\storagevolume2 microsoft/windowsservercore:latest
```

The preceding command adds two named volumes to the container, each available under C drive as shown here:

```
C:\>dir
 Volume in drive C has no label.
 Volume Serial Number is 961B-B7B6

 Directory of C:\

10/10/2016  06:20 AM             1,894 License.txt
07/16/2016  01:18 PM    <DIR>          PerfLogs
11/19/2016  10:18 AM    <DIR>          Program Files
07/16/2016  01:18 PM    <DIR>          Program Files (x86)
11/19/2016  10:18 AM    <SYMLINKD>     storagevolume1 [\\?\ContainerMappedDirectories\7485450D
11/19/2016  10:18 AM    <SYMLINKD>     storagevolume2 [\\?\ContainerMappedDirectories\EC8D942F
11/19/2016  10:18 AM    <DIR>          Users
11/19/2016  10:18 AM    <DIR>          Windows
               1 File(s)          1,894 bytes
               7 Dir(s)  21,181,784,064 bytes free
```

Sharing volumes

While sharing a folder with a container we use a physical path available on the host machine such as C:\temp. If we try to create another container with the same physical path, it does not mean containers share the same physical folder c:\temp. This is because every time we attach a volume to a container, Docker creates a new folder under c:\programdata\docker\volumes so physical storage paths on the host shared across containers are not physically shared. Does that mean we cannot share volumes across containers? No: Docker provides a special way to share volumes across containers using named volumes; we can point multiple containers to the same named volume so that the files can be shared. This is possible because named volumes or volumes in general are outside the layered filesystem:

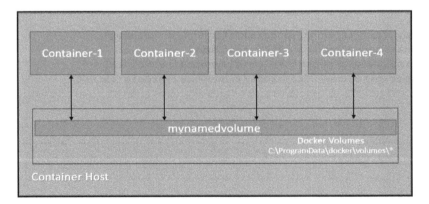

A named volume or volume created using the -v option which is already mounted to a container can be shared with another container using the -volumes-from flag. While using the -volumes-from flag the target container should be in running state. For example, the following command shares the volume(s) attached to a container with an ID. Any updates to the filesystem made from containers or the host will be visible across the containers.

```
docker run -it --volumes-from cd8f3b00ccc5 microsoft/
windowsservercore:latest
```

Music Store—store images using volumes

The *Music Store* application allows you to create new albums and upload images as album covers. We have not created any persistent layer for *Music Store* to store album images.

Let us now upgrade the *Music Store* web application to use storage volumes to store images of newly created albums. The samples for this section are available under https://github.com/vishwanathsrikanth/learningwsc/tree/master/chapter6/musicstore-volumes.

 If you have cloned the repository make sure the solution for this section is available under C:/learningwsc/chapter6/musicstore-volumes/ (here the drive letter can be anything). This is because the DockerTask.ps1 within the solution will publish the build out using the path of the solution file. You can choose any other folder to copy the source. Make sure DockerTask.ps1 is updated with path to publish the build output.

There are some noticeable updates to the solution which makes the storage possible; the first one is the Create action under Areas/Admin/Controllers/StoreManagerController.cs:

```
    // POST: /StoreManager/Create
      [HttpPost]
      [ValidateAntiForgeryToken]
      public async Task<IActionResult> Create(
          Album album,
          [FromServices] IMemoryCache cache,
          CancellationToken requestAborted)
      {
          if (ModelState.IsValid)
          {
              //upload file to volume
              string imgUrl = "~/Images/{0}";
```

```
            var uploads = _appSettings.StorageLocation;
            var file = Request.Form.Files.Count > 0 ?
                Request.Form.Files[0] : null;
            if (file != null)
            {
                string fileName = ExtractFileName(file);
                using (var fileStream = new
                    FileStream(Path.Combine(uploads, fileName),
                    FileMode.Create))
                {
                    await file.CopyToAsync(fileStream);
                }
                album.AlbumArtUrl = string.Format
                    (imgUrl, fileName);
                    album.Created = DateTime.UtcNow;
            }

            //add album to in-memory database
            DbContext.Albums.Add(album);
            await DbContext.SaveChangesAsync(requestAborted);
            var albumData = new AlbumData
            {
                Title = album.Title,
                Url = Url.Action("Details", "Store",
                    new { id = album.AlbumId })
            };
            cache.Remove("latestAlbum");
            return RedirectToAction("Index");
        }
        ViewBag.GenreId = new SelectList(DbContext.Genres,
            "GenreId", "Name", album.GenreId);
            ViewBag.ArtistId = new SelectList(DbContext.Artists,
            "ArtistId", "Name", album.ArtistId);
            return View(album);
    }
```

The preceding code uses the `StorageLocation` configured in the `config.json` file as shown in the upcoming piece of code to save the images to a folder inside the container. The build output is copied to `c:\app` folder as per instructions in Dockerfile and the images are referred from the `Images` folder under `wwwroot`:

```
{
  "AppSettings": {
    "SiteTitle": "Music Store",
    "CacheDbResults": true,
    "StorageLocation": "c:\\app\\wwwroot\\Images\\"
  },
```

Perform the following steps to run and test the newly upgraded feature:

1. Press *Ctrl* + *Shift* + *B* to build an updated `musicstore` image and ensure the updated image is listed using `docker images` command. Run the following command to create a new volume for storing `musicstore` images:

   ```
   docker volume create musicstoreimages
   ```

2. Create a new container and mount the `musicstoreimages` volume to the folder mentioned in the `config.json` section inside the container using the following command:

   ```
   docker run -d -p 80:80 -v c:\programdata\docker\volumes\
   musicstoreimages:c:\app\wwwroot\Images\albums --name musicstore
   learningwsc/musicstore:1.0.0 dotnet musicstore.dll
   ```

3. Navigate to the web application using the host's address.

4. Click on the **Login** link and log in with the default admin credentials stored in `config.json`.
5. Click on the **Admin** link on the footer to navigate to the admin area.
6. Click on **Create New**.

7. Create a new album and upload the album cover image from your machine as shown in the following screenshot. Click **Create**:

8. Click the **Store** dropdown on the top menu and select **Rock.**
9. Scroll to the end of the page to find a new album created with name `Death Magnetic`.
10. Click on the image to open the details section as shown here:

11. On the host machine, you will find the image we should uploaded under
    `C:\Programdata\docker\volumes\musicstoreimages`, which is
    successfully mounted to the `musicstore` container.

If you're running multiple `musicstore` containers, as we do in the production
environments, the `musicstoreimages` volume can be shared by mounting the same
volume across containers or by using the `-volumes-from` option. You can also mount
multiple volumes to the container using the `-v` option multiple times. Another great use of
mounting volumes is that we can put the source code of the application on the host and run
from the container. By doing this we can edit the source files or configurations
independently. Multiple containers using the shared volumes can corrupt data, so we must
make sure the applications are designed to handle all conditions. We created container
images earlier using Dockerfiles and `docker build` command. Creating volumes can be
incorporated in Dockerfile using the `VOLUME` command. The following Dockerfile creates a
new volume:

```
FROM microsoft/windowsservercore
VOLUME ["c:/vol"]
```

Once the image is created any containers created using the image will have a new volume
created and mounted automatically. The `-v` flag can also be used to mount a single file as
shown in the following command. The difference between `VOLUME` in a Dockerfile and `-v` is,
`-v` will mount an existing file(s) from your OS inside your Docker container and `VOLUME`
will create a new and empty volume on your host and mount it inside your container.

Deleting volumes

A Docker volume persists even after the container is deleted, using `docker rm` to delete a
container will leave a lot of orphan values. Docker never garbage collects any unattended
volumes so make sure you clean unused volumes. The following options are available to
delete volumes:

- You can delete a volume by specifying `-rm` to the run command as shown in the
  following command. This command removes `volume1` and `volume2` when the
  container is stopped. `docker rm` is used to automatically clean up the container
  when the container exists. When we use the `-rm` flag Docker also removes the
  volumes mounted on the container when the container is destroyed:

  ```
  docker run --rm -it -v c:/volume1 -v c:/volume2
  microsoft/windowsservercore powershell
  ```

- By using `docker volume rm`, the following command removes the container, `mycontainervolume`:

```
docker volume rm mycontainervolume
```

Volumes can be deleted only if certain pre-conditions are satisfied. Volumes are only deleted if the container is stopped and no other container links to it. Volumes linked to user specified directories are not deleted by Docker. Docker tags unlinked volumes as dangling volumes (like dangling images), and we can list dangling images using the dangling flag using the following command.

```
docker volume remove -f dangling=true
```

Relational databases and SQL Server container

Designing applications using microservices approach is the best way to increase ROI and agility, breaking down your application into silos and letting each time manage a silo increases the delivery momentum. Up to this point, we have learned building web applications as containers which can be scaled up or updated within minutes. We have also seen how to build applications using scalable storage facilities. However, in reality, no application deals in all in non-relational data, so this section focuses on building applications using relational database containers like SQL Server. Database containers help raise the delivery velocity by a great extent, and they can be used to create test/development environments, isolated and sandboxed environments at increased speed. Database containers are also a great help when you are building multi-tenant applications: each tenant's database can be independently managed and scaled per usage. Each tenant can also be onboard within minutes if the complete environment is built using microservices or containers.

Microsoft has released Windows Container image on Docker Hub which can be used right away to build and deploy database containers. It also allows you to attach existing databases using JSON configuration passed in as parameters. The next series of steps will explain the process of creating a SQL Server 2016 Express container and connect using database tools like SQL Server Management Studio:

1. Let us pull the latest SQL Server 2016 Express image from the Docker Hub using the following command:

   ```
   docker pull microsoft/mssql-server-2016-express-windows
   ```

2. The default port for accessing SQL Server is 1433, if you are using Azure you need to define the inbound security rule for this port. Login to https://portal.azure.com and select the network interface created for the machine (for resource manager machines; for classic VMs click **Endpoints** section), navigate to **Network security groups** | **All settings** and click **Inbound security rules**. Add a new rule to allow connections to port 1433 from any destination.

3. Run the following command on container host to open the port 1433 on firewall:

   ```
   if (!(Get-NetFirewallRule | where {$_.Name -eq "SQLServer
   1433"}))
   {New-NetFirewallRule -Name "SQL Server 1433"
   -DisplayName "SQL Server 1433" -Protocol tcp -LocalPort 1433
   -Action Allow -Enabled True}
   ```

4. The following command creates a new instance of SQL Server 2016 database container and opens an interactive session using PowerShell (-it flag):

   ```
   docker run -it -p 1433:1433 microsoft/mssql
   -server-2016-express-windows powershell
   ```

5. To connect to the database container, we would need a command-line utility called **SQL command** or **SQL Server Management Studio** (**SSMS**). The preceding command opens a PowerShell session which can be used to connect to the SQL Server running inside the container as shown in the following image:

```
PS C:\> sqlcmd
1> SELECT @@VERSION
2> GO

------------------------------------------------------------------

------------------------------------------------------------------
Microsoft SQL Server 2016 (RTM) - 13.0.1601.5 (X64)
        Apr 29 2016 23:23:58
        Copyright (c) Microsoft Corporation
        Express Edition (64-bit) on Windows Server 2016 Datacenter 6.3 <X64> (
```

6. Let us run the following commands using `sqlcmd` to enable `sa` login and configure a password:

```
ALTER LOGIN [sa] ENABLE
ALTER LOGIN [sa] WITH PASSWORD=N'NewPassword'
```

7. The second method is to connect using SSMS. Download and install SSMS from `https://msdn.microsoft.com/en-us/library/mt238290.aspx`.

8. Open SSMS and connect using the following parameters:

   - **Server name**: IP address or DNS Name of the machine
   - **Login**: `sa`
   - **Password**: Value given for environmental variable `sa_password`

The SQL Server database container can now be used to create a database or even use ORM frameworks like **Entity Framework Code-First** to create and test application databases during runtime.

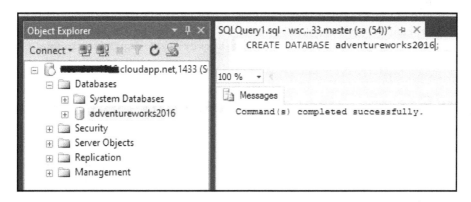

9. You can also connect to the database container using `sqlcmd` from anywhere using the following command:

```
sqlcmd -S tcp:<IP Address>,1433 -U sa -P Password@123
```

We have been using a pre-built SQL Server image but it isn't too tough to create one from scratch. Microsoft provides enough options to alter the configuration of the database. Let us say you already have a database (`*.mdf` file), you can attach the database using the `attach_dbs` JSON value as shown here:

```
docker run -p 1433:1433 -v C:/temp/:C:/temp/ --env attach_dbs="
[{'dbName':'adventureworks2016','dbFiles':
['C:\\temp\\adventureworks2016.mdf',
 'C:\\temp\\adventureworks2016_log.ldf']}]"
microsoft/mssql-server-2016-express-windows
```

You can also customize further by editing the Dockerfile used for creating the SQL Server container available on Docker Hub. SQL Server 2016 Express is an entry level database, which is a free edition and so it contains certain limitations; for instance, we can only build small data-driven applications with database size up to 10 GB. This is more suitable only for building dev/test environments or multi-tenant architectures. Microsoft has open-sourced the Dockerfile used to build the SQL Server 2016 Express container which can be extended to build any custom SQL Server Container. The source code and the Dockerfile instructions for the above image are available at: `https://github.com/Microsoft/mssql-docker/tree /master/windows/mssql-server-windows-express`. To know what SQL Server features are supported on Windows Server Core go to `https://msdn.microsoft.com/en-us/library/hh231669.aspx`.

We can also create Hyper-V Containers using an on premise installation of Windows Server 2016 SQL Server 2016 Windows Container image using the following isolation command. Notice that the environmental variable used here for `sa_password` is the admin (`sa`) password of the database container:

```
docker run -d -p 1433:1433 --env sa_password=<YOUR_PWD>
--isolation=hypervmicrosoft/mssql-server-2016-express-windows
```

Music Store—store data using SQL Server container

In the earlier section, we upgraded *Music Store* to store binary data using volumes. In this section we will build a `musicstore` image which will use SQL Server 2016 Express container to store data. The completed sample for *Music Store* is available under the GitHub repository: `C:/learningwsc/chapter6/musicstore-sqlserver`.

The following are the updates done to the *Music Store* application to enable data storage:

- `DockerTask.ps1`: In the earlier section, we used volumes to create images, the following changes are made to the `DockerTask.ps1` to create and use volume as part of the build and run process:

```
#Create Docker Volume
docker volume create musicstoreimages
#Creates a Music Store Container
docker run -v d:\temp\uploads -p
$HostPort&grave;:$ContainerPort -v
c:\programdata\docker\volumes\musicstoreimages:
c:\app\wwwroot\Images\albums $ImageName&grave;:
$Version dotnet musicstore.dll
```

- `Config.json`: The `defaultconnection` parameter in `config.json` now points to the SQL Server container using the following connection string:

```
"DefaultConnection": {
    "ConnectionString": "Data Source=<IPAddressOrDNSName>,
    1433;Initial Catalog=MusicStore;User ID=sa;
    Password=Password@123"
}
```

- `Startup.cs`: In the previous chapter, we have used in-memory databases to store data. The following code configures the *Music Store* application to use the database connection configured in `config.json`. The *Music Store* application uses Entity Framework Code-First approach to create and seed data:

```
services.AddDbContext<MusicStoreContext>(options =>
options.UseSqlServer(Configuration
[StoreConfig.ConnectionStringKey.Replace("__", ":")]));
```

Perform the following steps to run and test the *Music Store* application with storage capability:

1. Open the update *Music Store* solution from `Chapter6/musicstore-sqlserver`.
2. Open `Config.json` and replace `<IPAddressOrDNSName>` with the DNS name or IP address of your container host.
3. Press *Ctrl + Shift + B* to build the solution and create a *Music Store* image. The build process also creates a volume by name `musicstoresvolume` and uses this volume to store images.

 These steps assume the SQL Server data container we created earlier is already running on the IP address and port number configured in `config.json`. We will learn the process of creating multi-container environments in the next chapter.

4. Ensure **Docker** is selected as the run profile as shown following and press *F5*.

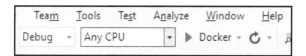

5. Wait for the dotnet process to create and seed the *Music Store* database with sample data. At the end of the process the following log will be shown on the console window:

```
Stopping conflicting containers using port 80
3275d4492603
musicstoreimages
Hosting environment: Production
Content root path: C:\app
Now listening on: http://*:80
Application started. Press Ctrl+C to shut down.
```

6. Connect to the SQL Server container using Management Studio and notice that the *Music Store* database is created and test data is pre-created. You can now use the *Music Store* application to test. As you might have noticed, it just takes a couple of minutes to create new environment which helps development teams to deliver at light speed:

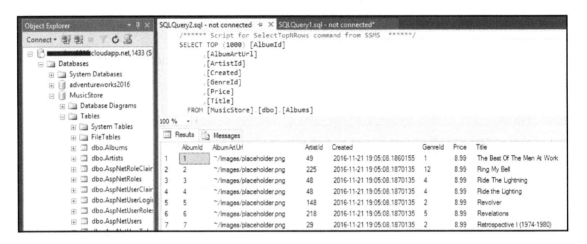

SQL Server container also supports `docker volumes`, the following command can be used for mounting a folder from the host inside the container. This can be used for saving databases outside the container. Microsoft has published SQL Server 2016 image for Linux environment as well which can be download from `https://hub.docker.com/r/microsoft/mssql-server-linux/`.

Over time databases get large, which means we might need a scalable storage to store the physical files. With Windows Containers, the storage is not just restricted to space on the containers. We can extend the storage by using scalable storage devices like storage spaces. If you're using Azure VM as the host, Azure provides storage options at a cheaper price. We can use Azure storage to create additional disks, or use Azure file share to store database logs and data on separate scalable locations as shown in the following image. Azure also provides local redundancy and global replication on a pay-per-use basis which can be used for backups and archiving.

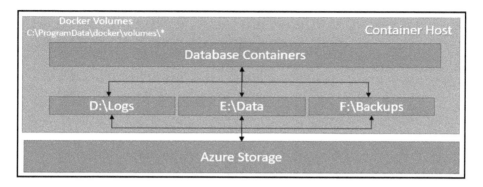

In this chapter, we used a pre-existing container but we can create any database container like MySQL, SQLLite, MongoDB or Oracle. From this point, you can manipulate database containers as you need, save an image and upload to the Docker Hub, which can later be used to create environments dynamically within minutes. Using container technology, we can spin up hundreds of SQL container instances within minutes and destroy them after use. There will not be any need to create a SQL Server environment from scratch for dev/test environments.

Summary

We covered the following topics in this chapter:

- Docker volumes can be used to share folders or files from the host with the container(s).
- Containers can share volumes using named volumes or `-volumes-from` flag.
- Applications using shared volumes should make ensure that multiple containers do not write to a shared file at once or else the data might end up corrupted.
- Relational databases can also be run and configured as containers.
- Volumes attached to a container in running state cannot be deleted. The container should be stopped first to delete the volume.
- Multiple volumes can be attached to one container.
- `VOLUME` is a Dockerfile instruction which can be used to create volumes as part of the build process.
- Microsoft provides a container image for SQL Server Express 2016 and 2014 which can be readily used.
- We can use Azure storage for Azure container hosts or storage spaces for on-premises container hosts while using database containers to configure scalable storages.

7
Redis Cache Containers

Performance is a critical measure for all enterprise/public facing data-centric applications. A persistent storage sub-system where the application stores critical data and performs frequent hops should be as near as possible to the application physically to reduce latency and improve the responsiveness of the application. Web applications on the other hand can be designed to be always by using intelligent traffic routing mechanisms, but they still all point to one database server or storage. So, it is not always possible for the database to be as near as possible to the applications. Other reasons could be data center availability in a region (especially if the data owner is against placing data in a specific geographical region), and compliance and data-integrity policies. As a database size grows, the performance of read or write operations deteriorate. This is due to the amount of data that should be scanned to fetch or update a row(s). In these cases, it makes sense to have a cache server which caches the recently used data and impose appropriate expiration policies for freshness; this reduces the latency for every fetch. Provisioning a cache server is a big deal which involves provisioning infrastructure, installing software and configuring master/slave and several other storage related configurations. Cloud vendors provide caching capabilities which relieve the pain of provisioning, but they are charged on pay per use basis. The operating costs for development and test environments increase as we move to the cloud due to uncleaned up resources which sit idle after tests are run or for development environments which are not used all the time. Cache containers will be a saving grace in all the previous scenarios. The benefits are enormous,: they can be spun in seconds and, since they are on the same host, the operational costs for development and test environments can be reduced. Once the application is moved to the production environment, the connections can be switched to real servers or you can continue using the same server by adding more CPU and scalable storage capacity to an existing container-based environment. Developing an application in silos or containers provides great agility for the development and operational teams. This chapter introduces building Redis Cache containers, configuration, and integration ASP.NET Core application.

The following scenarios and topics will be covered in this chapter:

- Creating Redis Cache containers
- Operating Redis Cache containers
- Persistent Redis containers
- Configuring master/slave environments for high availability
- Integrate web applications with cache containers

Creating Redis Cache container

Redis is an open-licensed (BSD licensed: `http://redis.io/topics/license`) software which can be used not just as a cache server but also as a data store and messaging platform. Apart from a mere key-value cache store, Redis supports complex data structures like hashes, lists, sets and sorted sets with range queries, bitmaps, hyperlogs, and geospatial indexes with radius queries. Redis comes with built-in replication, so we can configure one master and multiple slaves for high availability. Redis also offers various tools to manage Redis containers like **Redis Sentinel** which helps in configuration and monitoring related activities. **Redis Desktop Manager** is a GUI tool for managing data stored in Redis Cache databases.

There is no officially supported version of Redis on Windows. **Microsoft Open Tech** group developers maintain a Redis version for Windows 64/32-bit machines.

> For building 32-bit versions, download the source from GitHub repository and build. For instructions on building the 32-bit version please visit the repository `https://github.com/MSOpenTech/redis`.

The source code repository for Redis on Windows is available on GitHub at `https://github.com/MSOpenTech/redis`. The following diagram shows a sample design of Redis acting as a cache server with master-slave topology:

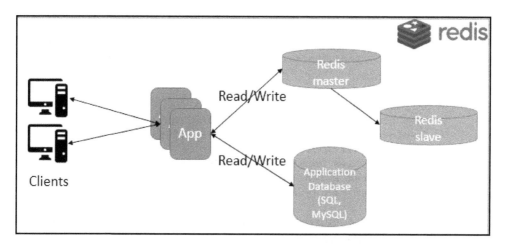

Let us quickly create a Redis Server image which can be deployed on a Windows Server 2016 platform as Windows Container or Hyper-V Container. You can use an Azure or on-premise version of Windows Server 2016 for the following exercise. The key step in creating a Redis Cache image is authoring a Dockerfile. We can use either MSI or zipped release of Redis on Windows from `https://github.com/MSOpenTech/redis/releases`. The following steps explain each command which goes into the Dockerfile. The complete Dockerfile can be downloaded from `https://github.com/vishwanathsrikanth/learningwsc/blob/master/chapter7/redis-server/Dockerfile`:

1. Create a new folder path on your container host with the following path: `c:\learninwsc\chapter7\redis-server`.
2. Create a new Dockerfile under `c:\learninwsc\chapter7\redis-server`. Ensure Dockerfile is created with no extension.
3. Open Dockerfile in any text editor and add the commands mentioned ahead.
4. The first line apparently is to select the base OS image. The following statement sets latest the `windowsservercore` as the base image:

```
FROM microsoft/windowsservercore
```

5. Since we will be using Windows PowerShell to execute commands, add the following command to Dockerfile which sets PowerShell as the default shell. If not specified, the default shell for Windows (CMD) will be used:

```
SHELL ["powershell"]
```

6. The following command downloads the latest release of Redis on Windows (version 3.2.100) in zipped format, extracts it to a default installation location (c:\Program Files\Redis) and cleans up the downloaded ZIP file. Add the following command to Dockerfile:

```
RUN $ErrorActionPreference = 'Stop'; \
    wget https://github.com/MSOpenTech/redis/releases/
    download/win-.2.100/Redis-x64-3.2.100.zip -OutFile
    Redis-x64-3.2.100.zip ; \
    Expand-Archive Redis-x64-3.2.100.zip -dest
    'C:\\Program Files\\Redis\\' ; \
    Remove-Item Redis-x64-3.2.100.zip -Force
```

7. Add the following command to set the PATH variables required for Redis without having to specify the whole path:

```
RUN setx PATH '%PATH%;C:\\Program Files\\Redis\\'
WORKDIR 'C:\\Program Files\\Redis\\'
```

8. Redis on Windows comes with a configuration file under the default installation path C:\Program Files\Redis\redis.windows.conf, which contains configuration for the Redis Cache, like the networking binding, ports, persistent store settings, replication configuration, and so on. The following command creates new configuration files called redis.unprotected.conf (and an intermediate file redis.openport.conf) which removes the default network binding configuration. The following script also disables the security protection which is on by default. Add the following command to Dockerfile:

```
RUN Get-Content redis.windows.conf | Where { $_ -notmatch
'bind 127.0.0.1' } | Set-Content redis.openport.conf ; \
Get-Content redis.openport.conf | Where { $_ -notmatch
'protected-mode yes' } | Set-Content redis.unprotected.conf ; \
Add-Content redis.unprotected.conf 'protected-mode no' ; \
Add-Content redis.unprotected.conf 'bind 0.0.0.0' ;
```

By default, if no binding information is present in the Redis configuration file, Redis Server will bind to all the available network interfaces available on the server when invoked. This is not a recommended approach for production environments because this exposes the server to the Internet. For production environments use the `bind` command to bind to specific IPs separated by a space, for example: `bind 127.0.0.1 123.33.xx.xx`. We can also use the server's firewall settings for blocking connections from unlisted clients. Protected-mode can be used in conjunction with bind to add more security for the Redis Cache container for highly secure environments.

9. The following command exposes the default port `6379` for the container. If the Windows Container host is provisioned on Azure, ensure the endpoints are created on the host for allowing remote connections on port `6379`. Also, port `6379` is unblocked on the firewall of the container host:

```
EXPOSE 6379
```

10. Adding the following command will start the service with `redis.unprotected.conf` as the configuration file on port `6379`:

```
CMD .\\redis-server.exe .\\redis.unprotected.conf
--port 6379 ; \
Write-Host Redis Started... ; \
while ($true) { Start-Sleep -Seconds 3600 }
```

This completes the Dockerfile for building the Redis Cache server image.

Creating Redis image and container

The previous Dockerfile contains all the basic setup to create a Redis container image for Windows. The following commands build a Redis image and create a Windows Container. The same image can also be used to create a Hyper-V Container by using the -isolation option.

1. Open a new PowerShell command window as **Administrator**, navigate to `C:\learningwsc\chapter7\redis-server`.

2. Run the following command to build the Redis Server Windows Container image with the name `learningwsc/redis-server`. Ensure the image is successfully built by checking for the message `Successfully built <IMAGEID>`.

```
docker build -t learningwsc/redis-server .
```

3. Create a detached container and map port 6379 to the container host with the following command:

```
docker run --name redis-server -d -p 6379:6379
learningwsc/redis-server
```

Since the container is created in detached mode, the Redis server container will be running even if the invoking process has shut down. Docker on Windows does not perform any automatic clean-up of resources unless specified. We can also use the -rm option while creating a container to automatically clean resources once the container is stopped/ killed.

Operating Redis Cache containers

With the previous example Redis Cache container is running on the host and ready to accept connections on port 6379 (from any PC). To connect to Redis Server from Windows (or Linux) we can use the **Redis client** command-line utility. Redis client can be installed on any Windows machine using the MSI installation available at https://github.com/MSOpenTech/redis/releases. The default install location on Windows is C:\Programfiles\Redis. The following steps should be used to connect to Redis Cache container from any Windows machine:

1. Open a PowerShell or Windows command-line utility window.
2. Navigate to C:\Programfiles\Redis.
3. Run the following command by replacing the <IPAddressOrHostName> with the hostname or IP address of the container host which was used earlier to launch the container:

```
\redis-cli.exe -h <IPAddressOrHostName> -p 6379
```

4. The following image shows the Redis client connected to the remote Redis Server container running on Windows Server 2016 (container host) on Azure:

5. We can also test the connectivity by using the command PING [Message], the server should respond with the message if the connection is successful as shown in the following screenshot:

```
                 .cloudapp.net:6379> PING HelloWorld
"HelloWorld"
                 .cloudapp.net:6379>
```

Redis Desktop Manager

Redis also offers a cross-platform GUI tool called **Redis Desktop Manager** (**RDM**) which can be downloaded from `https://redisdesktop.com/download`. The RDM tool offers tree view, CRUD operations on keys, and an option to execute commands via Shell. Download and install the tool from the previous link. The following steps show how to connect to Redis container from RDM:

1. Open RDM as administrator.
2. Click on the **Connect to Redis Server** button in the bottom-left corner.
3. Fill the connection properties as explained here:

   - **Name**: `RedisContainer`
   - **Host**: IP address or DNS name of the container host
   - **Port**: **6379** (default port)

4. Click on **Test Connection** and ensure the connection is successful.
5. Click on **OK** to connect to the Redis container.

 RDM can also be used to connect to Redis Cache server securely using Password/SSL.

Let us add some key-value pairs to the Redis container and test a few basic functionalities:

1. Double-click on the RedisContainer on the left panel. The tree now expands and shows all the available databases.
2. Right-click on db0 and click **Add New Key**.
3. Fill in the parameters for the **Add New Key** window as shown here and click **Save**:

   - **Key:** Test
   - **Type: string**
   - **Value:** HelloWorld from Redis Container!!

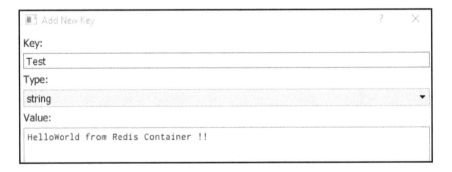

Open a Windows command-line utility and connect to the Redis container as explained in the preceding section. Type the following command to select the database and get the key-value pair added using RDM:

```
Select 0
get Test
```

Publishing Redis container

So far, we have learned to create Redis containers with basic configurations which can be used to provision Redis Cache server instances in seconds. Let us now push the image to the Docker Hub so that we can re-use it to deploy both Windows or Hyper-V Containers. Run the following commands to publish the image to Docker Hub. Optionally, you can also version the image based on a different Redis configuration, so that you can run and deploy based on the usage:

```
docker login –username <username> --password <password>
docker push learningwsc/redis-server
```

Persistent Redis containers

By default, Redis Server saves snapshots of the data on disk using a binary file called `dump.rdb` as configured in the default configuration file. The Redis containers we've created so far are not persistent. For example, if the container is removed or stopped all the data saved by the container is lost. Sometimes we would want to have a copy of the database even after the container exits. Redis provides an option to alter the offline database file location (and name) so that we can backup/archive the latest database before the container exits. This provides a very good disaster recovery mechanism because all we need to backup is a single compact file which can be easily transferred and restored in a different location. In the previous chapter, we have learnt to use the host's storage to build scalable storage spaces called volumes which can be managed outside the running container from the host's filesystem. The following steps show how to use volumes to create persistent Redis containers:

1. Create a new folder under `c:\learningwsc\chapter7\redis-server-volumes`.
2. Copy the Dockerfile from `redis-server` folder to `redis-server-volumes`.
3. Open Dockerfile from `redis-server-volumes` in a text editor.
4. The Redis default configuration file stores the location of the binary file using the `dir` configuration key. Adding the following command to the Dockerfile will replace the default location with new location as `c:\redisdatastore`:

```
RUN (Get-Content redis.unprotected.conf).replace
('dir ./', 'dir c:\redisdatastore') | Set-Content
redis.unprotected.conf
```

5. [*Optional*] The default name of the binary file is `dump.rdb`, although this step is optional, renaming the file will help identify application-specific cache. The following command replaces the default name with `redisdata.rdb`. You can replace the name with an application name in *Production Environments*:

```
RUN (Get-Content redis.unprotected.conf).replace
('dbfilename dump.rdb', 'dbfilename redisdata.rdb')
| Set-Content redis.unprotected.conf
```

6. The completed version of the Dockerfile after the preceding updates should be as shown here:

```
FROM microsoft/windowsservercore

SHELL ["powershell"]

RUN $ErrorActionPreference = 'Stop'; \
    wget https://github.com/MSOpenTech/redis/releases/
    download/win-.2.100/Redis-x64-3.2.100.zip -OutFile
    Redis-x64-3.2.100.zip ; \
    Expand-Archive Redis-x64-3.2.100.zip -dest 'C:\\Program
    Files\\Redis\\' ; \
    Remove-Item Redis-x64-3.2.100.zip -Force

RUN setx PATH '%PATH%;C:\\Program Files\\Redis\\'

WORKDIR 'C:\\Program Files\\Redis\\'

# Change to unprotected mode and open the daemon to
listen on all interfaces.
RUN Get-Content redis.windows.conf | Where { $_ -notmatch
'bind 127.0.0.1' } | Set-Content redis.openport.conf ; \
  Get-Content redis.openport.conf | Where { $_ -notmatch
  'protected-mode yes' } | Set-Content
  redis.unprotected.conf ; \
  Add-Content redis.unprotected.conf 'protected-mode no' ; \
  Add-Content redis.unprotected.conf 'bind 0.0.0.0' ; \
  Get-Content redis.unprotected.conf

EXPOSE 6379

CMD .\\redis-server.exe .\\redis.unprotected.conf
--port 6379 ; \
    Write-Host Redis Started... ; \
    while ($true) { Start-Sleep -Seconds 3600 }
```

7. Run the following command to create an updated version of Redis Container image. Let's call it `learningwsc/redis-server-volumes`:

```
docker build -t learningwsc/redis-server-volumes .
```

8. Before running the container. Create a new volume called `redisdatastore` using the following command:

```
docker volume create redisdatastore
```

9. Run the following command to create a persistent Redis container (in interactive mode). The following command maps the volume created previously to the container using the -v option and opens an interactive PowerShell window for the container:

```
docker run --name redis-server-volumes -it -p 6379:6379
-v c:\ProgramData\docker\volumes\redisdatastore:C:\
redisdatastore learningwsc/redis-server-volumes powershell
```

10. Navigate to `Redis Installation` folder on the container using the following commands:

```
cd\
cd "C:\Program Files\Redis"
```

11. The following command starts the Redis server using the configuration file which contains the updates made to the storage location:

```
\redis-server.exe redis.unprotected.conf
```

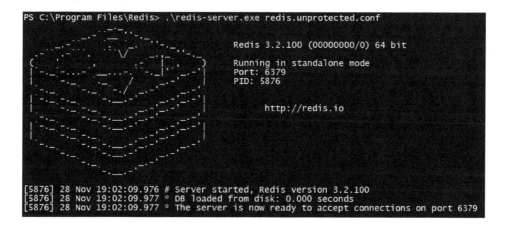

12. Connect to the Redis server using Redis command-line client using the IP address of the host as shown here:

```
\redis-cli.exe -h wsc-dev-1016.cloudapp.net -p 6379
```

13. Add a new key-value pair to the Redis Cache store using the following command:

```
Set Greeting "Welcome to Persistent Containers"
```

13. The Redis `Save` command will force save the cache data to persistent file storage. Run the following command on the Redis console window to force save:

```
Save
```

14. The preceding command saves the data to a single file with the name and location configured in the Redis configuration file used while starting the server. The following command, when run from Redis command-line client connected to remote server, shows the database filename and location of the file:

```
.cloudapp.net:6379> config get dbfilename
1) "dbfilename"
2) "redisdata.rdb"
                     .net:6379> config get dir
1) "dir"
2) "c:\\redisdatastore"
```

Since the target directory `c:\\redisdatastore` is mounted from the container host, the database file will be saved on the host at the default location mentioned here:

C:\ProgramData\docker\volumes\redisdatastore\redisdata.rdb.

We should now be able to extend the life of the cache data by ensuring secure backup strategies are applied for the folder containing the database file. Let's say the cache container gets destroyed; we can still spin up a new container within seconds which points to the database file saved on the host. If you are hosting the container using an Azure VM, Azure provides options to add more data disks to existing machines with global replication and high network bandwidth which can be used here to store cache data files.

The following commands create a new container pointing to the old `redisdata.rdb` file, notice that the old key-values are still available:

```
docker run --name redis-server-new -d -p 6379:6379
-v c:\ProgramData\docker\volumes\redisdatastore:C:\
redisdatastore learningwsc/redis-server-volumes
```

The following images show that the key-value is still retained by the new container:

Redis saves data to a database file as configured in the Save Points section of the configuration file. Save Points define how frequently the data should be persistent, for example, 5 100 configures the server to save data every 5 minutes and 100 writes. This could result in data loss if the container crashes in between the intervals. Redis provides a different type of persistence mechanism called the AOF file. The AOF type of persistence saves all the write operations to the cache store so that they can be replayed when the server start up reconstructing the original dataset. The disadvantage of this approach is that the start-up time of the new container can be huge if there are too many replays to be performed before the container is ready to use.

Master-slave configuration

Each of the solutions discussed previously have their own pros and cons. If a Redis container configured to save data to file fails, there are chances of losing the data; on the other hand, if it is configured to use AOF type persistence the new container might take more time to replay the logs. To build reliable and high performance web applications, the underlying sub-systems should also be available and performing as well. The ideal solution for promising round-the-clock availability is replication. Redis contains a built-in replication feature which is simple yet effective. Redis allows the master to save exact copies of itself as slaves. It uses asynchronous replication while copying data to slaves which increases the reliability of the cache service: since master is not kept busy during replication, the performance of the upstream systems during replication are not impacted. Further slaves can also talk to other slaves in a cascading style so that writes to a slave can be copied down the line in an asynchronous fashion. A Redis configuration file contains a variety of options to configure the master-slave relationship as per needs. For example, we can configure the master to stop accepting writes when the slave is not in synchronization, further we can also use slaves to distribute reads using the old data while the slave is still synchronizing.

So far ,we have built a Redis container image which we have used to create a Redis container as master and attached data volumes for persistence beyond container's life time. In this section, we will use the same image to create a new container using the same Redis image and configure it as a slave and further sync to master container. To configure an instance of Redis server as a slave, we should know the IP of the master, so in the following section we create the master first, fetch the IP of the master, and use the same to create and configure the slave:

1. Run the following command which creates a Redis Cache container named `learningwsc/redis-server-master` and use the default port `6379` for the master:

```
docker run --name redis-server-master -d -p 6379:6379
-v c:\ProgramData\docker\volumes\redisdatastore:C:\
redisdatastore learningwsc/redis-server-volumes
```

2. Run the following command to fetch the unique ID of the container created in the preceding step:

```
docker ps
```

3. The following command uses the master's container ID to get the IP address of the container. Running the following command writes the configuration of the container to the console window in JSON format, look for a property called **IP Address** under the **Networks** section as shown in the following image:

```
docker inspect <containerid>
```

```
"Networks": {
    "nat": {
        "IPAMConfig": null,
        "Links": null,
        "Aliases": null,
        "NetworkID": "b20a2fcc56a2767f2b3f2abf4dc
        "EndpointID": "00211161b5973435fdf47421c2
        "Gateway": "",
        "IPAddress": "172.30.28.30",
        "IPPrefixLen": 16,
        "IPv6Gateway": "",
        "GlobalIPv6Address": "",
        "GlobalIPv6PrefixLen": 0,
        "MacAddress": "00:15:5d:2b:3d:07"
```

`docker inspect` also prints the location of the log file (within the container's filesystem) which will be used by the container to store container specific logs. Check for the attribute `LogPath`.

4. Create a new Redis Cache container which will act as a slave to the master. Ensure the master is already running. The newly created container uses the IP address of the master and the port to connect with the master and synchronize. The Redis command-line console provides an option of passing the master's IP using the `-slaveof` argument, the same can also be achieved by replacing the master's IP and port in the configuration file:

```
docker run --name redis-server-slave -it -p 6380:6380
-v c:\ProgramData\docker\volumes\redisdatastore:C:\
redisdatastore learningwsc/redis-server-volumes
.\\redis-server.exe .\\redis.unprotected.conf --port
6380 --slaveof 172.30.28.30 6379
```

The following log from Redis console shows that the slave connected to the master successfully:

```
[7616] 01 Dec 19:02:42.780 # Server started, Redis version 3.2.100
[7616] 01 Dec 19:02:42.884 * DB loaded from disk: 0.000 seconds
[7616] 01 Dec 19:02:42.929 * The server is now ready to accept connections on port 6380
[7616] 01 Dec 19:02:42.935 * Connecting to MASTER 172.30.28.30:6379
[7616] 01 Dec 19:02:42.964 * MASTER <-> SLAVE sync started
[7616] 01 Dec 19:02:42.974 * Non blocking connect for SYNC fired the event.
[7616] 01 Dec 19:02:43.027 * Master replied to PING, replication can continue...
[7616] 01 Dec 19:02:43.036 * Partial resynchronization not possible (no cached master)
[7616] 01 Dec 19:02:43.432 * Full resync from master: 204735319cac62d21ed48e5c462316ebeba3fac0:1
[7616] 01 Dec 19:02:43.967 * MASTER <-> SLAVE sync: receiving 134 bytes from master
[7616] 01 Dec 19:02:44.017 * MASTER <-> SLAVE sync: Flushing old data
[7616] 01 Dec 19:02:44.018 * MASTER <-> SLAVE sync: Loading DB in memory
[7616] 01 Dec 19:02:44.029 * MASTER <-> SLAVE sync: Finished with success
```

We can also connect to the master cache container running on the container host from any Redis client and run the following command to get the number of slaves connected to the master.

`docker logs` command followed by the container ID prints all the logs written to the standard error log.

```
          .cloudapp.net:6379> info replication
# Replication
role:master
connected_slaves:1
slave0:ip=172.30.28.99,port=6380,state=online,offset=239,lag=1
master_repl_offset:239
repl_backlog_active:1
repl_backlog_size:1048576
repl_backlog_first_byte_offset:2
repl_backlog_histlen:238
```

Redis provides numerous configurable options for manipulating the relationship between master and slave(s). Few of those commands which can run from client are:

- `role`: Returns the role of the instance in the context of the replication
- `sync`: Internal command used for replication
- `wait`: Wait for the synchronous replication of all the write commands

In the preceding example, we have used the same container host to deploy the slave but in production environments the slave containers should be provisioned on a different container host so that availability is guaranteed beyond host's downtimes. Redis 2.8 and higher versions support diskless replication, when the data must be replicated to new slave(s) the RDB file is copied to the slave over the wire instead of just replaying the writes this increases the performance and turn up times for the cache service. Diskless replication can be setup using the argument `repl-diskless-sync` while starting the service or by using the configuration file.

The line between engineers and site operations is thinning; it is the responsibility of the application developer also to design solutions which can be configured, deployed and operated independently irrespective of the environment conditions. Docker on Windows aids in building configurable systems and sub-systems like Redis which are configurable by nature, and which enhance the deployment experience. Designing applications which can seamlessly integrate with container sub-system speeds up the delivery process and deployments per day.

Integrating Redis containers with Music Store

We started off with *Music Store* as a monolithic application and our goal was to break it down into multiple sub-systems which can be independently deployed as quickly as possible. Each of those sub-systems should be configurable for operations teams increasing the agility of the service. In the previous chapter, we added database storage features to *Music Store*. The database containers are provisioned on separate host which eases off maintenance activities and helps in adding additional resources like CPU power and storage on demand. Applications which depend hugely on data perform frequent data transactions, each of the transactions adds to cost and latency. Performance of an application can be improved by placing the frequently used data close to the application use distributed cache stores. In this section, will use Redis Cache containers to store frequently used data. *Music Store* is built using C# and ASP.NET Core and entity framework as the repository layer. The solution contains various third party which help in development; each of them is installed using the NuGet package manager. The Microsoft team maintains a NuGet package `Microsoft.Extensions.Caching.Redis.Core` which can be used to integrate with Redis Cache servers for .NET Core projects.

We will start this section with the *Music Store* solution from `Chapter 6`, *Storage Volumes*, which uses SQL Server container to store the album data and add Redis Cache features. This chapter, like all other chapters, assumes that the source code is downloaded and extracted to `c:\learningwsc\`. The completed solution is available at `c:\learningwsc\chapter7\musicstore-redis\completed`:

1. Open the Visual Studio 2015 *Music Store* solution at `c:\learningwsc\chapter7\musicstore-redis\begin`.
2. As explained previously we need to add the C# Redis library to be able to connect and save data to the cache store. Right-click on the **References** section of the *Music Store* project and click **Manage NuGet references**.
3. Click **Browse** and search for `Microsoft.Extensions.Caching.Redis.Core`.
4. Click on the search result and install the latest version (version 1.0.3 is used in the completed version).

5. Open `config.json` and add the new following configuration, under the **App Settings** section. Replace the `<IPAddressOrDNSNameofHost>` with the IP address or DNS name of the container host, the default port number can also be replaced if required. For example: `"RedisConnection":` `"samplehost.cloudapp.net:6379"`.

```
"RedisConnection": "<IPAddressOrDNSNameofHost>:6379"
```

6. AspNet Core features inbuilt dependency injection which is used to inject responsibility chains into the constructors. To inject the Redis Cache service into the constructors we must register it as a variant of `IDistributedCache`. Open `Startup.cs` and add the following code to the `ConfigureService` function. `ConfigureService` is called as part of the application life cycle.

```
services.AddDistributedRedisCache(option => {
    option.Configuration = Configuration["AppSettings:
    RedisConnection"];
    option.InstanceName = "master";
});
```

7. [*Optional*] The following code registers in-memory cache as service. We can either comment it or use it to store data in-memory as per need:

```
services.AddMemoryCache();
```

8. Open `HomeController.cs` and update the signature of the `Index` method with the following code. This code constructs and injects the Redis Cache object we registered in the preceding step:

```
public async Task<IActionResult> Index(
    [FromServices] MusicStoreContext dbContext,
    [FromServices] IDistributedCache cache)
```

9. Replace the contents of the `Index` function with the following code:

```
// Get most popular albums
    var cacheKey = "topselling";
    List<Album> albums = null;
    //try get top selling albums from cache
    var cachedalbums = cache.Get(cacheKey);
    if (cachedalbums == null)
    {
        //Get albums from database
        albums = await GetTopSellingAlbumsAsync(dbContext, 6);
        if (albums != null && albums.Count > 0)
```

```
        {
            if (_appSettings.CacheDbResults)
            {
                // Refresh it every 10 minutes.
                cache.Set(cacheKey,
                    Encoding.ASCII.GetBytes
                    (JsonConvert.SerializeObject(albums)),
                new DistributedCacheEntryOptions() {
                        AbsoluteExpiration =
                    DateTimeOffset.UtcNow.AddMinutes(10) }
                );
            }
        }
    }
    else
    {
        //deserialize cached albums
        albums = JsonConvert.
            DeserializeObject<List<Album>>
                System.Text.Encoding.UTF8.
                GetString(cachedalbums));
    }
    return View(albums);
```

The preceding code tries to get the top selling album from the cache store, which a request is made to the database store to get the top selling albums. The results of the database call are saved to the cache store so that subsequent requests can use the cached data. Before we run and test *Music Store* with caching capabilities we should create the dependent containers:

1. Run the following command to create a SQL Server container and configure for sa login. Please refer Chapter 6, *Storage Volumes* for more information:

    ```
    docker run -it -p 1433:1433 microsoft/
    mssql-server-2016-express-windows powershell
    ```

2. Run the following commands to configure sa login:

    ```
    SQLCMD
    ALTER LOGIN [sa] ENABLE
    GO
    ALTER LOGIN [sa] WITH PASSWORD=N'Password@123'
    GO
    ```

3. The second sub-system we need here is the Redis Cache container (master); the following command creates the first cache container. If you're planning to use a non-default port for Redis Cache, make sure *Music Store* is updated with the corresponding port in the `Config.json` file.

```
docker run --name redis-server-master -d
-p 6379:6379 -v c:\ProgramData\docker\volumes\redisdatastore:
C:\redisdatastore learningwsc/redis-server-volumes
```

4. Run the following command which creates a slave to the master container we've just created and exposed using port6380. Remember we can also connect to the slave container using Redis client and `run` commands.

> A full reference of Redis commands is available at
> `https://redis.io/commands`.

```
docker run --name redis-server-slave -it -p 6380:6380
-v c:\ProgramData\docker\volumes\redisdatastore:
C:\redisdatastore learningwsc/redis-server-volumes
.\\redis-server.exe .\\redis.unprotected.conf --port
6380 --slaveof <IPAddressOfRedisMasterContainer> 6379
```

5. Create container volumes for Redis and SQL Server to store data on the host using the following commands:

```
docker volume create redisdatastore
docker volume create musicstoreimages
```

Now we have the environment ready to create an updated image of *Music Store* and check the improved performance while rendering the top albums. Press *Ctrl + Shift + B* to build an upgraded `musicstorage` image with caching capability. Ensure `Docker` is selected as the run profile as shown screenshot and press *F5*:

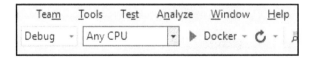

Wait for the .NET process to create and seed *Music Store* database with sample data. At the end of the process the following log will be shown on the console window:

```
Stopping conflicting containers using port 80
3275d4492603
musicstoreimages
Hosting environment: Production
Content root path: C:\app
Now listening on: http://*:80
Application started. Press Ctrl+C to shut down.
```

Open any browser and browse the home page of the application using the IP address or DNS name of the container host. We should be able to see a difference in response times between the first and second request, though the difference is in milliseconds. In real-time applications, which store large amounts of data, the difference in response times will be significant. We can witness the new key-value added to the Redis Cache container using the RDM as shown in the following screenshot:

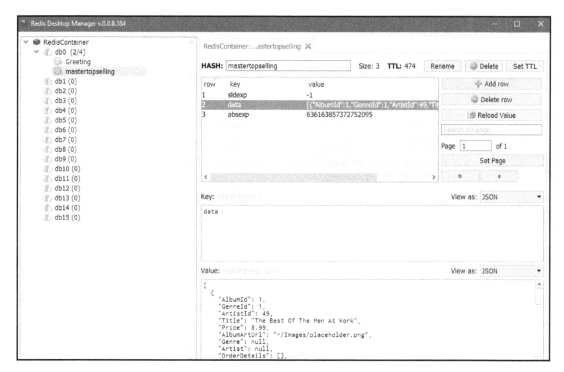

With the previous example, we have successfully added another sub-system to the *Music Store* solution. The new sub-system Redis is containerized and we can now provision cache containers in seconds and quickly configure them so that development teams can work in an agile fashion at greater speed. Redis offers other third-party tools for management, availability, and performance like Redis Sentinel and RDM. Redis also supports a variety of programming languages. Containerization reduces the cost of running the development and test infrastructure; multiple teams can work in parallel by quickly provisioning custom containers on the same shared host with isolation.

Summary

We covered the following topics in this chapter:

- Redis is an open-licensed software which can be used as cache server (and data store). Redis Cache server can be configured and deployed as Windows Container or Hyper-V Container.
- Redis provides wealth of configuration options which help customize the container deployment and configuration. Redis configuration options can be passed via a command line argument as part of the Dockerfile or by using the Redis configuration file.
- Windows Container volumes can be used to store Redis Cached data using RDB file or AOF persistence mechanisms. Volumes store data on the container host, and the volume data can be backed up or archived which increase the data availability and redundancy.
- .NET applications can use existing NuGet package libraries `Microsoft.Extensions.Caching.Redis.Core` for building applications using Redis Cache server.
- Redis contains in-built replication features, a Redis Cache deployment can contain one master and multiple slave(s). Slaves are synchronized using synchronous or asynchronous mode of communication. Redis configuration file can be used to manipulate the master-slave relationship properties.

8
Container Network

An application consists of many layers such as data repository layer, business component layer and a web layer which basically forms the interacting surface for the user. Each of these layers are typically deployed using a multi-subnet secured network topology so that communication across layers can be controlled individually at a subnet level. Every application is designed keeping the network topology, scalability and extensibility features in mind but, during the normal course of application development, these features are hardly tested. This is due to the time and effort required for setting up the required infrastructure. Developers test the application in isolation using a single instance without the network restrictions applied. During this cloud era, it is important for applications to be tested (at least occasionally) in a near production-like environment so that the security, scalability and performance expectations match the real environments. Testing in a production-like environment, which includes all the network related settings configured like subnets, firewalls and ACLs. This widens the scope/area of testing and unveils the security and extensibility loop holes, if any. The line between application engineers and operations team is thinning, it is hard for the operations/deployment teams to create and maintain such environments for every development cycle. It is also prone to increase the infrastructure costs of the application either on private data-center or on public clouds. Thankfully Windows Server 2016 Containers and Docker on Windows Server 2016 have come together to solve the above problem, Windows Server 2016 allows you to create virtual networks inside a container host using Docker commands or PowerShell scripts. You can configure security and setup communication channels across containers as per your application's requirements, and this is going to be the focus of this chapter. We will learn how virtual networks work inside a Windows Server 2016 host and how to configure complex networks across containers and across hosts for better security at reduced costs.

The following topics will be described in this chapter:

- Introduction to Windows Containers network management stack
- Configuring container networks
- Networking modes, multi-container networks
- Multinode container networks
- Deploying *Music Store* as a microservice
- Manage Docker, using PowerShell for Docker

Introduction to Windows networking

The networking requirements of an application are as critical and complicated as the business problem you are trying to solve. It is important and essential to follow the industry's best practice and guidelines on network configuration so that your application performs well during peak loads without breaking, and so that it is secured from any security breach which might intend to kill the application or, even worse, steal customer-sensitive data. Security can be controlled by adhering to strong networking policies and firewalls restrictions so that communication can be controlled, throttled and monitored across a group of machines (called subnets) and at each instance level. Network configuration also brings in logical isolation for a single tenant in a multi-tenant environments.

Deploying containerized applications using a virtualized network is quite like deploying virtual machines in a network. Any typical enterprise web application consists of a web tier which is made up of HTML, CSS and some scripts; a middle tier REST API or SOAP based web service, composed with business rule engines and application logic; and a database tier, which consists of a database with a relational database, replication, jobs and backup policies applied. Each tier consists of one or more virtual machines running identical deployment. Virtual machines in each tier are configured in a logical group called subnet, access control policies are applied at a subnet level so that communication across tiers can be completely controlled using the IP, port number and inbound/outbound combination.

For example, Azure offers pay-per-use virtual network service which can be used to split virtual machines into logical subnets. Azure virtual networks offer additional security across tiers using **Network Security Groups** (**NSG**), help solve specific IP requirements using custom subnets and allow access to be controlled to Internet and on-premises networks at a subnet/machine level. Further Azure also provides a programmable load balancer which can be used to configure custom policies to balance the load across identical deployments using tenant based policy. For example, in a multi-tenant model, routing patterns can be applied such that premium customers are always directed to high configuration machines so that they can be serviced fast.

The following picture shows a sample virtual network with multiple subnets, ILBs, and access restrictions applied across subnets using NSGs. Notice that the web tier is accessible from the Internet, but the middle tier is seized away from the Internet which gives an additional layer of security. The business logic is only accessible from the web tier and not directly from the Internet, and by configuring access to the middle tier using whitelisted IPs (which fall under the web tier subnet only), we have controlled access to the most important part of our application. The database tier is accessible only by the middle tier, thereby sealing away direct access from the Internet and, at the same time, the database tier can also be connected to the on-premises network so that data can be backed up and continuous monitoring can be setup using existing on-premises tools.

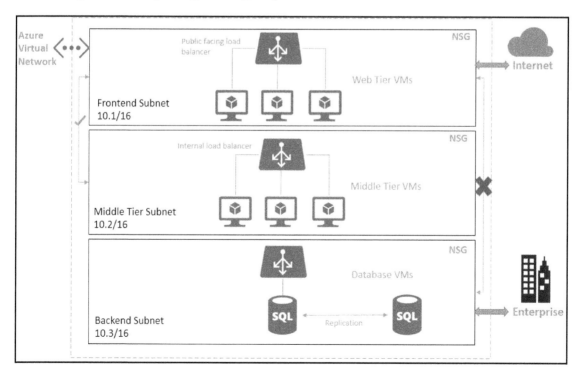

Windows Containers--network management stack

Windows Containers networking is very similar to the preceding configuration. Windows Container host machines which could be a Windows Server 2016 server on a physical server, virtual machine or even a Windows 10 client machine, and can extend their networking capabilities to the containers. If the container host is connected to the Internet using some type of channel like Ethernet or WiFi using a **Network Interface Card** (**NIC**), the containers running inside the host can latch onto the network using Virtual NICs (vNICs). The containers connect to the host's network using vNICs installed on each container and each vNIC is in turn connected to the **Virtual Switch** (**vSwitch**) of the container host. The type of vNIC installed on each container depends on the isolation type of the container, Windows Containers use Host vNIC while Hyper-V Containers use synthetic vNIC. In a non-container world, synthetic VM NIC is the default network adapter for virtual machines created using Hyper-V, and they have an additional advantage of being Hyper-V aware and are not exposed to the utility VM.

The Hyper-V switch provides the connectivity from the containers to the physical network of the container host. An additional layer 3 network configuration is also required for the container host to forward packets to the designated container based on IP address and protocol, such as TCP/UDP and port numbers. Layer 4-7 services like DNS, DHCP, HTTP and SMB are also required for containers to be useful in a wide variety of scenarios. Windows Containers networking stack supports all the previously mentioned requirements. The following picture shows how the container's networking stack works within a container host:

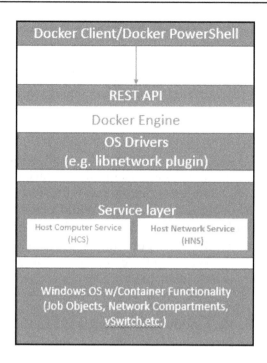

Windows Container host's network management stack consists of the layers described in the following points and each layer is responsible for the creation and configuration of virtual networks using the Docker command-line client, Docker REST API or Docker PowerShell.

- **Windows OS Container layer**: Windows OS Container layer consists of job objects, vSwitch and network compartments which provide the core features of creating and managing networks.
- **Services layer**: The services layer consists of two main components called **Host Compute Service** (**HCS**) and **Host Network Service** (**HNS**). HNS provides the necessary plumbing service using the underneath core components described here. For example, HNS is responsible for creating the firewall rule on the host whenever is created using the Docker Service.
- **Docker extension layer**: The Docker extension layer consists of the Docker Engine, Docker Rest API and the OS Drivers. Docker uses the Windows HNS for creating and configuring networks. Docker is the default and only management stack for a Windows Container network. The **Docker Engine** communicates with HNS using `libcontainer` plugin as shown in the preceding image.

The `libcontainer` plugin is the execution driver for Docker, which decouples itself from depending on underlying kernel features there by making it platform independent.

> Prior to `libcontainer`, Docker depended upon the Linux kernel features like LXC and CGroups to provision containers within Linux, with the introduction of `libcontainer` Docker is now supported on multiple platforms.

The Docker team created `libcontainer` to move away from being only Linux-Centric technology. `libContainer` provides a standard interface which can be used to create containers inside any Host OS. Containers can interact with Host OS resources, security and controls in a predictable way using `libcontainer`. With Docker Engine using `libcontainer` to interact with Windows HNS, users no longer have to worry about creating static mapping between the host's port and the container's port. Docker creates the port mapping automatically when creating the container, it also enables the firewall rules for the container (this feature is only available from Windows Server 2016 Containers TP5 onwards).

The default internal IP prefix for windows containers is `172.16.0.0/12`. Docker Engines create this network when the service starts for first time, the default name of the network is NAT. Any new container's IP falls under this default network if nothing is specified while creating the container using the Docker `run` command or `dockerfile`. Container's endpoints will also be created automatically attached to the NAT network.

> If the host's IP matches with the default IP prefix of the NAT network, the default IP prefix should be changed. Steps to customize network configuration will be described in further sections.

Configuring container networks

Windows Container network management stack can be managed using Docker commands or Docker PowerShell. Docker also exposes a REST API which can be used to manage the stack (we will learn about interacting with REST API in next chapter). We can also connect to a remote Docker host using remote connection as explained in the earlier chapters.

The following are a few commands which can be used while managing container networks using the Docker command line:

docker network

```
PS C:\> docker network

Usage:  docker network COMMAND

Manage networks

Options:
      --help    Print usage

Commands:
  connect       Connect a container to a network
  create        Create a network
  disconnect    Disconnect a container from a network
  inspect       Display detailed information on one or more networks
  ls            List networks
  rm            Remove one or more networks

Run 'docker network COMMAND --help' for more information on a command.
```

Docker creates default nat network when the service starts, the list of available networks on a Docker host can be found out using the docker network ls command as shown in the following screenshot:

```
PS C:\> docker network ls
NETWORK ID          NAME                DRIVER              SCOPE
70bd0e6a326c        nat                 nat                 local
434654b99817        none                null                local
```

The default network configuration of the host can be found out by inspecting the network using the `docker network inspect <network_name>` as shown in the following screenshot. The following command shows the subnet (`172.30.16.0/20`) and gateway IPs of the NAT network which are used by container by default:

```
docker network inspect nat

"Name": "nat",
"Id": "70bd0e6a326cae6910de85fe865df6e873bc511930a24edd2cca26f71991ae51",
"Scope": "local",
"Driver": "nat",
"EnableIPv6": false,
"IPAM": {
    "Driver": "default",
    "Options": null,
    "Config": [
        {
            "Subnet": "172.30.16.0/20",
            "Gateway": "172.30.16.1"
        }
    ]
},
"Internal": false,
"Attachable": false,
"Containers": {},
"Options": {
    "com.docker.network.windowsshim.hnsid": "95779b39-d7f8-4433-b01b-4088e674ee49",
    "com.docker.network.windowsshim.networkname": "nat"
},
"Labels": {}
```

Network Address Translation (**NAT**) is the default networking mode for the Windows Container host. It is the simplest form which uses the host's IP and NAT for providing an IP range for containers. It is the most apt networking mode for development environments. Microsoft offers a few other networking modes like transparent network and L2 bridge and L2 tunnel, which are explained in the next section. NAT allows containers or even virtual machines on the host to share the Public IP of the host to connect to an outside network. It creates a private network within the host which is used by all the containers (and VMs too if the host supports nested virtualization). When a new container is created, and attached to the NAT network (this happens by default) the container is assigned an IP from an IP range allocated to Nat and on any new connection like browsing www.bing.com. NAT translates the private IP assigned to the container to public IP address of the host and creates a new entry in the NAT flow state table on the host. When a connection is made from outside to a container on the internal network, NAT uses the flow state table to translate the connection to the internal IP of the container.

The same concept can be extended to virtual machines, and it is quite possible to create a hybrid environment consisting of Windows Server Containers, Hyper-V Containers, and traditional VMs, all sharing the same IP of the host, as shown in the following image:

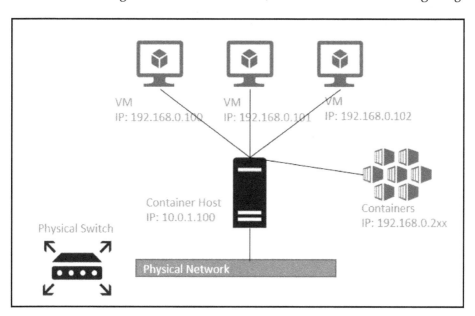

NAT is the default network for any new containers, the `--network` flag should be used to specify the networking driver to be used while creating containers, so the following command is equivalent to not using the `--network` flag at all since it is obvious in this case:

```
docker run -it --network nat microsoft/windowsservercore cmd
```

Let us create a new network called `mynetwork` using the following command and assign a new subnet range `172.20.81.0/24` and gateway `172.20.81.1`:

```
docker network create -d nat --subnet=172.20.81.0/24
--gateway=172.20.81.1 mynetwork
```

Windows containers use the networking compartment on each container to use the host's networking stack to connect with external network. Hyper-V containers use the vmNIC as Hyper-V Containers are already enclosed in an optimized VM, which has its own network stack. The gateway IP used in the preceding command is assigned to the vNIC which utilizes the WinNAT for NAT and the TCP/IP stack in the container host for external connectivity. The following picture explains the network connection for the preceding command:

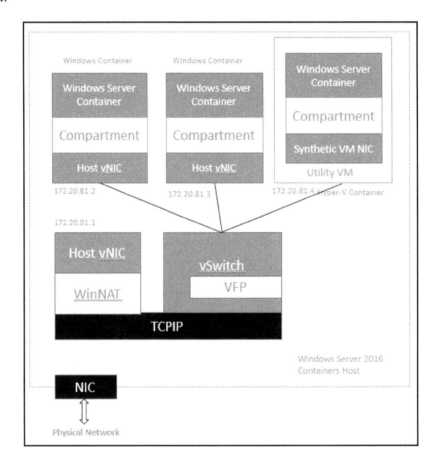

While creating containers, we can use the network shown in the preceding image to join containers to the subnet range specified in the command. The following command creates a container in the new network named `mynetwork`:

```
docker run -it --network mynetwork microsoft/windowsservercore cmd
```

The IP configuration of the newly created container can be verified as shown in the following screenshot. The IP range of the container falls within the range of the subnet we've previously created, and the default gateway is also the same.

```
C:\>ipconfig

Windows IP Configuration


Ethernet adapter vEthernet (Temp Nic Name):

   Connection-specific DNS Suffix   . : wsc-dev-1016.i7.internal.cloudapp.net
   Link-local IPv6 Address . . . . . : fe80::504b:5625:8050:c80f%24
   IPv4 Address. . . . . . . . . . . : 172.20.81.21
   Subnet Mask . . . . . . . . . . . : 255.255.255.0
   Default Gateway . . . . . . . . . : 172.20.81.1
```

We can also create containers and attach to an existing network as shown:

```
docker run -d --name natcontainer microsoft/windowsservercore
docker network connect mynetwork natcontainer
```

If your application is dependent on any specific IP, the `docker network` command provides an option to specify the IP address for the container which is attached to the network using the `--ip` flag. The container should be stopped momentarily before assigning the IP address, because Windows does not support updating the network configuration of a running container:

```
docker network connect --ip 172.20.81.2 mynetwork natcontainer
```

We can also rename the container inside a network using the alias flag, for example the following command assigns a static IP to the container and renames it to `mynetworkcontainer` so that it can be resolved using the aliased name within the network:

```
docker network connect -ip 172.20.81.2 -alias mynetworkcontainer
mynetwork natcontainer
```

If the container's IP address is specifically mentioned, as in the preceding example, the container tries to retain the IP beyond restarts. If the IP address is no longer available, the container fails to start. The ideal way to guarantee availability of the IP always is by specifying an `-ip-range` while creating the network and using a static IP outside the range. This ensures the IP is not given to any other container when this container is not in the network. We can pause, stop, and restart the containers connected to a network, and containers try to reconnect corresponding networks when they run. For example, the following commands specify an IP range and use a static IP outside the range to maintain a static IP for the container:

```
docker network create -subnet 172.20.0.0/16
-ip-range 172.20.240.0/20 mynetwork
docker network connect
-ip 172.20.128.2 mynetwork container1
```

Static port mappings

For the applications to be accessible on the container host's IP, a port mapping should be created between the container's port and the host's port. These mappings should be created while creating the container or when the container is stopped. TCP/UDP ports will be translated using **Port Address Translation (PAT)** so that traffic received on the external port of the host can be translated to an internal port using these mappings as shown in the following image:

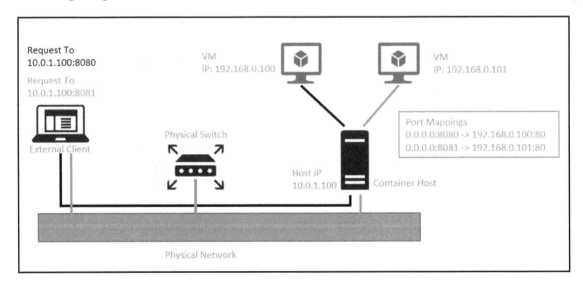

The following command maps the container host's port 80 to port 80 on the container. Take, for example, an IIS web server running on the container on port 80, any requests made to port 80 on the container's host from an external client using the host's IP or DNS name will be translated to port 80 on the container.

```
docker run -it -p 80:80 microsoft/windowsservercore cmd
```

It is not mandatory for the ports to be identical on the container and the host. For example, the following command maps port 8082 on the host to port 80 on the container:

```
docker run -it -p 8082:80 microsoft/windowsservercore cmd
```

Docker on Windows also supports dynamic ports using the -p parameter or the EXPOSE command in Dockerfile using the -p parameter. If not specified, an available random port on the container host will be selected. The random port selected by docker can be verified using the docker ps command as shown:

```
docker run -itd -p 80 windowsservercore cmd
```

```
PS C:\> docker ps
CONTAINER ID        IMAGE                          COMMAND        CREATED             STATUS             PORTS
6ca3d9f3c557        microsoft/windowsservercore    "cmd"          About a minute ago  Up About a minute  0.0.0.0:61310->80,
```

From Windows Server 2016 TP5 and Windows insider builds greater than 14,300, the Docker Engine creates a firewall rule for the port numbers used on the NAT network. This firewall is global to the container host and not specific for the container or network adapter.

Disconnecting containers from network

A container can be removed from the network using the following command. Remember to stop the container before disconnecting from the network. If we try to restart the stopped container after disconnecting from the network, it tries to reattach to the same network. To change the network of the container, use the connect command mentioned in the preceding code snippet:

```
docker network disconnect mynetwork <containername>
```

Use docker network rm to clean up the network completely, and clean up any Hyper-V virtual switches and NATs:

```
Docker network rm mynetwork
```

Limitations of WinNAT network implementation

WinNAT is the most preferable networking mode for development environments. However, it might be feasible to use the same in UAT/production environments because of the following limitations:

- **Multiple subnet is not allowed**: Let us say you have a multi-tenant environment or you have discrete applications running as containers on a host. All these applications/tenants should share the same internal subnet because WinNAT does not allow multiple internal subnet prefixes. All containers/VMs should coordinate between each other by using multiple partitions within a single subnet and making sure we create a larger subnet (for example: /18) might be required to host a multitude of containers/VMs. For applications sharing a container host, the static port mapping facility provided by NAT configuration will impose a restriction on port availability because external host ports can only be mapped to one internal port. If the container hosts two discrete web server containers like IIS, only one of them will be reachable using the host's IP or port 80.

- **Overlapping IPs**: The subnet range used by NAT on the container host cannot overlap with the host's external IP assigned by the network. For example, if the subnet range selected by NAT is 172.16.0.0/24, the host's IP cannot fall under this subnet, for example 172.16.1.208. If the container hosts IP is assigned dynamically and it falls under the subnet range of the NAT network the internal IP prefix of the NAT network should be modified accordingly.

- **Accessing internal endpoints from host**: Internal endpoints assigned to a container cannot be accessed using the static port mappings from the container host. For example, if we create a container using Microsoft/IIS image and if it is assigned an IP from NAT like 172.16.1.100 and assuming we configure port forwarding on port 8080, we will not able to access the web server from the Container host using the host's IP and static port 8080; although the web server will be accessible using container's IP like http://172.16.1.100:8080. As explained earlier, when the Docker service starts for the first-time, a NAT network is created automatically. This can be avoided by starting the docker service (dockerd) with -b none option as shown in the following command:

```
dockerd -b "none"
```

Networking modes

Windows Containers can use any of the four available networking modes (or drivers) to expose containers to the outside world. The networking mode chosen by the container decides how the container will be accessible from outside, how IP addresses are assigned and how networking policy can be applied. Apart from NAT networking mode, we've learned that the Windows Server 2016 networking stack offers three more modes for networking: transparent, L2 bridge and L2 tunnel. These are described in the next section.

Transparent

In transparent networking mode, each container is directly connected to the host's network (unlike NAT where containers use container host's IP to connect to the outside network). This mode is most familiar to Hyper-V users. Containers use the VM switch to connect to the network connected by the switch as shown in the following image:

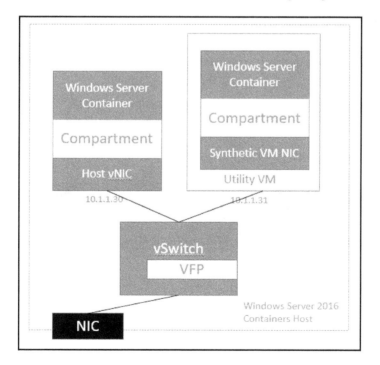

Traffic is routed from the containers to the NIC via the v-Switch directly. Containers can be assigned IP addresses statically or dynamically by using a DHCP server. **Dynamic Host Configuration Protocol** (**DHCP**) is a client/server protocol which can provide an IP address to an IP host and other configurations, like subnet mask and default gateway. Without DHCP devices on a network, every device is assigned an IP addresses manually and these addresses should be manually reclaimed when the device leaves the network. DHCP maintains a pool of IP address which are leased to the network device and claimed automatically when the device leaves the network.

The following command creates a simple transparent network, but this network cannot be used for accessing containers since we have not configured any subnet or gateway:

```
docker network create -d transparent transparentnetwork
```

If the idea is to assign static IPs manually to containers, you must ensure that the gateway and subnet information is specified while creating the network. The following command creates a transparent network with subnet and gateway details:

```
docker network create -d transparent --subnet=10.123.174.0/23
--gateway=10.123.174.1 transparentnetwork
```

 If you are connected to a container host remotely, there might be a small interruption while the network is being created.

The newly created network will be listed under the networks section with transparent driver as shown in the following screenshot:

```
PS C:\> docker network ls
NETWORK ID          NAME                DRIVER              SCOPE
d49146542f9c        mynetwork           nat                 local
b6b0a50a8a53        nat                 nat                 local
875a672583a5        none                null                local
b63ef5c76d0d        transparentnetwork  transparent         local
```

The following command creates a container under the transparent network:

```
docker run -it --network=transparentnetwork
--ip 10.123.174.105 microsoft/windowsservercore cmd
```

Since the container has access to the physical network of the container host it is not required to map ports for the container. We should be able to ping the container directly using the IP address provided using the `--ip` flag in the preceding code snippet.

If the container host is virtualized and if you are planning to use DHCP for assigning IP addresses automatically then MAC address spoofing should be enabled on the virtual network adapter using the container host. The network traffic will be blocked from the containers if MAC address spoofing is off:

```
Get-VMNetworkAdapter -VMName ContainerHostVM | Set-VMNetworkAdapter
-MacAddressSpoofing On
```

The preceding command will not work on Azure since it is not possible to enable `MacAddressSpoofing`. Azure only supports the NAT network driver.

L2 bridge or L2 tunnel

Under this networking mode, each container's endpoint will be created using the subnet of the container host. The IP address must be assigned statically from the container host's subnet. All the container endpoints will have the same MAC address due to Layer-2 address translation. Network traffic between any two containers on the same subnet will be bridged to the container host while network traffic between containers on different IP subnets or different hosts are forwarded to the physical host's virtual switch. While sending packets out of the container the MAC address will be replaced by the MAC Address of the container host. For incoming packets MAC address is re-written using the container's address. This type of networking mode is usually suitable for public and private cloud networks.

To create a new network using the L2 bridge, use the following command:

```
docker network create -d l2bridge --subnet=192.168.1.0/24
--gateway=192.168.1.1 bridgenetwork
```

L2 bridge and L2 tunnel use Microsoft **Software-Defined Networking (SDN)** stack to connect container endpoints to tenant's virtual network.

 These networking modes do not work on Azure, since there is no way to connect container endpoints to tenant virtual network.

Before understanding how L2 bridge or L2 tunnel mode works, it is important to understand another important component of Windows Server 2016 called SDN. SDN is a new technology which comes with Windows Server 2016 Datacenter edition, System Center 2016, and Microsoft Azure. It helps configure and manage physical and virtual networking devices like routers, switches, and routers in data center. Just as Hyper-V helps virtualize the servers, SDN provides virtualization over a physical network so that you can work with your applications or any other component in a consistent manner using the abstraction created by SDN. SDN allows you to define network policies and manage them centrally. SDN works across the physical network and virtual network, and it allows you to implement policies or apply restrictions seamlessly while adding or removing new applications or workloads from an existing infrastructure like a physical or virtual network.

The following are the core software components which define SDN:

- **Network Controller** (**NC**): Network controller is a highly scalable and highly available server role which provides a programmatic interface (API) to interact, configure, manage, and monitor both physical and virtual networks in a private data center. The network controller uses a programmatic API called southbound API to communicate with the underlying network. It provides another API called northbound API to communicate with the network controller. Using a REST API, PowerShell or any custom-built management client we can interact with NC to manage Hyper-V VMs, virtual switches, physical virtual switches, firewalls, VPN gateways, load balancers, and so on.
- **Hyper-V virtualization**: As the name implies, Hyper-V virtualization allows you to run virtual networks over an existing physical network. Virtual networks provide isolation and improve resource utilization in a multi-tenant environment. Virtual networks are also compatible with VLANs. More information on Hyper-V Virtualization is available at: `https://technet.microsoft.com/windows-serve r-docs/networking/sdn/technologies/hyper-v-network-virtualization/hy per-v-network-virtualization`.
- **Hyper-V virtual switch**: We have come across this term while discussing the NAT network. The Hyper-V virtual switch is a programmable and software based Layer-2 ethernet network which can be used to configure VMs or containers running inside a host to connect to the physical or virtual network in a variety of ways. Most importantly, this feature can be programmatically managed to enforce security policies, isolation and service levels across group of VMs or containers. More information on Hyper-V Virtual Switch is available at: `https://technet.microsoft.com/windows-server-docs/networking/techno logies/hyper-v-virtual-switch/hyper-v-virtual-switch`.

- **Internal DNS Service**: **Internal DNS Service** (**iDNS**) acts as a DNS name resolver (local name or internal resources) for tenants within their own network or external networks. More information on iDNS is available at `https://technet` `.microsoft.com/windows-server-docs/networking/sdn/technologies/idns-` `for-sdn`.

- **Network function virtualization**: Network function virtualization comes with a variety of technologies like **Software Load Balancing** (**SLB**), NAT, data center firewall and an RAS gateway, which provide a convenient way of interacting with virtualized network hardware appliances like load balancers, firewalls, routers, and so on.

 Windows Containers also form part of the **Software-Defined Networking** (**SDN**) of Windows Server 2016.

Windows Server 2016 is a perfect platform for implementing a **Software-Defined Data Center** (**SDDC**). The idea is that servers are virtualized to mimic CPU and Memory where CPU is shared across virtualized machines on a host and expandable memory is virtualized as disks. Network virtualization is a natural progressive in the virtualization pattern which helps you control the network components using programmatic APIs. Network hardware is being virtualized to create virtual networks with routers, switches and load balancers so that you can host multi-tenant applications in your software defined or say programmable data center. SDDC provides business isolation across workloads and helps network administrators configure policies with great agility and flexibility, combining this with containers, which is the fastest way to deploy application packages and can create wonders going forward.

How does the SDN work across hosts? Well the answer is explained in the following image which shows the programmable surface:

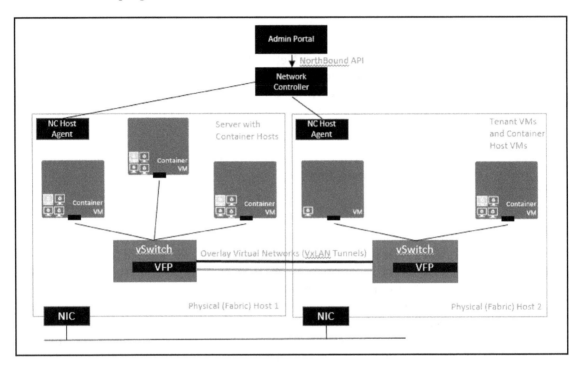

In a virtualized environment, the container runs on a virtual machine which is hosted on a physical server. The network controller will send a policy to the host agent running on the physical server using the southbound API via the OSVB protocol. The host agent will then apply the policy into the **Virtual Filtering Program** (**VFP**) extension of the physical server. This policy is specific to each IP and each endpoint. This helps in defining granular policies to configure traffic to multiple containers running on a single container host using a single network adapter.

With L2 bridge networking mode, all the traffic from the container is forwarded to the container host's VM from where it is forwarded to vSwitch. The VFP extension installed on each vSwitch applies the networking policy. This allows containers to communicate across container hosts using overlay networks like VxLAN in a multinode cluster as shown in the preceding image.

How do we apply L2 bridge network to container endpoints? L2 bridge or L2 tunnel networking modes require a private cloud setup with SDN, and therefore it is beyond the scope of this book to provide a working example. However, this section provides the guidelines to set up such network using containers. The following are the set of pre-requisites to setup L2 bridge container networking mode:

- An SDN infrastructure with a network controller
- Tenant virtual network
- Tenant virtual machine deployed with Windows Containers feature, Docker and Hyper-V role enabled (Hyper-V is required only for deploying Hyper-V Containers)

 More information on configuring container endpoints using overlay network on a private cloud is available at
https://technet.microsoft.com/en-us/windows-server-docs/networki ng/sdn/manage/connect-container-endpoints-to-a-tenant-virtual-network.

The basic difference between L2 tunnel and L2 bridge is that, L2 tunnel uses physical Hyper-V host to direct all network traffic from the container endpoints where L2 bridge forwards only cross-subnet network traffic to the physical Hyper-V host. Network policy is applied for both cross-subnet and cross-host traffic using the network controller or network resource provider.

Multiple container networks

Creating multiple container networks is possible by using either an external switch, as in transparent, L2 bridge or L2 tunnel networking mode, or by using NAT mode. In NAT mode, multiple container networks are possible on a single container host using logical partitions.

The following command shows the `InternalIPAddressPrefix` which can be used to create two or more logical NAT networks falling under the same IP prefix:

```
get-netnat
```

As shown in the following screenshot, the `InternalIPAddressPrefix` of the container host is `172.20.80.1/20`:

```
PS C:\> get-netnat

Name                           : H971db7ae-da9a-4872-a360-6d16476383e6
ExternalIPInterfaceAddressPrefix :
InternalIPInterfaceAddressPrefix : 172.20.80.1/20
IcmpQueryTimeout               : 30
TcpEstablishedConnectionTimeout : 1800
TcpTransientConnectionTimeout  : 120
TcpFilteringBehavior           : AddressDependentFiltering
UdpFilteringBehavior           : AddressDependentFiltering
UdpIdleSessionTimeout          : 120
UdpInboundRefresh              : False
Store                          : Local
Active                         : True
```

Run the following command to create two NAT networks and a gateway:

```
docker network create -d nat --subnet 172.20.81.0/24
--gateway 172.20.81.1 natnetwork1
docker network create -d nat --subnet 172.20.82.0/24
--gateway 172.20.82.1 natnetwork2
```

While creating containers in any subnet, the appropriate network can be chosen using the –network flag.

Container network routing

The following table summarizes the behavior of container traffic when connected in different networking modes.

Single node

The following table explains how a container network is routed across container hosts in a single networking mode:

	Container-container traffic	Container-external traffic
NAT	Connection is established using Hyper-V virtual switch.	Routed via WinNAT using MAC Address translation.
Transparent	Connection is established using Hyper-V virtual switch.	Containers have direct access to the physical network of the host.
L2 bridge	Connection is established using Hyper-V virtual switch.	Containers have direct access to a physical network with MAC address translation.

Multinode

The following table explains how a container network is routed across container hosts in different networking modes:

	Container-container traffic	Container-external traffic
NAT	Traffic is routed using the container host's IP and endpoint using WinNAT.	Traffic is routed using the container host's IP and endpoint using WinNAT.
Transparent	Container IP can be accessed directly.	Containers have direct access to the physical network of the host.
L2 bridge	Container IP can be accessed directly.	Containers have direct access to physical network with MAC address translation.

Multi-subnet deployment of Music Store

We started developing *Music Store* as a monolithic application which were containerized and later componentized by adding a database layer and a caching layer in previous chapters. We will further breakdown the *Music Store* application by adding an API layer, which will be responsible for holding the business logic of the application. *Music Store* API is an ASP.NET Core Web API project which acts as a RESTful service layer for *Music Store* data and business logic. 3-layered architecture is very common among many enterprise applications. *Music Store* is one such sample with a web front-end built using the ASP.NET Core MVC project, which contains the HTML, CSS and some JavaScript files; a middle tier API layer, which contains the business components and caching; and finally a database tier, which is responsible for storing data.

Having a layered architecture is beneficial in many ways: each layer can be individually managed; security and auto-scaling policies can be applied or monitored centrally; and it supports an independent deployment model. In a microservices environment, each team can focus on design, development and distribution of applications or service without impacting the other parts of the application. On the other hand, monolithic designs hinder progress in many ways, and any small change to the application requires a 360-degree testing, regression and a full deployment cycle, which consumes a lot of time and effort. microservices is the new way of designing applications or services, and this section focuses on deploying MusicStore as a set of independently deployable and scalable units. Apart from showcasing a distributed deployment approach this section also focuses on creating a Production/UAT kind of environment at less cost but providing the same scalability and security feature set. This helps in testing the application during development within a production-like environment, which is usually cost and time effective to create for every product increment cycle.

 To help understand the concepts of distributed deployment and networking, a few features of the MusicStore application have been eliminated from the source code: for example, the authentication and admin logins screens. Since this chapter deals with breaking down an application into silos and networking concepts around it, the business functionality is not strongly coupled to the deployment model. The same model can be extended to any given enterprise application with multiple silos.

Let us start with creating new images for the updated MusicStore application. The code samples for this section can be found under `c:\learningwsc\chapter8\musicstore` (assuming you've extracted the source code to `c:\learningwsc`).

The following image shows the new solution structure with the MusicStore WEB and API components:

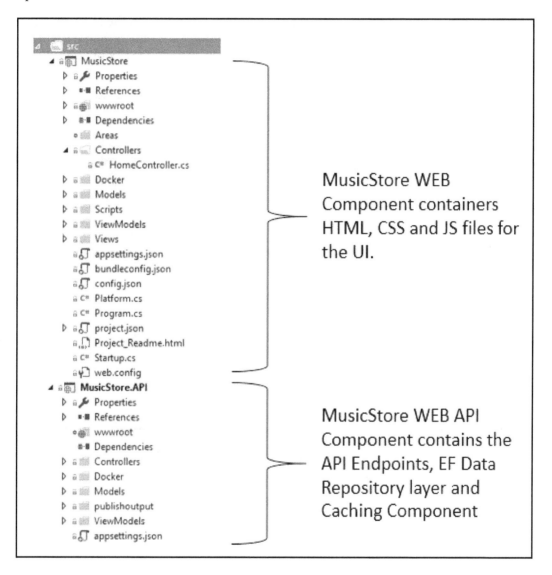

The next image shows the proposed deployment model of MusicStore using Windows Server 2016 Containers Networking Stack in NAT mode.

> The IPs and Subnet samples used here are dependent on the NAT IP of the host and are demonstrated for illustration purposes only. When working your own, replace the IP with `InternalIPAddressPrefix` of your container host.

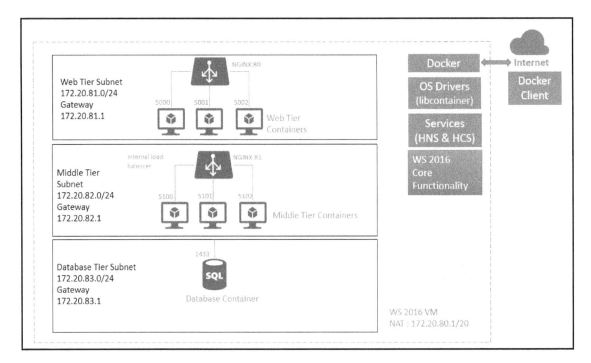

The following exercise goes through the steps involved in deploying MusicStore as explained in the preceding diagram:

1. Let us start building the MusicStore Web and API images. Open the MusicStore solution in Visual Studio.

2. Right-click on the `MusicStore.API` web project and click on **Build**. As explained in previous chapters, the build step is customized and extended to perform additional tasks using the `project.json` file as shown:

```
"scripts": {
    "prepublish": [ "bower install", "dotnet bundle" ],
    "postcompile": [ "powershell -executionpolicy
                     bypass ./docker/dockertask.ps1 -build
```

```
                    -projectname '%project:name%'
                    -configuration '%compile:configuration%'
                    -version '1.0.0'" ],
        "precompile": [ "powershell -executionpolicy
                    bypass ./docker/dockertask.ps1 -clean" ]
    }
```

Post successful compilation the PowerShell script kicks-in calling the build function with default parameter values. The first step shown publishes the binaries and resources to the folder C:/learningwsc/chapter8/musicstore/musicstore.api/publishoutput. The target publish folder can be updated at your convenience:

```
dotnet.exe publish --framework netcoreapp1.0
--configuration $Configuration
--output /learningwsc/chapter8/musicstore/musicstore.api/publishoutput
--no-build
```

Ensure the following folder is created and the latest binaries are copied. The next step creates a musicstore API image with name learningwsc/musicstore.api versioned 1.0.0. In this case the image name is prepended with learningwsc to make the publishing process easy (learningwsc is the account name/username of my Docker Hub account), the image and other parameters can be controlled by passing as parameter values while invoking the PowerShell script or by updating the default parameters. Ensure the build is successful and musicstore API image is created as shown in the following screenshot:

1. The next step is to build the latest musicstore web container image. Right-click on the MusicStore project and click on **Build**. The build process follows the same process as mentioned here; the only difference would be in the image name. Ensure image learningwsc/musicstore is created as shown in the following screenshot:

The musicstore web or API is designed to clean up any existing images before building a new image using pattern recognition. If you want to keep an older version, you can avoid the cleanup process by versioning your images using different version numbers assigned to the $Version PowerShell variable.

2. You can publish these images to your Docker Hub account if you intend to use them on a different container host by using `docker publish` command.

3. Ensure the container host being used for this exercise has the following ports open: `81`, `5100-5103`, `5000-5002`, `1433`, and `6379`. If you are using Azure VM login to the management portal to create the preceding endpoints. For on-premise hosts ensure traffic is allowed on the preceding mentioned ports.

4. Apart from `musicstore` Web and API images we are also dependent on SQL Server and Redis cache images. Unlike the SQL Server Express image that we used in an earlier chapter, we will be using Microsoft's SQL Server vNext container image which comes with an evaluation period of 180 days. More details regarding the image are available at `https://hub.docker.com/r/microsoft/mssql-server-windows/`. Run the following command to pull the latest Microsoft SQL Server image:

```
docker pull microsoft/mssql-server-windows
```

5. Ensure you have a Redis Server image available on the hos. You can either download the image from my Docker Hub account by running the following command, or learn to build the image as explained in `Chapter 7`, *Redis Cache Containers*.

```
docker pull learningwsc/redis-server:1.0.0
```

6. Run the following command to get the internal IP interface address prefix of your container The following screenshot shows the NAT configuration of the container host. Note the value for the property `InternalIPInterfaceAddressPrefix`. The value in my case is `172.20.80.1/20`:

```
PS C:\> Get-NetNat

Name                             : H971db7ae-da9a-4872-a360-6d16476383e6
ExternalIPInterfaceAddressPrefix :
InternalIPInterfaceAddressPrefix : 172.20.80.1/20
IcmpQueryTimeout                 : 30
TcpEstablishedConnectionTimeout  : 1800
TcpTransientConnectionTimeout    : 120
TcpFilteringBehavior             : AddressDependentFiltering
UdpFilteringBehavior             : AddressDependentFiltering
UdpIdleSessionTimeout            : 120
UdpInboundRefresh                : False
Store                            : Local
Active                           : True
```

7. In this exercise, the NAT network is divided into three logical subnets: the web tier, the middle tier, and the database tier. This can be extended to any number within the bounds of the host's address prefix. You can also create a larger NAT network if you intend to create large number of subnets. The following is the configuration of the three logical subnets. Dividing any given address prefix into multiple subnets requires an understanding of how prefixes and hosts per subnet are calculated. For more information on forming logical subnets visit https://technet.microsoft.com/en-us/library/cc958832.aspx.

Tier	Subnet	Gateway
webtier	172.20.81.0/24	172.20.81.1
middletier	172.20.82.0/24	172.20.82.1
datatier	172.20.83.0/24	172.20.83.1

8. Run the following command to create the network configuration as described in the preceding table:

```
docker network create -d nat --subnet 172.20.81.0/24
--gateway 172.20.81.1 webtier
docker network create -d nat --subnet 172.20.82.0/24
--gateway 172.20.82.1 middletier
docker network create -d nat --subnet 172.20.83.0/24
--gateway 172.20.83.1 datatier
```

9. Let us first deploy a database container into the datatier subnet, which will host the MusicStore database using the following command. The following docker command uses the new SQL Server vNext image to create a SQL database container with SA login and password configured as part of the command. The NAT network of the container is selected using the -network command and the IP of the container is configured by using -ip command as shown here:

```
docker run -d -p 1433:1433 --network datatier
--ip 172.20.83.2 -e sa_password=Password@123
-e ACCEPT_EULA=Y microsoft/mssql-server-windows
```

10. Ensure you can connect to the SQL Server container using SSMS or any other management client. You can connect to the container using the host's IP address or DNS name followed by the IP. Use the default SA login to connect to the container using `sa` as username and `Password@123` as password.

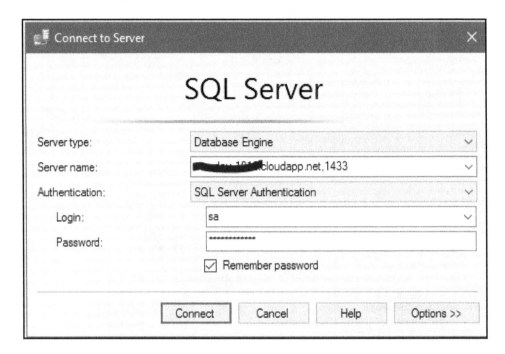

11. Let us now deploy an instance of Redis cache container on the middle tier subnet: run the following command to create a Redi cache container. Ensure the Redis cache image specified in the command is available on the host or else Docker will try to download it from public repositories:

```
docker run -d -p 6379:6379 --name redis-server
--network middletier
--ip 172.20.82.5 learningwsc/redis-server
```

12. We will deploy three instances of the *Music Store* API container using ports `5100`, `5101`, and `5102` of the host mapped to the container's port `80`. Run the following command to create three instances of API container in the `middlertier` network as shown:

```
docker run -d -p 5100:80 --name musicstoreapi1
--network middletier
--ip 172.20.82.2 learningwsc/musicstore.api:1.0.0
dotnet musicstore.api.dll
docker run -d -p 5101:80 --name musicstoreapi2
--network middletier --ip 172.20.82.3
learningwsc/musicstore.api:1.0.0 dotnet musicstore.api.dll
docker run -d -p 5102:80 --name musicstoreapi3
--network middletier --ip 172.20.82.4
learningwsc/musicstore.api:1.0.0 dotnet musicstore.api.dll
```

13. Assuming you have extracted the source code of this book to `C:\learningwsc`, under the path `C:\learningwsc\chapter8\musicstore\Deploy\MusicStore.API` you would find a Dockerfile and `Nginx.conf` file. We will be using these two files to create a custom NGINX container, which will load balance the requests across the three web API containers. Replace the `<dnsnameorip>` tag in the `nginx.conf` with the DNS name or host name of the container host.

14. Open a PowerShell window and navigate to `C:\learningwsc\chapter8\musicstore\Deploy\MusicStore.API`.

15. Run the following command to create an NGINX image for a web API:

```
docker build -t learningwsc/nginx.musicstore.api:1.0.0 .
```

16. Run the following command to create a container using `learningwsc/nginx.musicstore.api` image which listens on port `81` and forwards the requests to port `5100`, `5101`, and `5102` using least connection algorithm.

```
docker run -d -p 81:81 learningwsc/nginx.musicstore.api:1.0.0
```

17. Verify that the API is deployed and you can receive the data using the URL `http://<dnsnameoripaddress>/api/album`. Replace the `<dnsnameoripddress>` tag with the IP address or DNS name of your host. The result should be a JSON containing album data as shown in the following screenshot. The initial page load might take some time because it initiates database creation and seeding steps.

```
[
  - {
        albumId: 1,
        genreId: 1,
        artistId: 49,
        title: "The Best Of The Men At Work",
        price: 8.99,
        albumArtUrl: "~/Images/placeholder.png",
        genre: null,
        artist: null,
        orderDetails: [ ],
        created: "2016-12-28T13:35:22.8839055"
  },
  - {
        albumId: 2,
        genreId: 12,
        artistId: 225,
        title: "Ring My Bell",
        price: 8.99,
        albumArtUrl: "~/Images/placeholder.png",
        genre: null,
        artist: null,
        orderDetails: [ ],
        created: "2016-12-28T13:35:22.8844785"
  },
```

18. The *Music Store* API provides another endpoint which responds with details of a single album as shown by the following screenshot. The endpoint is reachable by appending the previous a URL by `albumId`. For example, `http://<dnsnameoripaddress>/api/album/1`.

```
{
    albumId: 1,
    genreId: 1,
    artistId: 49,
    title: "The Best Of The Men At Work",
    price: 8.99,
    albumArtUrl: "~/Images/placeholder.png",
  - genre: {
        genreId: 1,
        name: "Pop",
        description: null,
        albums: [ ]
    },
  - artist: {
        artistId: 49,
        name: "Men At Work"
    },
    orderDetails: [ ],
    created: "2016-12-28T13:35:22.8839055"
}
```

19. Run the following command to create three containers of `musicstore` Web UI under the web tier:

```
docker run -d -p 5000:80 --name musicstore1 --network webtier
--ip 172.20.81.2 learningwsc/musicstore:1.0.0 dotnet
musicstore.dll
docker run -d -p 5001:80 --name musicstore2 --network webtier
--ip 172.20.81.3 learningwsc/musicstore:1.0.0 dotnet
musicstore.dll
docker run -d -p 5002:80 --name musicstore3 --network webtier
--ip 172.20.81.4 learningwsc/musicstore:1.0.0 dotnet
musicstore.dll
```

20. From a PowerShell command prompt, navigate to
    `C:\learningwsc\chapter8\musicstore\Deploy\MusicStore`. Run the
    following command to create a NGINX image for the `musicstore` web UI which
    routes the requests to any of the three containers using the least connection
    algorithm:

    ```
    docker build -t learningwsc/nginx.musicstore:1.0.0 .
    ```

21. Run the following command to create an instance of `musicstore` NGINX image:

    ```
    docker run -d -p 80:80 learningwsc/nginx.musicstore:1.0.0
    ```

22. The **Music Store** home page should be reachable using port 80 of the container
    host `http://<dnshostoripaddress>` as shown in the following screenshot:

This completes our exercise of deploying *Music Store* as independently deployable microservices in a production-like environment at a reduced cost. The isolation level of the containers can be increased by deploying as Hyper-V Containers by just *adding -isolation = Hyper-V*. With the above design application, it can also be tested for security, scalability and performance, which is normally not feasible due to the additional costs, time, and resources required in provisioning such an environment. You can instantly scale the application by creating more containers and check how the application performs as the load increases and apply security policies using subnet IPs. Although we have performed many manual steps to provision the above environment, the next chapters focus on dealing with automated builds and deployments involving containers, and orchestrating composite deployments using container management tools like Docker Compose.

Managing Docker networks using Windows PowerShell for Docker

We have so far used docker commands to manage Windows Containers networking stack. Windows also offer PowerShell commands to manage the stack. However the PowerShell package is still in development and available as open source. Docker PowerShell uses the Docker REST API to connect to Docker service. The decision whether to use docker or REST API is purely a matter of choice. Use the following process to install the PowerShell management stack for creating and managing windows containers:

1. Open PowerShell windows as administrator.
2. Run the following command to install the development build of Docker PowerShell:

```
Register-PSRepository -Name DockerPS-Dev -SourceLocation
https://ci.appveyor.com/nuget/docker-powershell-dev
Install-Module Docker -Repository DockerPS-Dev -Scope
CurrentUser
```

3. Run the following command to get the list of containers running using the PowerShell command:

```
Get-Container
```

4. If you want to update the Docker PowerShell module to newer builds, run the following command:

```
Update-Module docker
```

More details on Docker PowerShell module is available for reference at https://github.com/Microsoft/Docker-PowerShell/tree/master/src/Docker.PowerShell/Help.

Summary

Windows Server 2016 provides four networking modes: NAT, transparent, L2 bridge and L2 tunnel. NAT is the default networking mode for the Windows Container host. It is the simplest form, which uses the host's IP and NAT for providing an IP range for containers. NAT networking mode is suitable for development environments. Windows Server 2016 HNS creates a firewall rule automatically when a new container is created using NAT mode. Windows Containers Networking stack can be used to create isolated tenants, apply security policies and custom routing. Windows Server 2016 provides an abstraction layer over physical networks called SDN which can be used to programmatically create and manage networks.

L2 bridge and L2 tunnel use SDN and is the most preferred way of networking in private clouds. Cross-Subnet and cross node connections are possible using all four networking modes but Transparent, L2 bridge/L2 tunnel are preferred because NAT poses restrictions on port usage. The host port in a NAT network mode can only be used by one container.

Deploying an application as set of microservices spread across multiple subnets brings isolation and scalability benefits. Microsoft is also working on PowerShell for Docker, which use the Docker REST API to interact with the Docker service running on a container host.

9
Continuous Integration and Delivery

Separating a monolithic application into functionally separate processes or microservices is just one side of the success story. Microservices bring a lot of agility to the overall development process, at the same time also provide new opportunities. One such opportunity is the ability to perform **continuous integration** (**CI**) and **continuous delivery** (**CD**). Continuous integration and delivery is the most recommended and common development practice among agile teams. Microservices allow each microservice to be independently deployed; configuring a continuous integration and testing pipeline increases the flexibility and speed in deployment, which means we can deliver tested and reviewed code at a faster pace. CI and CD are the key practices of DevOps culture with the goal of delivering features to the customer at a faster pace in smaller chunks so that customer's feedback can be collected and corrections can be applied as the product matures. Continuous testing is also a critical process of DevOps which should be included within CI for quality analysis, continuous testing is a process of setting up continuous tests with a good percentage of code coverage for every code checked-in by the developers so that teams are aware of the code quality and can be assured that new code does not introduce any new issues or cause regression issues.

This chapter focuses on the process of enabling a continuous integration and delivery pipeline for containerized application on a Windows platform using **Visual Studio Team Services** (**VSTS**), a pay-per-use service provided by Microsoft, and also available as part of an Azure subscription. This chapter deals with integrating build and publish (to the Docker Hub) process every time code is pushed to the source control.

The following topics will be covered in this chapter:

- Introducing Visual Studio Team Services
- Continuous integration
    - Sign up for a VSTS account
    - Uploading code to a VSTS code repository
    - Creating and configuring custom agents
    - Configuring automated builds
    - Automating Docker publish with CI
- Continuous delivery
    - Creating environment(s) using ARM templates
    - Deploying containers to Azure VMs and configuring SPN
    - Integration tests and web performance tests
    - Promoting deployments and code promotion workflow

Introduction to Visual Studio Team Services

Continuous integration and continuous delivery is a process which requires lots of tools and processes such as an online code repository for developers to submit code, version control, agents to build code every time a developer submits code to the repository, and finally a release agent which can deploy code to multiple environments. Apart from these, the management team would also need a reporting platform and dashboard which depict the status of development day-to-day. VSTS (formerly Visual Studio Online) is one tool which provides all the features described here, plus many more. VSTS integrates seamlessly with Visual Studio IDE creating a perfect development environment for our team. We can write code in any language and build applications targeting any platform. Since VSTS is a code repository and a build tool it can also be integrated with many application development tools used for any other language, such as Eclipse, Xcode, IntelliJ, Visual Studio Code, and Android Studio.

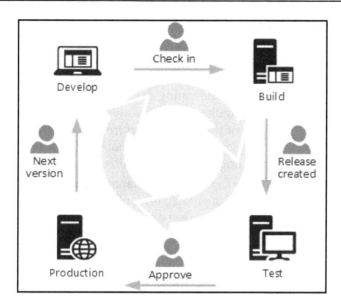

VSTS is backed by Azure and is part of any Azure subscription by default. The following are few salient features of VSTS:

- **Work item management**: VSTS can be used as a repository for storing product backlogs, user stories, tasks, bugs and even test cases. It can be used as a single repository for product owners to groom a single product backlog, prioritize work items, plan sprints, track execution, and deliver and collect feedback on the product from customers. VSTS supports multiple process templates such as agile, scrum and CMMI. It integrates seamlessly with other Microsoft Office products including MS Excel, Power BI and Project for bulk operations and custom reporting.

- **Source control**: At the heart of VSTS is the single code repository which can be used to store code of any language. VSTS supports two types of source control methods called **Team Foundation Version Control (TFVC)**, which is Microsoft's legacy source control engine and Git (from version 2013). Git is the recommended engine since it is supported across various operating systems, has amazing tool support and excellent versioning support. Conventional Git management tools or command line interfaces can still be used to manage VSTS with Git as source control engine. VSTS and Git provide an option to store multiple versions of the code base using the killer branching system introduced by Git. Git's branching model is extremely lightweight and makes branching operations easy and fast.

- **Continuous integration**: VSTS comes with a hosted build agent which can build the code as soon as the new code is checked in (continuous integration), apply policies, run analysis and tests, package and publish. It can also be used to publish reports on the overall health of the code, such as code metrics, tests results, code coverage, and versioning details. VSTS allows build customization using custom build executables (`.exe`) files which can be used added as part of the code and run as part of the build. Apart from the hosted agent, it also allows us to configure custom agents (a windows machine with VSTS agent installed) and agent pools for running customized builds.

- **Release management**: VSTS helps us to manage releases to various environments, each environment can be configured and managed independently. We can deploy applications to cloud or on-premise environments. Without VSTS, the approval and notification process during regular product release cycle is quite tedious, and VSTS eases these tasks by automating the approval process. At each stage a release to an environment can be reviewed using the various types of tests before promoting the deployment to the next stage. At every stage, approvers or environment owners are notified by e-mails and by using a live dashboard. It is also possible to revoke the approval and enable a continuous delivery pipeline to lower environments (for example, development) for every code that is checked-in.

- **Testing**: VSTS assists in building software with great quality using continuous testing and advanced testing mechanisms, such as exploratory testing. For regular coded tests, we can choose from a wide variety of tools such as MSTest, xUnit, coded UI, JUnit and so on. Irrespective of whether the application is deployed on cloud or on-premise, VSTS provides a test agent which can be used to run variety of tests before package or publishing and also deployment. Apart from Unit tests we can also use VSTS for running performance tests on cloud without worrying about configuring agents, we can use VSTS to simulate tests with multiple concurrent users and generate load from multiple regions as well. VSTS integrates with existing manual testing clients such as **Microsoft Test Manager** (**MTM**), and it can also be used for manual testing, defect logging and tracking. We can also log actionable defects using exploratory testing mechanism without authoring any tests cases. For more details on exploratory testing please visit `https://www.visualstudio.com/en-us/docs/test/manual-exploratory-testing/getting-started/perform-exploratory-tests`.

- **Reporting**: Sometimes it takes more than just few basic metrics to analyze the progress of a project life cycle. To gain better insight, product owners or stakeholders might need more data to be gathered to build custom reports. VSTS allows us to build custom dashboards, build tailored views, add widgets from the VSTS catalogue, and so on. We can also build our own custom widget and share across teams. VSTS data can be exported and integrated with Power BI, which is another Microsoft product that provides great support for building dynamic visual dashboards and drillable charts, to build more intelligent reports or dashboards. All teams can benefit from great insights and answers to otherwise unanswered questions using Power BI. The results can be integrated with artificial intelligence platforms such as Cortana or Azure cognitive services. For more information on VSTS and Power BI please visit `https://www.visualstudio.com/en-us/docs/report/powerbi/connect-vso-pbi -vs`.

VSTS features can also be made available for private data centers using an on-premise version of VSTS called team foundation server. TFS 2015 comes with all the preceding mentioned features, which run on private clouds. The latest version of TFS 2015 can be downloaded at `https://go.microsoft.com/fwlink/?LinkId=615439`.

The following diagram depicts the scenario we are trying to achieve in this chapter using VSTS, Git, custom build agents, Docker Hub and Windows Server 2016 VMs deployed on Azure. The same is also possible for on-premise environments using TFS and Windows Server 2016 on-premise with private Docker repository.

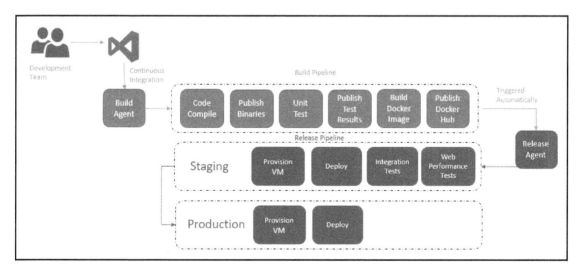

Continuous integration

Application Lifecycle Management (**ALM**) is the set of processes for delivering a product from idea to release and maintenance, and VSTS is a tool which facilitates the process. This section of the chapter focuses on continuous integration which includes building and publishing our sample music store application to the Docker Hub as a continuous and automated process. As part of this process we will go through the following steps:

1. Sign up for a new VSTS account and upload code to the online repository.
2. Create a custom build agent for building Docker images in a Windows environment.
3. Configure a build definition to build, test and publish images continuously.
4. Configure continuous integration.

Signing up for a VSTS account

A VSTS account offers free unlimited and private Git repositories which can be connected from your favorite development tools. A VSTS account can be setup using your personal Microsoft Account, which can be created at `https://signup.live.com`. We can register VSTS accounts using an organization's account configured in Azure Active directory. Although you can create any number of repository within a free account, the number of users associated with a repository has few limitations.

An Azure subscription is not mandatory for creating a VSTS account. However, VSTS only serves as an online code repository with hosted build and release agents. To build a custom build or release agent or for creating an environment (VMs, storage, and so on) for deploying the binaries we would need an Azure account. In this section, we will be using Microsoft Azure to create custom build agents using Windows Server 2016 machines to build binaries for the music store application. The following steps explain the process of signing up for a VSTS account.

 For this chapter, it is recommended that you use a personal Microsoft account which is also associated with Azure subscription.

1. Login to VSTS account using your personal Microsoft account by going to `https://go.microsoft.com/fwlink/?LinkId=307137&clcid=0x409`.

2. After successful login, we will be redirected to VSTS accounts page where we will be prompted to create a new VSTS account. All VSTS accounts have a common suffix `visualstudio.com`. Here I've chosen `musicstorecode` as my account name and **Git** as my version control.

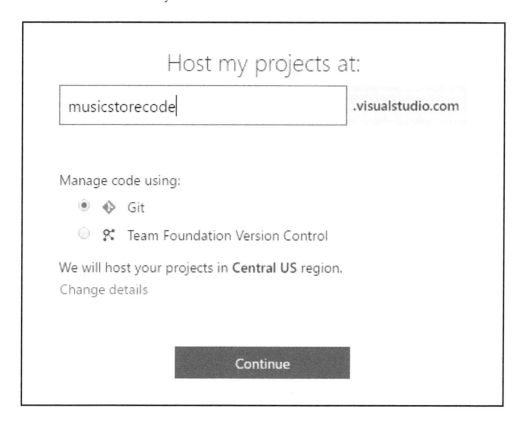

3. By default, VSTS hosts the code and projects in **Central US region**. Click on **Change** to change the default location, select development process (**Scrum**, **Agile** and CMMI) and name the default project as shown in the following image:

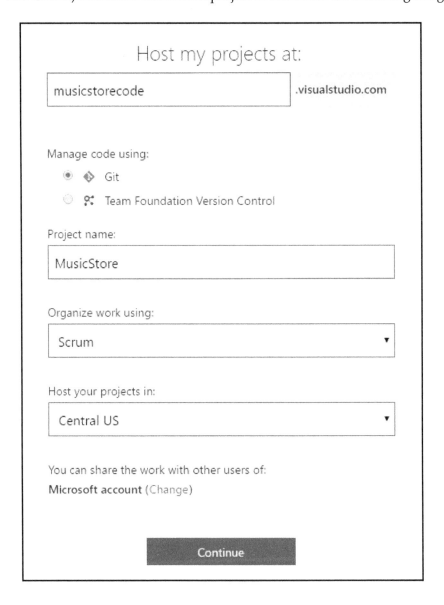

4. Click on **Continue** to create a VSTS account. We will be redirected to the home page of a newly created VSTS account as shown in the following image. The account will be reachable at: `https://musicstore.visualstudio.com`.

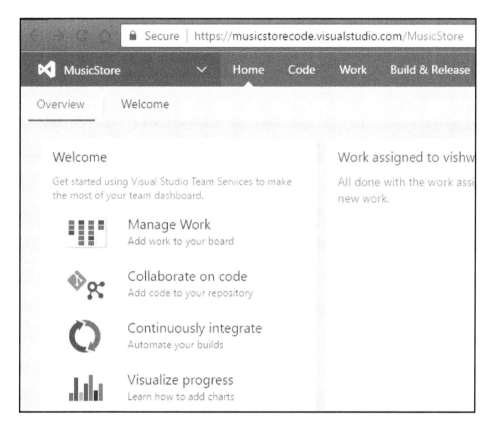

Likewise, VSTS account can be created by using an old management portal (`https://manage.windowsazure.com`) or by using an Ibiza portal (`https://portal.azure.com`) by navigating to **New** | **Developer Tools** | **Team Project**.

Uploading Music Store to VSTS

So far, we developed Music Store as microservices: one for the web platform and the other acting as an API layer. We have modified the ASP.NET core project to build Docker container images for a Windows platform when the solution or the project is compiled using Visual Studio. This is, in fact, time consuming for every build and can be avoided by building images only as part of the continuous integration process. In a DevOps practice, packaging an application should be the concern of the operations team, the application's design and developers should facilitate packaging in various forms so that the product can be packaged in any form; for example it could be an MSI, a zipped file, or a Windows Container. In this section, we will work with a modified version of music store which is completely decoupled from the image-building process. This helps developers develop and test code faster, and while they submit code to the central code repository, the custom build definition (which we will define in upcoming sections) will take care of creating and publishing the latest container images to the Docker Hub. This way, irrespective of the features added by the developers to the application layer, the packaging can be modified and developed independently in true DevOps style, where the DevOps team owns the packaging process and the development team is only responsible for developing the application. But again, DevOps is just a culture or a set of practices using a combination of tools. The most important success factor of a DevOps culture is the communication between the development and operations teams. A proper communication channel between the developers and the operations team is critical for a product's success. Every design discussion, be it at feature level or deployment level, should be known by every member of the team to contribute to an automated and error-free release pipeline.

So, the music store application used in this sample will have the build and deploy components separated from the main application features as shown in the following screenshot:

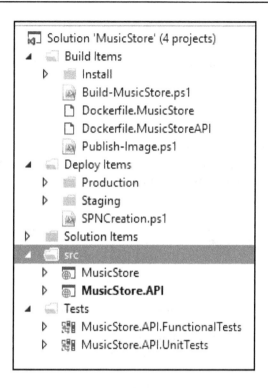

This version of the code also contains unit tests written using XUnit and Moq framework to show how we can automate running unit tests and functional tests at different stages of the deployment. Running the tests as part of the build and deployment qualifies the build and deployment, you can configure code coverage and publish test results to larger teams so that each update can be verified, promoted or failed based on how the tests perform automatically. In this chapter, we will learn to configure unit tests and functional tests as part of the continuous integration and delivery cycle. The code samples for this section are available under `C:\learningwsc\chapter9`.

Assuming the source code of this book is downloaded and extracted to `c:\`

To configure builds as part of the source code commits, the solution and related artefacts should be available in the VSTS code repository (we can also build images by using GitHub as the source repository). The following steps explain the process of adding an existing solution to VSTS:

1. Login to the VSTS account we created earlier: `https://musicstorecode.visual studio.com/`.

2. Notice that a new team project named `MusicStore` is already created; you can also create a new team project by clicking on the **New** button. Each VSTS account can contain multiple team projects. Click on `MusicStore` team project.

3. Click **Code** on the main menu as shown in the following screenshot:

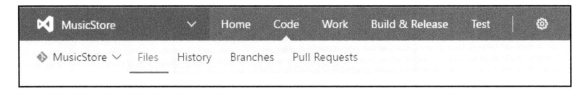

4. Copy the URL shown under **Clone** to your computer; the URL contains the VSTS account and team project name for example: `https://musicstorecode.visuals tudio.com/_git/MusicStore`.

5. Open **Visual Studio 2015** as **administrator** and navigate to **Team Explorer**. If Team Explorer is not visible, click on **View | Team Explorer** or press the combination of keys *Ctrl + \, Ctrl + M* (keyboard shortcut).

6. Click on the **Manage Connections** icon and then click on **Clone**.

7. Paste the clone URL copied earlier and choose the location on your development machine to store the code as shown in the following screenshot:

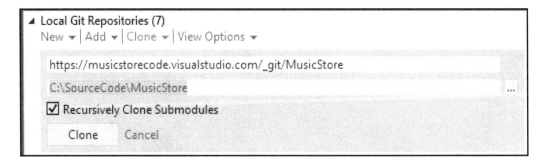

8. Click on **Clone** to start cloning the empty repository to the development machine.

9. Copy the code sample from `c:\learningwsc\chapter9` to the VSTS clone location which is `c:\sourcecode\musicstore`.

10. Open **Team Explorer** again and click on **Manage Connections**. Under the local repositories, double-click `MusicStore` to select as current repository context.

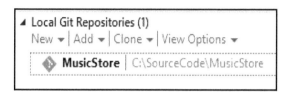

11. Visual Studio automatically identifies the solution files in the current repository, click on the `MusicStore.sln` under the **Solutions** section.

12. Ensure the solution builds successfully by clicking on **Build | Build Solution** or *Ctrl + Shift + B*. Notice that this time no Docker images are created as part of the build.

13. On the **Team Explorer**, click on **Changes** to validate the changes made to the local repository. Visual Studio shows all the newly added files as shown in the following screenshot:

14. Verify the files added and enter the commit message as appropriate and then click on **Commit All**.

15. Git repository contains a local and remote repository, the above action **Commit All** commits the code to local repository only. Click on **Sync** after a successful local commit to synchronize your changes to the remote repository. Alternatively, we can also say **Commit All** and **Push** instead of **Commit All** to push the changes to local and remote repositories together.

16. Click on **Push** in the outgoing commits section to push the code to the remote repository.

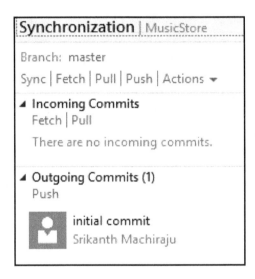

17. Push commits the changes to the remote repository using master branch. Once the Push command completes successfully the source code will be visible on our online code repository under the **Code** section as shown in the following screenshot:

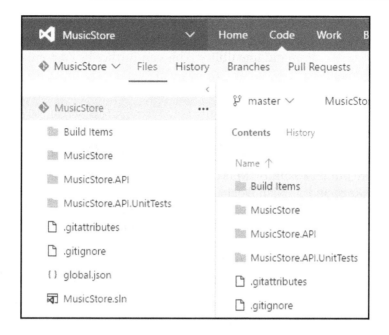

We have successfully added code to VSTS using Git repository to the master branch. Git manages multiple branches so that each code base can be versioned and deployed independently. The build and deploy mechanism shown in this chapter will be the same, irrespective of the branch used. For more information on Git branching go to `https://www.visualstudio.com/en-us/docs/git/tutorial/branches`. Git repositories can also be managed using the Git command line for Windows or Mac machines. Visual Studio 2015 comes with default extension for Git repositories. For more information on managing Git using Windows without using Visual Studio's support visit `https://git-for-windows.github.io/`.

Configuring automated builds

VSTS build definitions are used to build and package the code present in the repositories. However, it is not necessary for the code to be in a VSTS repository. We can use any third-party code repositories, such as GitHub, remote code repositories, or subversion. VSTS build definitions require an agent queue and a build agent, which is responsible for building the source code, preparing the binaries, publishing, running tests and so on. By default, VSTS provides a hosted build agent which can be used to trigger builds during the continuous integration process.

Since .NET Core and ASP.NET core are new additions to the .NET frameworks, Microsoft has released an online build agent for building any .NET core components which build the code using the `.dotnet` command line utility. This can further be customized by sending command line arguments to `dotnet.exe` or by even packing the .NET utility along with the code so that you can use a specific version of .NET.

Why do we need a custom build agent?

Like ASP.NET Core build capability, Microsoft has also released a Docker build agent for VSTS to build, package and publish Docker images to the Docker Hub or any custom Docker image repository. This extension is not available out of the box within VSTS. The Docker extension for VSTS should be explicitly added by installing from VSTS market place URL `https://marketplace.visualstudio.com/items?itemName=ms-vscs-rm.docker`. Clicking on **Install** will open a popup window where the user is required to select the VSTS account to which the extension should be installed as shown in the following screenshot:

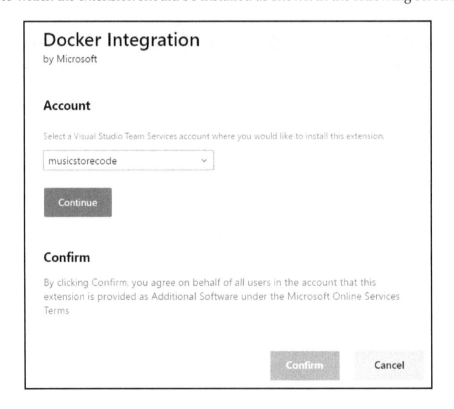

Click on **Continue** and then **Confirm** to add the extension to your VSTS account. This adds two additional tasks called **Docker** and **Docker Compose** (Docker Compose is a multi container deployment tool which will be covered in the next chapter) as shown in the following screenshot:

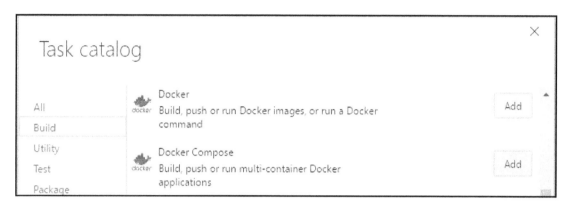

The Docker task can be used to build, push or run Docker images. However, the main problem with this approach as of writing the Docker Agent, which here runs on a Linux environment only. Windows Containers are created using Windows Server core base OS which cannot be installed on Linux machines. Because of this limitation, we would need a custom agent using Windows Server 2016 which will be capable of building Docker images in Windows environment. In future, Microsoft might release Docker build agents running on a Windows machine to overcome this limitation. The next section explains the process of creating and configuring custom build agent in VSTS.

Custom build agent

A VSTS build agent is any Windows machine which can run VSTS agent as service. The minimum OS requirement for installing VSTS agent are available at `https://github.com/Microsoft/vsts-agent/blob/master/docs/start/envwin.md`. In this section, we will build a custom build agent using Windows Server 2016 with containers that has the capability of building ASP.NET core applications and Docker for Windows.

Create Azure VM for build agent: Apply the following steps to create and configure the build agent:

1. The first step is to create a WS 2016 machine. We can use the Ibiza portal (`portal.azure.com`) or PowerShell to create the machine. Login to `https://portal.azure.com`

2. Click **New** and then click on **Compute**.

3. Search for image: **Windows Server 2016 Datacenter - with Containers**
4. Select the image and click **Create**.
5. The following picture shows **Basic** settings for creating a build agent machine named musicstoreagent.

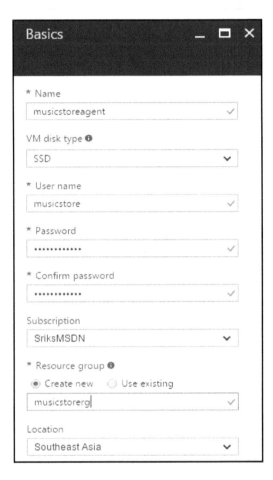

6. You can choose the VM size as appropriate from the recommended VM Sizes for example standard DS2 v2

7. The following image shows the default network configuration. Ensure the RDP port is enabled to configure the machine later. We can choose any virtual network and subnet as appropriate as we are not dependent on any virtual network or subnet configuration.

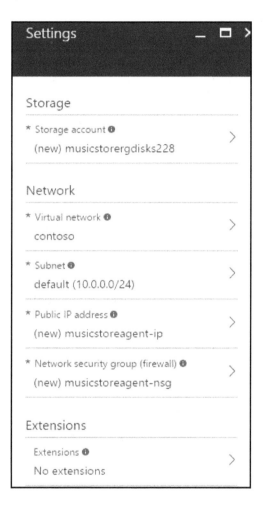

8. Here is a quick summary of the machine configuration:

Settings

Computer name	musicstoreagent
Disk type	SSD
User name	musicstore
Size	Standard DS2 v2
Storage account	(new) musicstorergdisks228
Virtual network	contoso
Subnet	default (10.0.0.0/24)
Public IP address	(new) musicstoreagent-ip
Network security group (firewall)	(new) musicstoreagent-nsg
Availability set	None
Guest OS diagnostics	Disabled
Boot diagnostics	Enabled
Diagnostics storage account	(new) musicstorergdiag981

9. Click **OK** to initiate the deployment and wait for the deployment to complete.

Configure access to custom VSTS agent: For running builds on a custom VSTS agent, the portal should be able to identify and authenticate with the machine. In this section, we will create a personal access token which will be used while configuring the agent on the agent machine:

1. Log in to your VSTS account https://musicstorecode.visualstudio.com.
2. Click on the **Security** tab under the **User Profile** button as shown in the following screenshot:

3. Click **Add**, under the **personal access token** section.
4. Fill in the **Description** and expiry date for the token. You can give full admin access to this token by choosing **All scopes** or choose the scopes to have a fine-grained access control.

5. Click on **Create Token** to create the token. Do not forget to copy the token has expired, or if we have forgotten the existing token.

Configure agent: The agent machine we've just created should be capable on building ASP.NET Core projects and building Docker images. WS2016 does not come with ASP.NET Core build capabilities, nor with other open source compilers such as Bower and Node.js, which are required to compile the music store application.

This section deals with configuring the agent with all the capabilities which are required to build, package and publish the music store application:

1. To download the VSTS agent, click on the **Settings** icon on the VSTS home page and click on **Agent pools**:

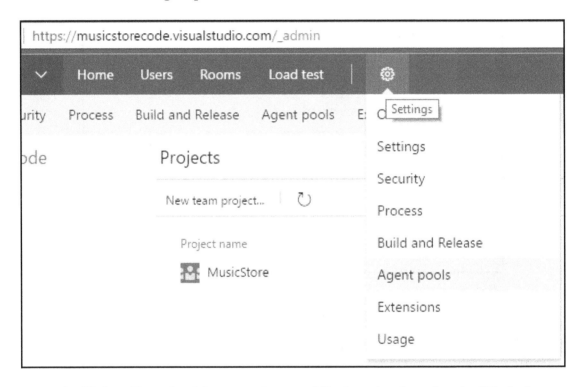

2. Click on **Download Agent**, and ensure Windows is selected as the OS platform and then click on **Download**. This downloads a zipped file named `vsts-agent-win7-x64-xx.zip` which contains the binaries for the VSTS agent.

3. Login to the **Music Store Agent** machine using **Remote Desktop** and the **Admin** credentials configured while creating the machine. The RDP file can be downloaded from the Ibiza portal by selecting the virtual machine and clicking on **Connect** icon.

4. Copy the ZIP file download above to the agent machine to `c:\`. Extract the ZIP file to `c:\agent`.

5. Open a new PowerShell command line window and navigate to `c:\agent`.

6. Run the following command on PowerShell command line:

   `.\config.cmd`

7. The window asks for VSTS URL. Enter the URL, for example
   `https://musicstorecode.visualstudio.com` and hit *Enter*.

8. Enter authentication type as `PAT` and hit *Enter*.

9. Enter the personal access token created earlier and hit *Enter*.

```
PS C:\agent> .\config.cmd

>> Connect:

Enter server URL > https://musicstorecode.visualstudio.com
Enter authentication type (press enter for PAT) > PAT
Enter personal access token > ********************************************
```

10. Before proceeding further, let's create a custom agent pool to differentiate between hosted agents and custom agents. Open the VSTS account in a browser and navigate to settings icon **Agent Queues**.

11. Click on **New Pool**. Enter the **Agent Pool** name as `WindowsDockerAgent` and click **OK** on the **Create Agent Pool** popup window.

12. Switch back to the agent machine's PowerShell command window. Enter the newly created agent pool name `WindowsDockerAgent` and hit *Enter*.

13. Hit *Enter* again to set the default name for the agent. At this point, the agent scans for capabilities installed on the machine and verifies the connection to the VSTS account. Ensure the following message is shown in the command-line window:

```
>> Register Agent:

Enter agent pool (press enter for default) > WindowsDockerAgent
Enter agent name (press enter for MUSICSTOREAGENT) >
Scanning for tool capabilities.
Connecting to the server.
Successfully added the agent
Testing agent connection.
```

14. Hit *Enter* again to make `c:\_work` as the default working folder for the agent.

15. Next press *Y* and hit *Enter* to run agent as a service.

16. To run the agent under the administrator account, enter the admin user name and press *Enter* and then enter the administrator password.

This completes configuring the custom agent, and the new agent should now be visible under the custom agent pool we created above on VSTS account under the **Settings** | **Agent queues** section as shown in the following screenshot:

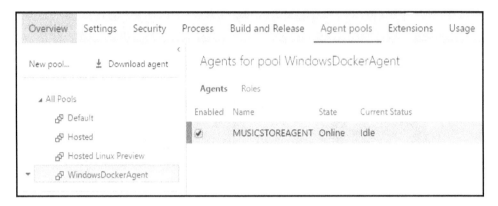

We are still missing a few key capabilities on the agent. Though it can create Windows Docker images inherently, it cannot compile .NET Core and the dependent components of music store. To build dependent components we should install other compilers, such as npm and bower. These dependent components may vary per application. The agent should have all the third-party components installed and configured in class path so that agent can run the custom commands during the build event. Apply the following steps to install the third-party components which are required to compile Music Store:

1. Download and install .NET Core SDK from https://www.microsoft.com/net/core#windowscmd.

2. Go to https://nodejs.org/en/download/ and click on Windows 64-bit MSI version to download the Node.js installer on the Windows agent machine.

 Internet Explorer enhanced security is ON by default on Windows Server 2016 machines deployed on Azure. This option restricts you from browsing remote URLs which are not added to your trusted sites zone. You can turn off this option by opening Server Manager and navigating to **Local Server** | **IE Enhanced configuration** and selecting **off** for administrators and users.

3. Install Node.js on the agent by double-clicking on the installer downloaded in the preceding steps. Use the default options while installing the software.

4. Open a new Windows command line and navigate to the installation path of Node.js, which is `C:\Program Files\nodejs\` by default.

5. Run the following command to install the `bower` component with global scope.

```
npm install -g bower
```

For VSTS agent service to register the newly added components, the service should be restarted. Open the Server manager and restart the service name VSTS Agent (`musicstorecode.MusicStoreAgent`). Verify the new capabilities are scanned and registered under the capabilities section for `WindowsDockerAgent` as shown in the following screenshot:

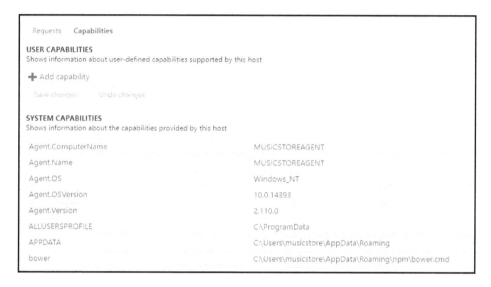

Create a build definition: A build definition consists of multiple tasks, each of which can be related to build, test, package and publish. VSTS provides a wide variety of pre-built tasks which can be added to the build definition and configured as required. In this section, we will create a build definition to build, test, package and publish music store to the Docker Hub using the custom agent created above. Since pre-built Docker tasks cannot be used, we will use PowerShell scripts to create and push the images to Docker Hub:

1. Click on **Builds & Release** and click on **Builds**.

2. Click on **New** definition and then choose ASP.NET Core Build as the template. Click **Next** to continue.

3. Select MusicStore as the repository and **master** branch as the default branch.

4. Click on the **Continuous Integration** checkbox to **enable CI**.

5. Select the custom agent queue we created earlier, WindowsDockerAgent, as the Agent queue.

6. Click **Create**.

7. We can use the default settings for restore, build and publish tasks already present in the build definition.

8. Update the Test definition to run only the unit tests and publish the results as .xml file as shown in the following image:

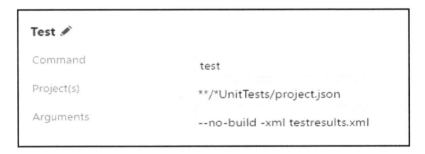

9. Click on Add Build Step and add the task called **Publish Test Results**. Configure the **Build** step as shown in the following image. Be sure to place this task before **Publish Artifact**.

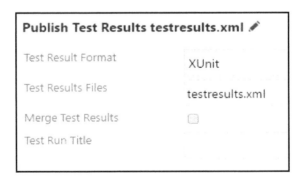

10. Click on Add build step and add a new step called **Copy Files** and configure the step as shown in the following image. This step copies the build PowerShell scripts to the drop location (which is special folder created on the build agent that contains the source code and binaries for each build). Be sure to place this task before **Publish Artifact.**

Copy Files to: $(build.artifactstagingdirectory) ✏️

Source Folder	musicstore/Build Items/
Contents	**
Target Folder	$(build.artifactstagingdirectory)

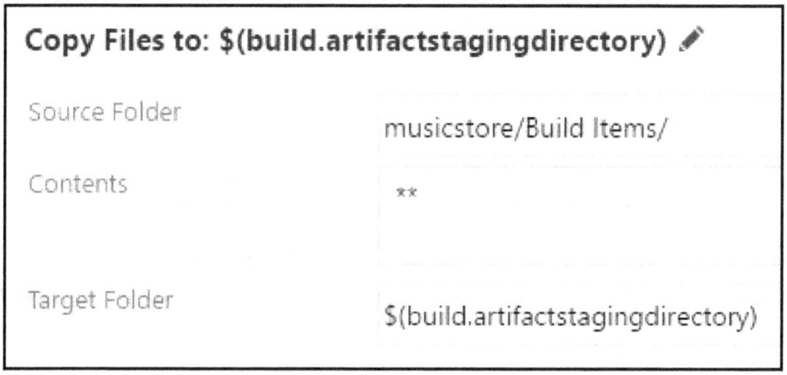

11. Click on Add build step and add a new step called **Copy Files** and configure the step as shown in the following image: This step copies the PowerShell scripts related to deployment to the drop location. Ensure this task is placed before **Publish Artifact.**

Copy Deploy Files to: $(build.artifactstagingdirectory) ✏️

Source Folder	Deploy Items
Contents	**
Target Folder	$(build.artifactstagingdirectory)

12. Click on Add build step and add a new step called **Copy Files** and configure the step as shown in the following image. This step copies the functional tests to the drop location. The functional tests, which become a part of the build drop after a successful build will be run on the staging environment post deployment. Ensure this task is placed before publish Artifact.

Copy Functional Test Files to: $(build.artifactstagingdirectory) ✎

Source Folder	MusicStore.API.FunctionalTests
Contents	**
Target Folder	$(build.artifactstagingdirectory)/FunctionalTests

13. Add a new build step to build definition called PowerShell. Configure the step using the following details. Name the task as `Build` Music Store API image:

   - **Type**: File path
   - **Script path**: `musicstore/Build Items/Build-MusicStore.ps1`
   - **Arguments**: `-ImageName "learningwsc/musicstore" -Version "$(ImageVersion)" -DockerfilePath "$(build.artifactstagingdirectory)/Dockerfile.MusicStore" -BuildContext $(build.artifactstagingdirectory) -ProjectName 'musicstore'`
   - **Advanced/Working Folder**: `$(build.artifactstagingdirectory)`

14. Add a new build step to the build definition called PowerShell. The following tasks including this one are dependent on publish artifact, so make sure this task and the next ones are placed after the publish artifact step, we can drag and drop the tasks to adjust the order. Configure the tasks as shown in the following points and name it `Build` Music Store image by clicking on the pencil icon. This step builds a Windows Docker image using the published binaries of the music store web component:

   - **Type**: File path
   - **Script path**: `musicstore/Build Items/Build-MusicStore.ps1`
   - **Arguments**: `-ImageName "learningwsc/musicstore.api" -Version "$(ImageVersion)" -DockerfilePath "$(build.artifactstagingdirectory)/Dockerfile.MusicStoreAPI" -BuildContext $(build.artifactstagingdirectory) -ProjectName 'musicstore.api'`

- **Advanced\Working Folder**:
  `$(build.artifactstagingdirectory)`

15. Add a new build step to build the definition called PowerShell. Configure the step using the following details. Name the task as `Publish` Music Store image:

    - **Type**: File path
    - **Script path**: `musicstore/Build Items/Publish-Image.ps1`
    - **Arguments**: `-ImageName "learningwsc/musicstore" -Version "$(ImageVersion)" -username $(DockerUsername) -password $(DockerPassword)`

16. Add a new build step to build the definition called PowerShell. Configure the step using the following details. Name the task as `Publish` Music Store API image:

    - **Type**: File path
    - **Script path**: `musicstore/Build Items/Publish-Image.ps1`
    - **Arguments**: `-ImageName "learningwsc/musicstore.api" -Version "$(ImageVersion)" -username $(DockerUsername) -password $(DockerPassword)`

17. Click on **Save** and name the definition as `MusicStore.CIBuild` and click **OK**.

18. Click on the **Variables** tab and add new variables as shown in the following image. You can replace the Docker username and password with the account details of your Docker Hub account. Ensure the image names are updated accordingly in the preceding configuration so that they can be pushed to your account.

19. Click on Save the save the new variables configured above.

The following screenshot shows the build definition with all the preceding steps configured:

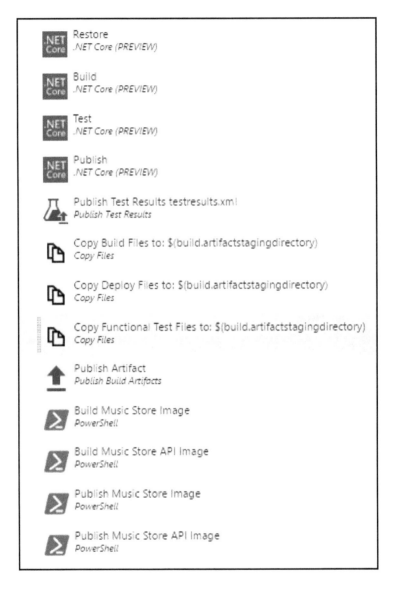

This completes the process of configuring automated builds for the music store application. From now on, any code commits made to the repository (master branch) will be automatically built and the Docker image will be published to the Docker Hub account. The following diagram depicts the overall continuous integration process:

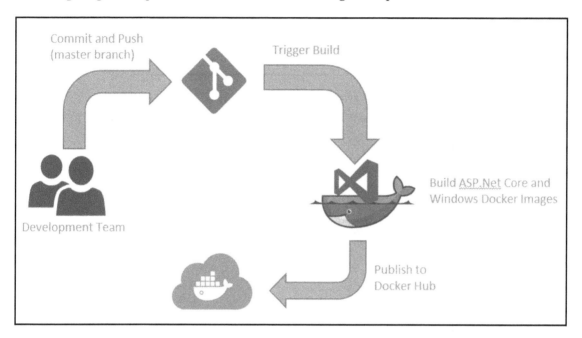

Queuing build

Apart from continuous integration builds, VSTS also allows you to trigger builds manually, and schedule nightly builds so that you are assured of a good quality builds on a daily basis, and that the team is notified of any failures. The Git branching strategy is one of the key reasons for its success, Git branching allows you to run multiple versions of the code. The master branch always represents the code deployed to production. Developers can work on a branch created from the master called, for example, Develop. Once a developed branch with new features is tested and deployed to the production environment, it is merged back into the master. This is one of many branching strategies. We can also configure scheduled builds from multiple branches using VSTS builds. Since VSTS also contains work item management we have an option to associate a work item with a failed build or failed test and assign it to the relevant team or person. This way, the build system shows the overall health of the system and acts as an application life cycle dashboard.

Let's queue a new music store build and verify the image publish process.

1. Log on to your VSTS account `https://musicstorecode.visualstudio.com`
2. Navigate to **Build & Release** | **Builds**
3. Click on the **Build** definition we just created called **MusicStore.CIBuild**.
4. Click on the **Triggers** tab and opt-in for continuous integration as shown in the following screenshot, you can also trigger scheduled builds in this section.

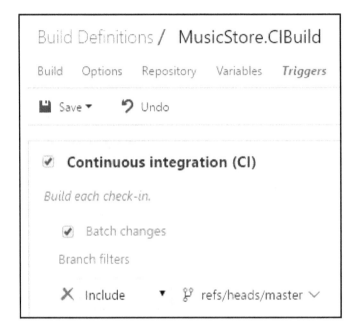

5. We can perform any check-in from Visual Studio using the master branch, as shown in the following screenshot, and then click **Commit All** and **Push** or trigger a build manually as explained in the next step:

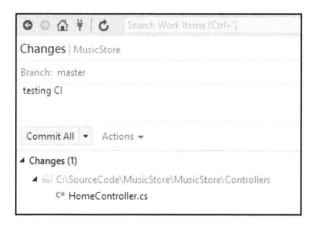

6. Alternatively, we can click on **Queue new Build**, verify the branch, and ensure **WindowsDockerAgent** is selected as the queue, as shown in the following image. You can change the image version before triggering the build.

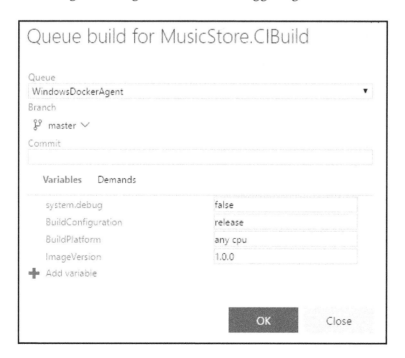

7. Click **OK** for the build to start and wait for the build to succeed.

8. Verify the running builds in the **Build Definitions** | **MusicStore.CIBuild** | **Summary.**

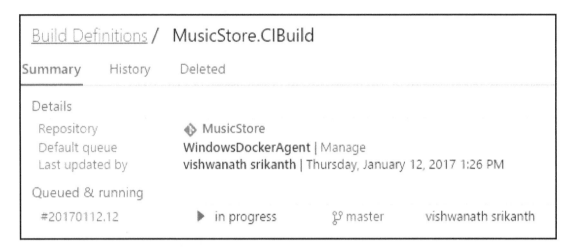

9. After a successful build, click on the **Publish Test Results** `testresults.xml` task to get the test results link. Click on the test results link to see the pass/fail percentage. A short summary of the tests is also shown on the build summary section as shown in the following image:

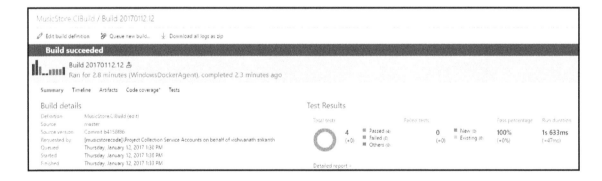

10. The next thing is to check published Windows Docker images. Login to your Docker Hub account and verify the updated image as shown in the following image:

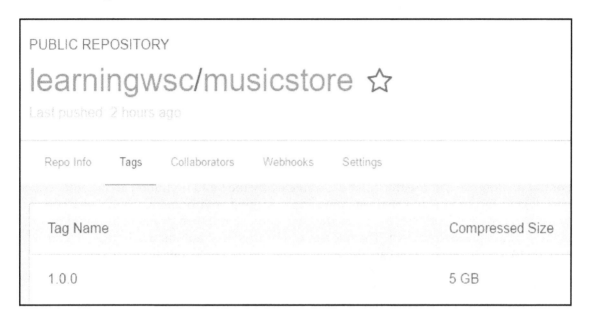

 The publish process to Docker Hub might not complete immediately; it depends on the network bandwidth allocated to the agent server.

Continuous delivery

Continuous delivery is the software engineering approach of extending the continuous integration pipeline to deploy the build output (or build drop) on an environment. Traditionally, every application's delivery pipeline consists of multiple stages, such as development, integration, UAT, and production. At each stage the build drop or build output goes through multiple stages of testing and finally release to production. Each stage/environment has a team responsible for validating the environment after applying the new update by running through multiple categories of tests, like acceptance tests, regression tests, integration tests, functional tests, load tests and performance tests. Continuous delivery makes the routine affair of deployments easy: by defining deployment in terms of code and configuration, we are making it less error prone and more predictable.

VSTS allows you to automate your release pipeline using the VSTS release management feature available under the **Releases** Tab. VSTS release management comes with various pre-created tasks which can used to deploy your code on any environment such as public or private cloud. The pipeline is defined using a release definition. A release definition consists of multiple environments, and each environment can have one or more tasks. Each task uses the build drop to deploy, test or certify the environment. At each stage the environment team has the option to configure pre- and post-approval. An approval forwards the deployment to the next level. VSTS notifies the status via e0mails as well, and the e-mail notification contains details of each release, such as the approval status, release pass/fail status, and so on. Variables can be stored specific to any environment and specific to the release definition so that they can be updated from one place. VSTS provides a hosted release agent per account to run the deployments, we can also build custom agents like we did for Build.

For this section, we will use the build drop created by the build definition above and deploy it to staging and production environments. In the staging environment, we will also run functional tests and load tests to certify the environment and then promote the build drop to the production environment. The releases can be triggered automatically whenever a new build is available or they can also be triggered manually to any environment on-demand. Continuous deployment (or delivery) is when a new release is created automatically in release management whenever a new build drop is available. The following diagram depicts the complete CI/CD pipeline:

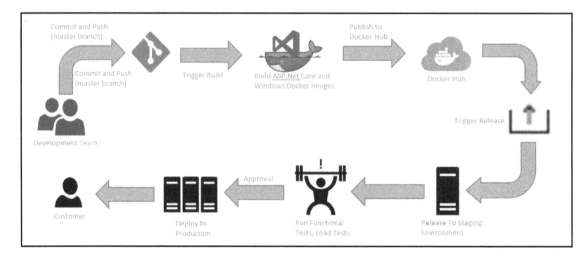

In the section, we will also create and configure Windows Server 2016 environments on Azure using ARM templates. **Azure ARM** (**Azure Resource Manager**) lets us define infrastructure as code, thereby automating the environment creation and configuration. For every release, the VSTS release agent either creates or updates the infrastructure defined as a JSON template in an incremental fashion.

The source code for deployment is placed under the `Deploy Items` folder as shown in the following image. Release definition also use music store functional tests which test the API layer using a test client and validates the response. Ideally these test results define whether the build can be promoted to the next stage. The source code is depicted in the following screenshot:

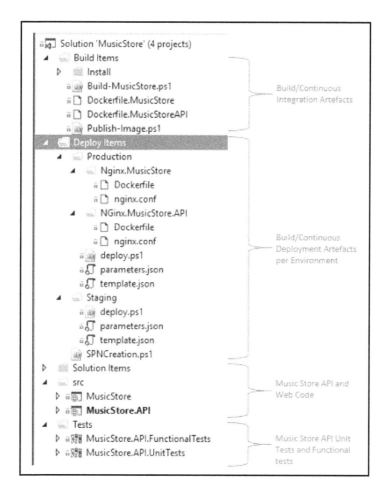

Configuring service principal name

For VSTS to create resources on the user's subscription, a new role must be provisioned in the Azure Active Directory account associated with the subscription so that VSTS agents can authenticate before creating the environments. The following section shows how to create Azure Resource Manager Service Endpoint. To authorize VSTS to create machines, we must create an AAD application and assign a service principal name with a role. To simplify the whole process a PowerShell script added under `c:\learningwsc\chapter9\musicstore\Deploy Items\SPNCreation.ps1` will be used. Run the script using a PowerShell command line as explained in the following steps before proceeding further.

1. Open a new PowerShell command line window as **Administrator**.
2. Navigate to **Deploy Items** using the command or you can also use the one added to the VSTS code repository cloned to your development machine:

   ```
   cd "C:\learningwsc\chapter9\MusicStore\Deploy Items"
   ```

3. Invoke the PowerShell script using the following command:

   ```
   .\SPNCreation.ps1
   ```

4. Enter the Azure subscription name and password (password here is the service principal key).
5. Log in with credentials associated with Azure subscription.
6. Ensure SPN role assignment completed successfully.
7. Note the details mentioned under **Copy and Paste below values for Service Connection** like **Connection Name**, **Subscription ID**, **Subscription Name**, **Service Principal ID** and **Tenant ID**. The service principalley is the password entered in *Step 6*.
8. Log in to your VSTS account at `https://musicstorecode.visualstudio.com`.
9. Click on the **Settings** section.
10. Click on **New Service Endpoint** and then select **Azure Resource Manager**.
11. A pop-up window will appear with **Title Add Azure Resource Manager Service Endpoint**, fill the details collected from *step 9*, name the connection as **MusicStoreConn** and click on **Verify Connection**.
12. Ensure the connection is verified and click **OK** to save the settings.

Configure staging environment

Follow the following set of steps to configure continuous deployment for music store application.

1. Login to VSTS account `https://musicstorecode.visualstudio.com`.
2. Select the team project **MusicStore** and navigate to **Build & Release | Releases** section.
3. Click on and then click on **Empty** (start with an empty definition). Select **Next** to continue.
4. Select **Team Builds**, **Project Name**, and **Build Definition** as shown in the following image. Check the option for continuous deployment to release every time a new build is available. Select **Hosted** agent as the release agent queue:

5. Click **Create** to create the release definition.

6. Click on the Pencil icon and rename the definition to `MusicStore.CD` and click on **Save**.

7. Rename `Environment 1` to `Staging`.

8. Click on **Add** task and add new task named Azure resource group deployment and click **Close**. This pre-built tasks creates or updates resources as defined in the `template.json` file under the staging environment. Fill in the values as shown in the following points:

   - **Azure Connection Type**: Azure Resource Manager
   - **Azure RM subscription**: Select the name of Azure Resource Manager Service Endpoint created above in this case `MusicStorConn`
   - **Action**: Create or update resource group
   - **Resource group**: `musicstorestagrg`
   - **Location**: Southeast Asia (or as appropriate, but ensure the location is the same everywhere)
   - **Template**:
     `$(System.DefaultWorkingDirectory)/MusicStore.CIBuild/drop/Staging/template.json`
   - **Parameter**:
     `$(System.DefaultWorkingDirectory)/MusicStore.CIBuild/drop/Staging/parameters.json`
   - **Override Template Parameters**: `-adminPassword (ConvertTo-SecureString -String '$(password)' -AsPlainText -Force)`
   - **Deployment Mode**: Incremental

9. Click on **Add Task** and add a new task called `Azure File` copy and configure the task as shown in the following image. Use the source as `$(System.DefaultWorkingDirectory)/MusicStore.CIBuild/drop/Staging/deploy.ps1`. Select any storage account as RM storage Account. This account will be used to upload the file momentarily before copying and running inside the virtual machine.

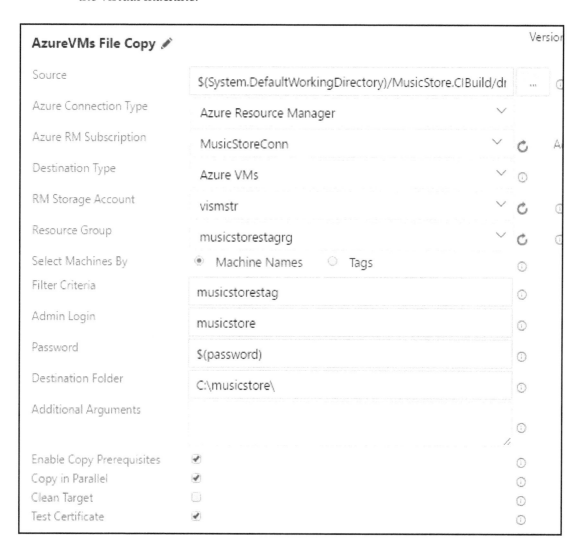

10. Click on **Add Task** and add a new task called PowerShell on target machines and configure the task as shown in the following image. This task calls the deployment PowerShell script which is copied to the target machine in the preceding step.

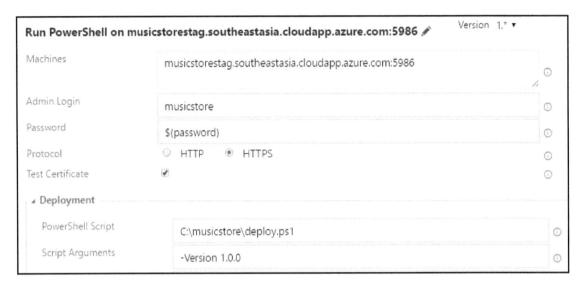

11. Click on **+Add Task** and add a new task called .NET Core Preview and configure the task as shown in the following image. This task restores the packages for the Music Store functional tests:

12. Click on **Add Task** and add a new task called .NET Core Preview and configure the task as shown in the following image. This task runs the music store functional tests. The results of the test will be available in the log for every release.

13. Now lets us add a Cloud based load testing task, which will generate the load as configured and report the status as part of the release logs. Click on **Add Task** and add a new task called Cloud-based web performance test and configure the task as shown in the following image:

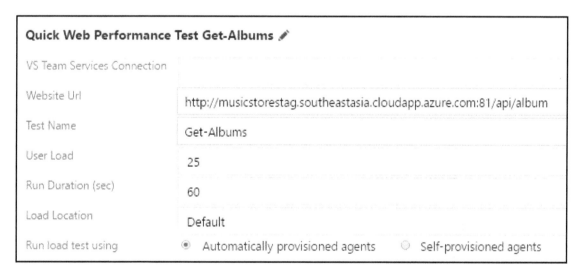

This completes the configuration for releasing the build drop to the staging environment including tests and environment creation. The next section shows the configuration for the production environment.

Configure the production environment

Once we configure an environment we can use the VSTS clone feature to configure similar environments. You can assign approvers at each stage, both before and after deployment. The following process explains the process of configuring the production environment.

1. Click on Ellipses of Staging environment and then click on **Clone Environment**.

2. Apply pre-deployment rules as appropriate. Check the auto-trigger on successful deployment to the staging environment if you would like the deployment to pass to the next environment. However, the deployment will be on hold if the pre-deployment approver is configured. Click on **Create** to create the environment.

3. Name the new environment as `Production`.

4. Update the Azure Resource Group Deployment task's configuration as shown in the following points. The remaining configuration details can be left intact:

   - **Resource Group**: `musicstoreprodrg`
   - **Template**:
     `$(System.DefaultWorkingDirectory)/MusicStore.CIBuild/drop/Production/template.json`
   - **Parameters**:
     `$(System.DefaultWorkingDirectory)/MusicStore.CIBuild/drop/Production/parameters.json`

5. Update the Azure File Copy task's configuration as shown here. The remaining configuration details can be left unchanged:

   - **Resource Group**: `musicstoreprodrg`
   - **Filter Criteria**: `musicstoreprod`

6. Update the PowerShell on the target machines task's configuration as shown here. The remaining configuration details can be left unchanged:

   - **Machines**:
     `musicstoreprod.southeastasia.cloudapp.azure.com:5986`

7. The remaining tasks which perform the functional and load tests can be safely deleted.

8. To configure the universal password, click on the **Variables** section on the release definition menu, and add a new variable under the variables section as shown in the following image:

9. Click **Save** to save the definition.

Testing CI/CD

With the above configuration, every check-in from a developer will trigger a build followed by deployment to staging environment. If the team size is huge and involves too many builds per day, we can batch the builds and schedule releases as required. By default, VSTS contains a 30-day' retention policy for the build drops, so any old drop can be deployed to rollback by selecting the build number from the history. The following picture shows the result of release trigger by the continuous integration process once a new build drop is available.

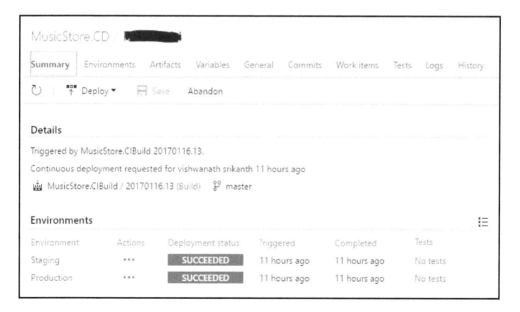

What makes an application great and successful? If having an automated, flexible and error-free build and release pipeline is one part of the answer, having a good telemetry solution which can help diagnose how the application is performing and how it is being used by the customers is another part. Telemetry solutions can capture the usage statistics, errors and application specific events from production environment which complete the full application life cycle which is from idea to implementation. Microsoft Application Insights is an excellent product as part of Azure PaaS offering which helps us understand how our application is performing or being used by various customers across the world. Application Insights generates deep insights and predictive alerts which can be used to further improvise the product. In the next chapter, we will learn to integrate our application with Application Insights and capturing key events.

Summary

Microsoft offers a code repository, build and release environment in a single suite called Visual Studio Team Services (VSTS) which is also part of the Microsoft Azure subscription. VSTS can be used for work item management, source and version control, automated builds, continuous integration, delivery and reporting. A similar setup can be achieved for a private cloud using TFS 2015. Windows Containers can be built and publishing using a continuous integration and deployment pipeline built using VSTS. Docker extension for VSTS uses Linux machines to build and create images which cannot be used to build Windows Container images. As of today, we should create a Windows agent using Windows Server 2016 to build and publish Docker images. Configuring CI and CD enables faster releases and tested builds using automation. Continuous release to the development or staging environments for every code checked in ensures that the application is regularly tested and that all the stakeholders are kept informed of the latest developments on a daily basis. VSTS can also be used to automatically create or update environments on Azure. Integrating an application with a good telemetry solution is also necessary for gathering insights on the usage and performance of the application.

10
Manage Resource Allocation and REST API

Windows Containers is a virtualization platform. Like any other virtualization platform, it comes with its own share of challenges: one such issue is managing resource utilization. Containers are a critical step towards maximizing resource utilization; but at the same time is very important to draw a line between how much CPU or memory a container can utilize on a shared environment. If there is no medium to control the resource usage, the few systems might exploit the shared infrastructure leading to errors or failures to other systems sharing the same infrastructure. In this chapter, we will learn how to manage the resource allocation of Windows Containers within a host. We will also learn how to use the Docker REST API to control and manage Windows Containers on Windows Server 2016. We have been using the Docker command line so far to build and run containers, but for some category of users it is a suboptimal way of handling systems: let us say you want to manage a container host from mobile application, or you want to control the host from within another application. This chapter shows you how to build a custom application to build and manage Windows Containers by using the Docker REST API.

The following topics will be covered in this chapter:

- Container resource allocation
- Monitoring using Operations Management Suite
- Optimizing Dockerfiles and image storage
- About the Docker REST API and the API Reference
- Listing containers using the REST API

- Starting and stopping a container using the REST API
- Building, listing and pushing images using the REST API
- REST API authentication
- Managing networks and volumes

Container resource allocation

When we create a container using `docker run`, the container host does not set any resource constraints on the container. If you are planning to build a multi-tenant system to host a set of microservices as containers, you would want all the services to perform well. Each service would have its own resource requirements: some services may run CPU intensive workloads, some may run memory intensive work loads, like in-memory storage, and few may bank on high bandwidth. In a multi-tenant environment or shared infrastructure, resource usage should be constrained to avoid problems like noisy neighbors. If it's not, a CPU-intensive service might eat into the host system, which impacts other services running on the same host. The following image shows a typical noisy neighbor problem:

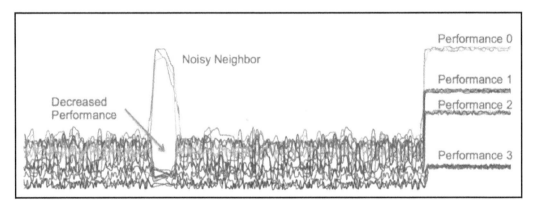

Noisy neighbor is a common problem in cloud-computing and shared infrastructure, where a co-tenant monopolizes bandwidth, disk, IO, CPU and other resources, and can negatively impact another tenant's application performance. They cause uneven resource distribution and the shutting down of systems without notice. One-way cloud-computing vendors avoid this problem is by declaring tiers. A tier is a logical group of resource allocations, so if you choose, say, Tier-1 your service has to abide to the rules of Tier A. Let us take SQL Azure for example: Azure provides three sets of tiers for using Azure SQL Database called Basic, Standard, and Premium, as shown in the following table:

	Basic	Standard				Premium				
		S0	S1	S2	S3	P1	P2	P4	P6/P3	P11
DTUs	5	10	20	50	100	125	250	500	1,000	1,750
Max database size (GB)	2	250				500				1,000
Max In-memory OLTP storage (GB)	N/A	N/A	N/A	N/A	N/A	1	2	4	8	14
Max concurrent workers	30	60	90	120	200	200	400	800	1,600	2,400
Max concurrent logins	30	60	90	120	200	200	400	800	1,600	2,400
Max concurrent sessions	300	600	900	1,200	2,400	2,400	4,800	9,600	19,200	32,000
Point-in-time restore	Any point last 7 days	Any point last 35 days				Any point last 35 days				
Disaster recovery	Active Geo-Replication, up to 4 readable secondary backups									

A **Data Transfer Unit** (**DTU**) is a unit of measure of the resources that will be allocated to the Azure SQL database. A DTU is a measure of CPU, memory, and bandwidth allocation.

A database falling under the basic tier can only store data up to 5 GB and cannot extend beyond it. A similar classification is available for all the resources on Azure. This strategy is applied by many other cloud vendors like Amazon and Google. They also offer options to easily switch between tiers on-demand or automatically as the application needs.

The Docker Engine on Windows facilitates a similar infrastructure. It allows you to allocate CPU, memory and network bandwidth per container. For example, running the following command on the Windows Container host creates a container with absolutely no resource allocation or say default resource allocation which is unlimited:

```
docker run -it microsoft/windowsservercore cmd
```

To check the CPU, memory and network resource allocated to this container run the following command in a new PowerShell window followed by the container ID. Run `docker ps` to fetch the container ID of a running container:

```
docker inspect <containerid>
```

Once we run the `docker inspect` command container resource information will be found under the host config section. The following image shows the default resource allocation for this container.

```
"Isolation": "process",
"CpuShares": 0,
"Memory": 0,
"CgroupParent": "",
"BlkioWeight": 0,
"BlkioWeightDevice": null,
"BlkioDeviceReadBps": null,
"BlkioDeviceWriteBps": null,
"BlkioDeviceReadIOps": null,
"BlkioDeviceWriteIOps": null,
"CpuPeriod": 0,
"CpuQuota": 0,
"CpusetCpus": "",
"CpusetMems": "",
"Devices": [],
"DiskQuota": 0,
"KernelMemory": 0,
"MemoryReservation": 0,
"MemorySwap": 0,
"MemorySwappiness": -1,
"OomKillDisable": false,
"PidsLimit": 0,
"Ulimits": null,
"CpuCount": 0,
"CpuPercent": 0,
"IOMaximumIOps": 0,
"IOMaximumBandwidth": 0
```

CPU resource allocation

Using Docker, we can control CPU percentage, CPU period, CPU quota, CPU shares, CPU set, and CPU Set Mems. The following command uses the `docker run` command to allocate CPU resources to the container.

```
docker run -it --cpu-percent=50 microsoft/windowsservercore cmd
```

If you run `docker inspect` followed by the container ID of the previously mentioned container, you would notice that the CPU percent is set to `50`, as shown in the following screenshot. Remember `CPU Percent` can only be an integer:

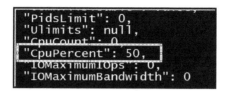

Similarly, you can set `--cpu-period` and `--cpu-quota` options to Completely Fair Scheduler's. The following table shows various other options which you can use to control the CPU allocation for any container:

Option	Data type	Description
`--cpu-percent`	Int	Set CPU percentage for container
`--cpu-period`	Int	Limit CPU **Completely Fair Scheduler (CFS)** period
`--cpu-quota`	Int	Limit CPU CFS quota
`--cpu-shares`	Int	Relative share of CPU to be allocated to the container compared to others. For example, you can assign CPU shares in the ration of 50:50, or 80:20.
`--cpuset-cpus`	String	CPUs in which to allow execution (0-3, 0,1)
`--cpuset-mems`	String	MEMs in which to allow execution (0-3, 0,1)

Memory allocation

We can also limit the RAM memory than can be allocated to Windows Container, a few containers which are memory intensive might require more amounts of RAM memory, as for example, the SQL Server. By default, every container is allocated all of the RAM memory available on the host. The following command restricts the memory allocation to 1 GB for the Windows Container:

```
docker run -it --memory=1024 microsoft/windowsservercore cmd
```

A few more options available for allocating memory to containers are shown in the following table:

Option	Data type	Description
--memory, -m	String	Memory limit
--memory-reservation	String	Memory soft limit
--memory-swap	String	Swap limit equal to memory plus swap: −1 to enable unlimited swap
--memory-swappiness	Int	Tune container memory swappiness (0 to 100)

Network allocation

Network bandwidth is also a key resource which should be throttled as required by the container. The following two options are available to control the network usage for the container:

Option	Data type	Description
--io-maxbandwidth	String	Maximum IO bandwidth limit for the system drive (Windows only)
--io-maxiops	UINT	Maximum IOps limit for the system drive (Windows only)

Docker resource allocation options are kernel specific; most of the commands were built keeping Linux in mind. Microsoft and Docker are working together to enable all the docker commands for Windows operating systems. Please read the updated support documentation before implementing any resource allocation strategies.

Insights and telemetry

When you run a multitude of systems on a virtualized environment, it is necessary to have a complete telemetry and monitoring solution which can be used to analyze how the containers are performing over time. In this section, we will learn about application and environment monitoring solutions which should be incorporated into every service for deeper insights into the application's performance and overall health of the system. Though most of these technologies are introduced by Microsoft, they do not yet support the Windows Container Ecosystem but it is worth understanding capabilities of each of the following systems so that you can plan to integrate it into your application topology when Microsoft announces support.

Application Insights

Visual Studio Application Insights for Docker helps you monitor containerized applications by collecting telemetry about performance of the application and the Docker host as well. Application insights capture all the activities performed by Docker and publish to the Insights Dashboard. Application Insights is a *Software-as-a-Service* offering which is available as part of the Azure subscription. Application Insights integrates seamlessly with .NET and other open source platforms. More information on integrating non-containerized applications with Application Insights is available at `https://docs.microsoft.com/en-us/azure/application-insights/app-insights-overview`. Application Insights can collect telemetry information from both mobile and web applications. The telemetry information captured from applications is transferred to Azure for processing and storage. The data can be viewed in pictorial format using charts, line graphs, sliced and diced, and various other forms.

Recently, Microsoft has launched full support for Docker containers by adding an Application Insights image to the Docker hub. Instructions for pulling and building on top of the Application Insights image for Docker is available at `https://hub.docker.com/r/microsoft/applicationinsights/`. Click on the **Dockerfile** tab to see the contents of Dockerfile, notice the image is built using a non-Windows based image. For enabling insights using the Docker image, pull the image and create a container on the Docker host. The agent here is responsible for sending the telemetry information captured from dockerized applications to the Application Insights account on Azure. The Docker agent captures the following information from the host:

- Captures telemetry information for the applications which are not integrated with Application Insights. For example, if you are running an ASP.NET Core web application on a Linux machine which is not integrated with Application Insights, you still be able to capture telemetry information from the application by installing the agent.
- If you're developing an application which will be deployed as a container, it is recommended to install Application Insights SDK into the application. If the application is composed as a set of microservices, you can direct all the telemetry data to one Application Insights resource and filter the data as need.
- Lifecycle events, performance counters originating from Docker host by image.
- Performance counters for all the container's CPU, memory, network usage, and more.
- Container events, error information.

To set up the Application Insights resource, log in to the Azure portal and create an Application Insights resource. Copy the instrumentation key and apply it to all the applications or microservices for which you want the telemetry information to flow to the insights account. Do not forget to add the Docker tile to the Application Insights dashboard as shown in the following screenshot:

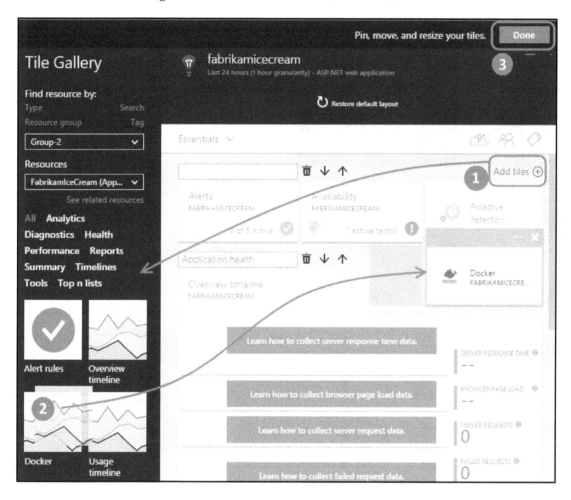

Image source: https://docs.microsoft.com/en-us/azure/application-insights/app-insights-docker

Provide the value for `ikey` using the key from the **Application Insights** dashboard and run the following command on any Linux Docker host to create the agent. If your application is spread across multiple hosts, you can repeat the command on every host.

```
docker run -v /var/run/docker.sock:/docker.sock -d
microsoft/applicationinsights ikey=<ApplicationInsightsKey>
```

A sample dashboard is shown in the following image, with telemetry information for the Docker host, per image, and Docker information, like the number of containers and images available on the host:

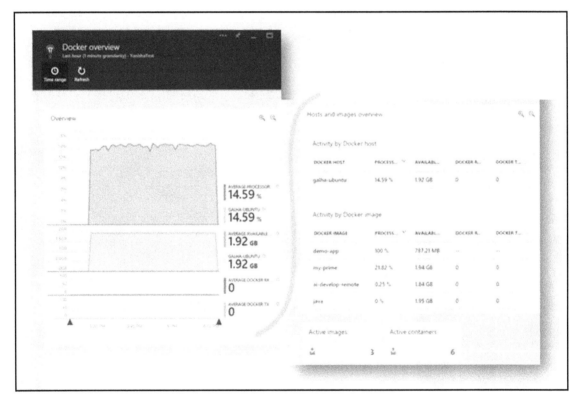

Image source: https://docs.microsoft.com/en-us/azure/application-insights/app-insights-docker

The following image shows the Docker custom events which show much granular data which can be used to investigate errors or critical events. Source code for application insights for Docker is available at
`https://github.com/Microsoft/ApplicationInsights-Docker`.

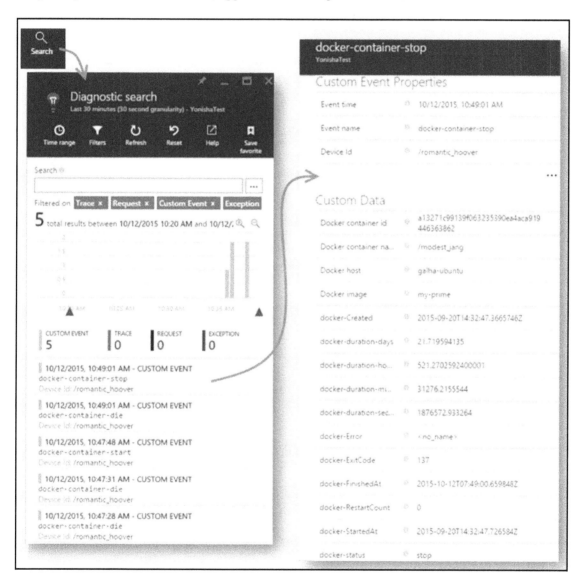

Operations Management Site

Azure Operations Management Suite offers functionality similar to Application Insights. OMS is a **Software as a Service (SaaS)** offering from Microsoft which allows Enterprise IT to manage a hybrid cloud. OMS helps you run log analytics by consolidating logs from various environments, automated deployments or jobs, backup and recovery and also makes sure you adhere to the security and compliance standards set by your organization. There are considerable differences between application insights and OMS. Application insights are an application monitoring tool, whereas OMS is an all-in-one cloud management solution which works across public and private clouds. OMS is the most suitable way to manage containers which are spread across hosts.

Similar to Application Insights for Docker, OMS containers solution is only supported on Linux OS. OMS too runs as an agent on the Container host, like Application Insights agent, OMS Dockerfile and image information is available at `https://hub.docker.com/r/microsoft/oms/`. Run the following command on the Linux container host to start OMS container:

```
sudo docker run --privileged -d -v /var/run/docker.
sock:/var/run/docker.sock -e WSID="your workspace id"
-e KEY="your key" -p 127.0.0.1:25225:25225 --name="omsagent"
-h=&grave;hostname&grave; --restart=always microsoft/oms
```

The following events can be captured using OMS:

- Number of container host VMs and their utilization
- Number of running containers
- Container and image inventory
- Container performance and container logs
- Docker daemon logs

In addition to this data, OMS can also capture information from standard error repositories like information or errors written to the System Viewer using Windows Diagnostics API. The following image shows OMS container solution for Linux:

The tile from the OMS dashboard shows the overall containers running or stopped on a container host or a combination of hosts:

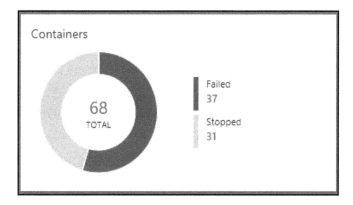

OMS has a custom querying syntax which can be used to filter results based on container hosts, image, container status and so on. The following image shows a sample search:

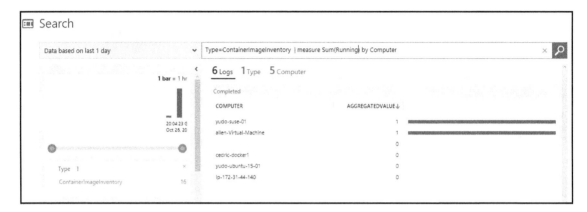

OMS or Application Insights integrate seamlessly with other Microsoft integration and Business Intelligence tools, like Office 365 and PowerBI.

Optimizing Dockerfiles

We have learned about building Windows Container images using Docker image files and also using Docker build. However, we have not yet learned how to build them efficiently. This section deals with important tips and tactics which can be used to optimize the image-building process. Before we learn to optimize a Dockerfile, let us first understand how Docker builds images.

The following Dockerfile creates a Windows image with IIS installed:

```
FROM Microsoft/windowsservercore
RUN dism /online /enable-feature /all /
featurename:iis-webserver /NoRestart
RUN echo "Hello World - Dockerfile" >
c:\inetpub\wwwroot\index.html
EXPOSE 80
CMD [ "cmd" ]
```

Docker consumes the above Dockerfile and, at the first instruction, where we select the base image `Microsoft/windowsservercore`, a temporary container is created. Thereafter at every instruction Docker updates the container and creates another temporary container which will be used by the next instruction. In this way, docker builds the image until the end of file is encountered. If you run the following `docker build` command for the above Dockerfile, you might be expecting three layers: one for the container OS image, a second for installing IIS and setting up the default page; and a third for exposing port 80.

```
docker build -t learningwsc/iis .
```

However, if you run the following command which shows the layers for any image, you'll notice that there are more than three layers:

```
PS C:\temp> docker history learningwsc/iis
IMAGE            CREATED          CREATED BY                                      SIZE
aef79f397d05     9 minutes ago    cmd /S /C #(nop)   CMD ["cmd"]                  22 MB
2280b9838275     9 minutes ago    cmd /S /C #(nop)   EXPOSE 80/tcp                273 MB
5007124eac46     9 minutes ago    cmd /S /C echo "Hello World - Dockerfile" ...   1.35 GB
bcad545c6f91     9 minutes ago    cmd /S /C dism /online /enable-feature /al...   7.33 GB
```

Each of these lines corresponds to a line in the Dockefile: the bottom layer `bcad545c6f91` is of 7.33 GB which consists of the based image; one layer above that is the IIS installation layer; and the one above that is the layer for exposing port 80. Dockerfiles can be written in a way that the number of layers are reduced and the build time and process improves. Dockerfiles should be readable as well, and in this section we will also learn how to increase the readability of the Dockerfile.

Optimizing image size

The image we created above consumes approximately 9 GB of memory. When we are building images on a container host, the image size becomes an important factor when we want to move the image from one host to another or while uploading to a registry. It is very important to learn about authoring Dockerfiles that dramatically reduce the size of the image.

The first step to reduce the image size is to group the RUN commands. As we have seen, each RUN command turns into a layer, if we can reduce the number of RUN commands, we should be able to reduce the number of layers. For example, let us compare two Dockerfiles which install Redis on Windows Server Core. The following file contains instructions spread out into multiple RUN commands:

```
FROM microsoft/windowsservercore
RUN powershell.exe -Command Invoke-WebRequest
https://github.com/MSOpenTech/redis/releases/download/
win-3.2.100/Redis-x64-3.2.100.zip -OutFile Redis-x64-3.2.100.zip
RUN powershell.exe -Command Expand-Archive Redis-x64-3.2.100.zip
-dest 'C:\\Program Files\\Redis\\'
RUN powershell.exe -Command Remove-Item Redis-x64-3.2.100.zip
-Force
EXPOSE 6379
CMD .\\redis-server.exe .\\redis.unprotected.conf --port 6379 ;
```

The resulting image shows five layers as shown in the following screenshot, one for each RUN instruction:

```
PS C:\redis> docker history learningwsc/redis
IMAGE           CREATED         CREATED BY                                          SIZE
fc661da00736    15 seconds ago  cmd /S /C #(nop)  CMD ["cmd" "/S" "/C" ".\...      52.8 MB
084c2ba92e7d    19 seconds ago  cmd /S /C #(nop)  EXPOSE 6379/tcp                   75.2 MB
a9b61af0c26f    25 seconds ago  cmd /S /C powershell.exe -Command Remove-I...      58.9 MB
af2b8d0ec366    51 seconds ago  cmd /S /C powershell.exe -Command Expand-A...      1.35 GB
b38955e7e0ae    About a minute ago  cmd /S /C powershell.exe -Command Invoke-W...  7.33 GB
```

Let us now try to reduce the number of layers, the following Dockerfile clubs all the RUN instructions into a single RUN instruction. For increasing the readability, you can split the instruction into multiple lines by using the ' \ ' character:

```
FROM microsoft/windowsservercore
RUN powershell.exe -Command Invoke-WebRequest
https://github.com/MSOpenTech/redis/releases/download/
win-3.2.100/Redis-x64-3.2.100.zip -OutFile Redis-x64-3.2.100.zip;\
    Expand-Archive Redis-x64-3.2.100.zip -dest 'C:\\Program
    Files\\Redis\\'; \
    Remove-Item Redis-x64-3.2.100.zip -Force
EXPOSE 6379
CMD .\\redis-server.exe .\\redis.unprotected.conf --port 6379 ;
```

The resulting image consists of lesser layers than the one above. Note that this did not reduce the image size; it just reduced the number of layers:

```
PS C:\redis> docker history learningwsc/redis
IMAGE            CREATED             CREATED BY                                                      SIZE
ccc6bed32eab     About a minute ago  cmd /S /C #(nop)   CMD ["cmd" "/S" "/C" ".\...    76.2 MB
a7ab9495427e     About a minute ago  cmd /S /C #(nop)   EXPOSE 6379/tcp                1.35 GB
2f6ce7491a9f     About a minute ago  cmd /S /C powershell.exe -Command Invoke-W...     7.33 GB
```

If you are installing any software while building an image, it is always good practice to delete the downloaded artefacts. This reduces the image size by an amount equal to the size of the software. Remember to put the instruction which removes the item in the same line where the software was downloaded and installed as shown in the above Redis example. Doing so removes the file from the lower level image layer.

Optimize build speed

On the contrary, we can optimize the build speeds if we split the instructions into multiple RUN commands. This is because each RUN instruction that is converted into a layer is cached by the Docker build system, while building an image. If Docker finds an instruction which is repeated, Docker uses the cached layer instead of creating a new layer. The result is that Docker's build speed is increased.

For example, the following Dockerfile downloads and installs the Visual Studio redistributable package and Apache, and then cleans up the files. Since this is all done in a single RUN instruction it creates only two layers:

```
FROM windowsservercore

RUN powershell -Command \

  # Download software ; \
  wget https://www.apachelounge.com/download/VC11/binaries/
  httpd-2.4.18-win32-VC11.zip -OutFile c:\apache.zip ; \
  wget "https://download.microsoft.com/download/1/6/B/
  16B06F60-3B20-4FF2-B699-5E9B7962F9AE/VSU_4/vcredist_x86.exe"
  -OutFile c:\vcredist.exe ; \
  wget -Uri http://windows.php.net/downloads/releases/
  php-5.5.33-Win32-VC11-x86.zip -OutFile c:\php.zip ; \

  # Install Software ; \

  Expand-Archive -Path c:\php.zip -DestinationPath c:\php ; \
  Expand-Archive -Path c:\apache.zip -DestinationPath c:\ ; \
  start-Process c:\vcredistexe -ArgumentList '/quiet' -Wait ; \
```

```
# Remove unneeded files ; \

Remove-Item c:\apache.zip -Force; \
Remove-Item c:\vcredist.exe -Force
```

The drawback of this is that if there are any minor changes to the preceding file, the whole instruction set will be re-run. On the contrary, if we try to split this Dockerfile into multiple instructions as shown in the following code, there are couple of advantages. The first advantage is that each layer is cached, which means if there is another Dockerfile that needs the Visual Studio Redistributable package, the layer is reused, which reduces download and installation efforts; The second advantage is that, if there is any change to one line in the Dockerfile, re-building the image will cost less because the remaining un-touched lines will be used from the cache. The following Dockerfile shows a similar file split into multiple RUN statements to increase the build speed:

```
FROM windowsservercore

RUN powershell -Command \
    $ErrorActionPreference = 'Stop'; \
    wget https://www.apachelounge.com/download/VC11/ \
    binaries/httpd-2.4.18-win32-VC11.zip -OutFile c:\apache.zip ; \
    Expand-Archive -Path c:\apache.zip -DestinationPath c:\ ; \
    Remove-Item c:\apache.zip -Force

RUN powershell -Command \
    $ErrorActionPreference = 'Stop'; \
    wget "https://download.microsoft.com/download/1/6/ \
    B/16B06F60-3B20-4FF2-B699-5E9B7962F9AE/VSU_4/ \
    vcredist_x86.exe" -OutFile c:\vcredist.exe ; \
    start-Process c:\vcredist.exe -ArgumentList '/quiet' -Wait ; \
    Remove-Item c:\vcredist.exe -Force

RUN powershell -Command \
    $ErrorActionPreference = 'Stop'; \
    wget http://windows.php.net/downloads/releases/ \
    php-5.5.33-Win32-VC11-x86.zip -OutFile c:\php.zip ; \
    Expand-Archive -Path c:\php.zip -DestinationPath c:\php ; \
    Remove-Item c:\php.zip -Force
```

The decision whether to split the instructions or to club them together depends on the content of the instruction. Let us say we are installing a generic piece of software like SQL Server, IIS or .NET framework: we can safely put them into separate RUN instructions provided we are anticipating building similar images in future. If the instructions are related to installing a custom application or configuring it, it is advisable to club the instructions so that the number of layers are reduced. Each of the image building guidelines have their own pros and cons, it is therefore a decision which should be taken based on need - *size vs speed*. If I'm getting ample storage space at a cheap price, I would prefer speed over concentrating on reducing the image size.

Ordering instructions

It is quite interesting to know how the caching process works. A Dockerfile is processed from top to bottom, and at every instruction the Docker engine checks if there is a cached layer. If the instruction contains a cached layer, Docker will just pick it up. If the instruction is something new, a new container layer is created and even if the next line is cached, Docker will still re-build a new layer because the previous line is not cached one. Because of this, the ordering of the instructions is very important. Place the instructions that will remain constant at the top of the Dockerfile. Place the instructions that may change at the bottom of the Dockerfile. This makes sure we are using the caching mechanism efficiently.

For example, the following Dockerfile creates four directories:

```
FROM windowsservercore

RUN mkdir test-1
RUN mkdir test-2
RUN mkdir test-3
RUN mkdir test-4
```

The resulting image contains five layers, one for the container base OS image and one for each RUN instruction. Now let us say we have another Dockerfile as shown here:

```
FROM windowsservercore

RUN mkdir test-1
RUN mkdir test-2
RUN mkdir test-5
RUN mkdir test-4
```

When Docker runs this file, for the first two RUN instructions Docker uses the cached version of layers. For the third RUN instruction Docker creates a new layer but for the fourth RUN statement Docker cannot use the cached layer because it has to build on the previous statement's layer.

An application stack might consist of multiple layers. It is always a good practice to decouple the application components into multiple containers. For example, an application might consist of a web application, a database layer and a caching layer; it is always advisable to prepare one image per component. As we have learnt at every step in the Dockerfile docker checks for existing containers using the instructions but or commands like ADD and COPY the content(s) of the file in the image are examined and checksum is calculated before reusing the cached layer. The last-modified and last-accessed time are ignored while calculating the checksums. If there is any change in the checksum, the cache is invalidation. There is a way to completely avoid cache layers while building an image using docker build, and that is by appending the command with `--no-cache = true`.

Docker REST API

We have been using the Docker command line or PowerShell to control containers, images or networks but there are few scenarios where you might want to integrate container operations into an existing application or build a custom client like a mobile application or chatbot to manage containers running in your environment. Integrating docker management tasks into a custom application using commands is a tedious task, so to solve this problem Docker offers a REST API called Docker Engine API.

A REST API stands for **Representational State Transfer** (**REST**). It is one way of providing interoperability among different services. RESTful services use HTTP/HTTPs to communicate with the service using operations mapped to HTTP actions like GET, POST, PUT, DELETE, and so on. The Docker engine API allows you to control every aspect of Docker from within your application. The Docker API client can be written in any language which can make a REST call like C#, Java, Go, Perl, JavaScript, Python and so on. Docker offers SDKs for C#, Java, Python and Go languages which makes it easier to interact with a REST API. For full list of SDKs or libraries available in any language visit `https://docs.docker.com/engine/api/sdks/`. These libraries are built and managed by the community outside Docker, and Docker team does not claim any ownership for issues raised, nor provide clarification for unsupported features. If you are looking for a feature which is not yet included in the SDK, you can always fall back to using the REST API. In this section, we will learn about using the REST API and C# SDK to perform most basic operations on Docker.

At the time of writing, the latest Docker Engine API available was 1.26. You can always target a particular version by including the version number in the REST call. Windows Server 2016 comes pre-installed with Docker. To interact with Docker Engine API the container host should start listing for remote requests. Run the following commands on the PowerShell command window to make Docker start listening on port 2375:

```
Remove-Item C:\ProgramData\docker.pid -Force
dockerd.exe -H 0.0.0.0:2375
```

In this section, I'm using a postman application to interact with Docker API on Windows Container host. Postman can be downloaded from `https://www.getpostman.com/`. The API calls mentioned in this section can be done using any programming language and client. For interacting with the Docker REST API one would need the IP or the host name of the docker container host. For example, the following URL shows the base URL for interacting with the API, where `musicstorehost.cloudapp.net` is the host name of the container host, `2375` is where the docker process is looking for connections. We are targeting version 1.24 in the following URL. The Docker Engine API responds using **JavaScript Object Notation (JSON)** syntax.

```
http://musicstorehost.cloudapp.net:2375/v1.24/
```

List containers

Listing containers is one of the most common operation which lists the containers available on the container host. To get a list of all containers running on the container, append `containers/json?all=1` to the base URL as:

```
http://musicstorehost.cloudapp.net:2375/v1.24/containers/json?all=1
```

We can further filter the results using the query parameter options as shown in the following table:

Query parameter	Data type	Default	Description
All	`boolean (0/1)`	`0 (false)`	Returns all containers, by default only running containers are shown.
Limit	`Int`	–	Limits the list to value provided, including the non-running containers.
Size	`boolean`	`false`	Return the size of the container as fields.
Filters	`String`		Filters the results using the JSON string. For example, `{"status": "paused"}` will return only paused containers.

The following is a sample request and response screenshot taken from Postman:

Create container

Append the query parameters `containers/create` to create a container. Remember `create container` is a post method which means we should pass the request parameters as a post body for creating the containers. The following is a sample request which creates a Windows Server Core container.

Since this is a `POST` request, the server might respond with a variety of response codes as shown in the following table, which should be handled gracefully:

Response codes	Description
201	Container created successfully
400	Bad parameter
404	No such image/container
409	Conflict
500	Server error

Start/stop container

You might want to conditionally start/stop a container to save on resources or for updates from a remote client. The following post request will help you start the container using the container ID. The container ID can be fetched by using the list container operation which is similar to the list images request we saw earlier:

```
Containers/{Id}/start
```

To stop a container, just replace the command with stop as shown in the following code:

```
Containers/{Id}/stop
```

The following image shows a sample start request from Postman:

Removing a container

The following image shows a sample request and response for killing a container. Notice the use of HTTP DELETE method for making a delete call:

Docker contains REST APIs for every function that can be performed from the command line. A full REST API specification is available at `https://docs.docker.com/engine/api/`.

Docker .NET SDK

When you are building clients using .NET, Docker.DotNet helps interact with Docker Remote API. Docker.DotNet is fully asynchronous, designed to be non-blocking and object-oriented way to interact with container host programmatically.

The library can be added to the project by running the following command in the NuGet Package Manager Console.

```
PM> Install-Package Docker.DotNet
```

Alternatively, right-click on your project in Visual Studio, choose **Manage NuGet Packages** and search for **Docker.Dotnet** and click **Install**. This section show you a few key methods using .NET library for Docker.

To start communicating with your Windows Container host, we should create a client first. The following code shows you how to create a Docker Client. `DockerClient` is part of the `Docker.Dotnet` namespace so include the `Docker.Dotnet` code in the namespaces section.

```
DockerClient client = new DockerClientConfiguration
(new Uri(containerHostUrl)).CreateClient();
```

The client object consists of the following properties: images, containers and networks. These properties offer operations like list, create, and remove on the docker artifacts. The container host URL in the preceding code is the host name plus the port number, for example, `http://your-docker-host:2375/`. You can also secure the connection using SSL/TLS certificate with:

```
var certificate = new X509Certificate2 ("CertFile", "Password");
var credentials = new CertificateCredentials(certificate);
DockerClient client = new DockerClientConfiguration("tcp://your-docker-
host:4243", credentials).CreateClient();
```

List containers

The following code shows how to get containers. The `containerslistparameters` contains properties for filtering the list of containers based on size, number, before/since a particular container ID and using custom filters.

```
/// <summary>
/// Lists all the containers running on a host
/// </summary>
/// <param name="limit">Limit number of containers</param>
/// <returns>A list of containers</returns>
private async static Task<IList<ContainerListResponse>>
ListContainers(int limit = 10)
{
    client = new DockerClientConfiguration(new
    Uri(containerHostUrl)).CreateClient();
    var containers = await client.Containers.
    ListContainersAsync(new ContainersListParameters()
    {
        Limit = limit,
        Size = true,
        All = true
    });
    return containers;
}
```

Creating a container

The following method creates a container using image `microsoft/windowsservercore`. `CreateContainerParameters` provides a lot of options for creating containers like setting up the working directory, Shell, port mappings and so on:

```
/// <summary>
/// Creates a Container
/// </summary>
private async static Task<CreateContainerResponse>
CreateContainer()
{
    client = new DockerClientConfiguration(new
    Uri(containerHostUrl)).CreateClient();
    return await client.Containers.CreateContainerAsync
    (new CreateContainerParameters()
    {
        Image = "microsoft/windowsservercore",
        Name = "mycontainer",
```

```
            Shell = new List<string> { "CMD" }
        }
    );
}
```

Starting a container

The following method starts a container by `Container Id`:

```
/// <summary>
/// Starts a container by Container Id
/// </summary>
/// <param name="id">Container Id</param>
private async static Task<bool> StartContainer(string id)
{
    client = new DockerClientConfiguration
    (new Uri(containerHostUrl)).CreateClient();
    return await client.Containers.StartContainerAsync
    (id, null);
}
```

Stopping a container

The following method stops a container, and we can configure a lead time before killing the container:

```
/// <summary>
/// Stop a container by Container Id
/// </summary>
/// <param name="id">Container Id</param>
private async static Task<bool> StopContainer(string id)
{
    client = new DockerClientConfiguration
    (new Uri(containerHostUrl)).CreateClient();
    return await client.Containers.StopContainerAsync
    (id, new ContainerStopParameters()
    { WaitBeforeKillSeconds = 10 },
        default(CancellationToken));
}
```

Removing a container

The following code force removes a container from the container host:

```
/// <summary>
/// Removes a container by Container Id
/// </summary>
/// <param name="id">Container Id</param>
private async static Task RemoveContainer(string id)
{
    client = new DockerClientConfiguration
    (new Uri(containerHostUrl)).CreateClient();
    await client.Containers.RemoveContainerAsync
    (id, new ContainerRemoveParameters()
    {
        Force = true
    });
}
```

Downloading an image

The following code creates an image by downloading the image from the Docker Hub if required:

```
/// <summary>
/// Creates a new Image by pulling from Docker Hub
/// </summary>
/// <returns></returns>
public async static Task<Stream> CreateImage()
{
    client = new DockerClientConfiguration
    (new Uri(containerHostUrl)).CreateClient();
    return await client.Images.CreateImageAsync
    (new ImagesCreateParameters()
    { Parent = "microsoft/iis", Tag = "webserver" }, null);
}
```

Few docker API endpoints stream responses; for example, creating images or monitoring docker events. We can obtain the events from the stream by using the following code:

```
CancellationTokenSource cancellation = new CancellationTokenSource();
Stream stream = await client.Miscellaneous.MonitorEventsAsync(new
ContainerEventsParameters(), cancellation.Token);
```

By default, we do not have to specify any version number in the API. However, if you intend to target a specific API you can pass the version parameter as:

```
var config = new DockerClientConfiguration(...);
DockerClient client = config.CreateClient(new Version(1, 16));
```

The following is a list of exceptions which will be thrown by the client library:

- `DockerApiException`: This exception is thrown when the Docker API responds with a non-success result. A few sub-classes of this exception are `DockerContainerNotFoundException` and `DockerImageNotFoundException`.
- `TaskCanceledException`: This is an exception thrown by the `HTTPClient` library in the case of a connection drop or timeout. The default request timeout is 100 seconds.
- `ArgumentNullException`: This exception is thrown when there is a required parameter missing/empty.

Summary

In a shared environment, CPU, memory and network resources used by each container should be controlled to avoid the noisy neighbor problem. Docker provides configuration options for setting up minimum and maximum limits on CPU, memory and CPU while creating containers. Microsoft provides telemetry solutions at application level and also at the host level. These can capture critical information on the container performance and the host performance. At present these technologies only support Linux-based container hosts.

Dockerfile contents are operated from top to bottom. In order to reduce the build time of an image one should club statements. Docker checks for cached layers for every instruction in the Dockerfile. To increase the re-usability or caching installations not specific to an application, they should be separated out. Ordering of the instructions is also important since any change in the intermediate layer invalidates the remaining cached layers, and Docker starts building the layer from scratch.

Apart from the command line, Docker also provides a REST API which comes pre-installed on every Docker host. Docker REST API supports all sorts of operations that can also be performed using the command line client. The Docker community provides wrappers or client libraries for interacting with the REST API in C#, Java, Python, Go, and many other languages.

11
Composite Containers and Clustering

Most of the enterprise applications are multi-tier, each application might consist of web app, services, database, caching, networking components, and so on. When it comes to deploying multi-tier applications as containers it is unproductive and often error prone to do it using the Docker commands. The sequence of the commands is also a matter of concern because there might be dependencies among the components, like say the web application would need the DNS name or IP and port number of the database container. In these circumstances, it is ideal to have a composite deployment tool which can be used to setup an environment and manage as a single unit instead of individual components. In this chapter, we will learn to compose multi-container deployments, manage and scale as a single unit. Likewise, container hosts can also grow by large number as organizations move from VM virtualization to containerization. It is tedious to maintain a set of discrete container hosts, controlling the up times, scheduling for cost optimization and managing updates. Virtualized environments are often backed up by management tools which help configure and monitor the large environments from one place. In this chapter, we will also learn to create and manage a cluster of container hosts using famous tools.

The following topics will be discussed in this chapter:

- Orchestrating multi-container deployment using `docker-compose`
- `docker-compose` file reference
- `docker-compose` CLI and commands
- Cluster management tools
- Docker Swarm architecture
- Setting up Swarm Cluster using ACS
- Docker Swarm features

Orchestrating multi-container deployment using docker-compose

Most of the applications in today's world are multi layered and cater to various form factors and hence contain more than one layer to meet the performance, scalability and reliability requirements. In a large and virtualized environment, it is necessary to have a composition tool to setup or tear down environments instantly as a single unit. For example, Azure offers compute, storage, and network as a service, when a customer wants to deploy a multi-layered/multi-resource application they must deploy each resource like web app service, Azure SQL and virtual networks in an order and connect them logically based on the dependencies. It is quite tedious and error prone to micro manage an application's environment. To solve this problem Microsoft introduced **Azure Resource Manager** (**ARM**) based deployments by using templates. ARM templates are used to compose the environment consisting of various resources and dependencies and deploy at once. Similarly, containers when there are too many logically forming a single application it is necessary to have a composition tool to setup large environments or to manage them. There are two ways to do this, one way is to compose all components into a single container -this isn't too scalable and reliable approach. A crash in a container can bring the whole application down; instead it is advisable to decompose the application into multiple containers and managing each one individually. But how do we manage or even create a multi container environment? Well, there are many tools available in the market which can help you orchestrate multi-container deployments, all of them take advantage of the Docker REST API which is built into each container host. But the best and the recommended one comes from Docker called `docker-compose`.

`docker-compose` is a tool for defining and running multi-container dockerized applications. We have learned authoring applications as containers using Docker image files, similarly `docker-compose` s uses a single file to define a multi-container environment. Once the file authoring is complete we can setup or tear down the environment using a single command. We can also micro manage each individual container or a sub-group of containers within the environment using `docker-compose` commands.

The following is a sample `docker-compose` file.

```
version: '3'
services:
 web:
  image: microsoft/iis
  ports:
   - "8080:8080"
 db:
  image: microsoft/mssql-server-windows
```

```
    ports:
      - "1433:1433"
    environment:
    - ACCEPT_EULA="Y"
    volumes:
      - c:\data
  networks:
   default:
    external:
     name: "nat"
```

The file should be named `docker-compose.yml` or `docker-compose.yaml`. The following things are happening in the `docker-compose` preceding file:

- In services section, we are building two containers a web server using image `microsoft/iis` and database server using `microsoft/mssql-server-windows`
- Setting up port forward for both the containers, port `8080` for web server and port `1433` for the database server
- Mount volume `c:\data` from the host to the database server
- Assigning the containers to a `nat` network

All the preceding is happening in a single file, whereas with Docker commands the same thing should be split a series of docker commands. Clearly, `docker-compose` allow us to spin up and environment with multiple containers and networking requirements in a single file. Now let us see how to setup this environment, name the preceding file as `docker-compose.yml` and place in under folder `C:\learninwsc\chapter11\simple-docker-container`. To build and run applications using `docker-compose` the CLI tool should be installed on the container host, follow the following steps to install `docker-compose` on a Windows Server 2016 machine.

In this section, we will install `docker-compose` using `chocolatey` packages. **Chocolatey** is a packaging software which is built on top of PowerShell and unattended installation. Chocolatey makes software installation easy and prompt-free. Open a PowerShell prompt in administrator mode and run the following command to install the latest version of chocolatey.

```
iwr https://chocolatey.org/install.ps1 -UseBasicParsing | iex
```

Next let us install `docker-compose` using `chocolatey` using the following command.

```
choco install docker-compose -y
```

We should now be able to invoke `docker-compose` commands as shown following.

```
PS C:\> docker-compose
Define and run multi-container applications with Docker.

Usage:
  docker-compose [-f <arg>...] [options] [COMMAND] [ARGS...]
  docker-compose -h|--help

Options:
  -f, --file FILE             Specify an alternate compose file (default: docker-compose.yml)
  -p, --project-name NAME     Specify an alternate project name (default: directory name)
  --verbose                   Show more output
  -v, --version               Print version and exit
  -H, --host HOST             Daemon socket to connect to

  --tls                       Use TLS; implied by --tlsverify
  --tlscacert CA_PATH         Trust certs signed only by this CA
  --tlscert CLIENT_CERT_PATH  Path to TLS certificate file
  --tlskey TLS_KEY_PATH       Path to TLS key file
  --tlsverify                 Use TLS and verify the remote
  --skip-hostname-check       Don't check the daemon's hostname against the name specified
                              in the client certificate (for example if your docker host
                              is an IP address)
```

Navigate to the folder where we saved `docker-compose.yml` earlier and run the following command to spin up the environment as defined in the file.

```
docker-compose up
```

The output would be as follows.

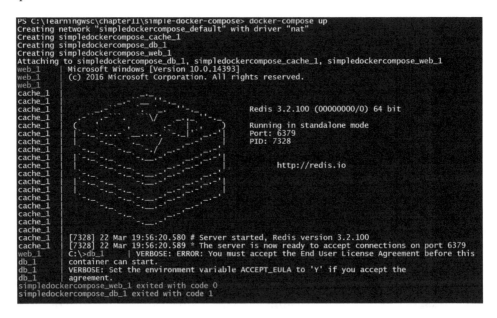

If you list the containers now, you would see that the `docker-compose` created three containers each for one section of the service defined in the compose definition.

```
PS C:\learningwsc\chapter11\simple-docker-compose> docker ps -a
CONTAINER ID        IMAGE                                    COMMAND                  CREATED
            PORTS                        NAMES
d9ff0635c2bc        microsoft/mssql-server-windows-express   "cmd /S /C 'powers..."   15 minutes ago
utes ago                                 simpledockercompose_db_1
1cda7c9503f4        webserver                                "c:\\windows\\system..."   15 minutes ago
utes ago                                 simpledockercompose_web_1
b31f7b8f1faf        learningwsc/redis-server                 "powershell '.\\\\re..."   15 minutes ago
seconds ago                              simpledockercompose_cache_1
```

Each of these containers are named by prepending the folder they are within followed by the service name and the instance Id. After running the `docker-compose up` command which is used to setup an environment you would notice that the services are running in the foreground and the containers would just run until the invoking process (in this case the command line) is killed. You can also run the services in the background in detached mode like we do for the containers using the following command.

> `docker-compose up -d`

The `docker-compose up` command's log contains the log for each service within the `yml` file with unique coloring. Each individual service can be individually monitored as a container or collective done using the `docker-compose` command line. For example, to list all the environments running you can use the following command.

> `docker-compose ps`

The `ps` command like for docker lists the environments that are running or stopped as shown following.

```
PS C:\learningwsc\chapter11\simple-docker-compose> docker-compose ps
            Name                       Command                   State       Ports
-------------------------------------------------------------------------------------
simpledockercompose_cache_1   powershell .\\redis-server ...   Exit 1067
simpledockercompose_db_1      cmd /S /C powershell ./sta ...   Exit 1
simpledockercompose_web_1     c:\windows\system32\cmd.exe      Exit 0
```

We can bring down the whole environment at once using the following command.

> `docker-compose down`

Use the `--volumes` option to remove the volume when shutting down the environment as shown following:

```
PS C:\learningwsc\chapter11\simple-docker-compose> docker-compose down --volumes
Removing simpledockercompose_db_1 ... done
Removing simpledockercompose_web_1 ... done
Removing simpledockercompose_cache_1 ... done
Removing network simpledockercompose_default
```

Now that is how we compose multi-container deployments and setup or shutdown environments using a single command. `docker-compose` is much more flexible and powerful, before we learn more about controlling environments using `docker-compose`, let us see how to compose the environments using various options in the compose file.

A docker-compose file reference

A `docker-compose` file is used to define services, networks and volumes for containers in an environment. The extension for the compose file can be either `.yml` or `.yaml`. You can use any of your favorite text editors to author a compose file. By default, `docker-compose` tool looks for the compose file in the current directory. `docker-compose` file is versioned; the latest version at the time of writing is version 3. A `docker-compose` file consists of `key:option:value` pairs, the `version:3.0 key:value` pair in the preceding example of the compose file tells the tool which version to use while validating the contents of the file. Following the indentation rules for a compose file is very important, if you consider the `docker-compose` file as a table of characters with rows and columns, every new `key:value` pair starts at column 0 in a compose file. The options for a key, like *web* in the preceding example starts at column 1 or say after leaving a space. Similarly, the options for *web* are prepended by two leading spaces. This indentation rules extend throughout the key-option-value chain.

The following image shows the indentation applied for the `docker-compose` file. Each dot represents an empty space in the following screenshot:

```
version:··'3'
services:
|·web:
··image:·microsoft/iis
··ports:
····-·"8080:8080"
·db:
··image:·microsoft/mssql-server-windows
··ports:
·····-·"1433:1433"
··environment:
····-·ACCEPT_EULA="Y"
··volumes:
····-·c:\data
networks:
·default:
··external:
···name:·"nat"
    □
```

Build options

Using `docker-compose` you can also build an image using the file options. For example, in the following `docker-compose` file we are building a custom web server and setting up the environment at once. In the following `docker-compose` we are providing the build context using the `build` key and the image name with tag using the `image` key.

```
version: '3'
services:
 db:
   image: microsoft/mssql-server-windows-express
   ports:
     - "1433:1433"
   volumes:
     - c:\data
 cache:
   image: learningwsc/redis-server
   ports:
     - "6379:6379"
 web:
   build: .
```

```
      image: webserver:latest
      ports:
        - "80:80"
      environment:
        - db_connection = db
        - cache_connection = cache
   networks:
    default:
     driver: nat
     ipam:
      driver: default
      config:
        - subnet: 172.20.81.0/24
```

If you are building multiple images in a single docker-compose file, the build context can point to multiple relative paths within the host or to a remote git repository. By default, docker-compose looks for the dockerfile within the build context however, we can point to a remote dockerfile instead as shown following. We can also pass arguments to the dockerfile using the args key-value option from a docker-compose file like we do using a docker run option.

```
web:
build: .
dockerfile: dockerfile-alternative
image: webserver:latest
ports:
  - "80:80"
args
  - buildversion: '1.0.0'
```

Naming containers

If you notice the container names for the preceding file are named using the folder name and name of the service. docker-compose gives you an option to adapt custom container names using the following option.

```
   web:
build: .
image: webserver:latest
ports:
  - "80:80"
Container-name: webcontainer
```

Dependencies

While setting up environments using multiple containers it might require to setup dependencies among the containers. For example, if a web container requires database connection string or cache connection string the database and cache containers should be built prior to the web container. `docker-compose` has the `depends_on` property can be used to setup dependencies among the containers as shown in the following code:

```
version: '3'
services:
 db:
  image: microsoft/mssql-server-windows-express
  ports:
   - "1433:1433"
  volumes:
   - c:\data
 cache:
  image: learningwsc/redis-server
  ports:
   - "6379:6379"
 web:
  build: .
  image: webserver:latest
  container_name: webcontainer
  ports:
   - "80:80"
  depends_on:
   - db
   - cache
  environment:
   - db_connection = db
   - cache_connection = cache
networks:
 default:
  driver: nat
  ipam:
   driver: default
   config:
    - subnet: 172.20.81.0/24
```

With the dependencies defined as preceding the services are started in the order of dependencies. In this case the `db` and `cache` containers are started first and then the `web` container. Remember, `docker-compose` will not wait for `db` or `cache` containers to attain the `ready` state before starting the web container. In a distributed environment where containers move across multiple hosts there is no guarantee for the resources to be 100% available all the times, the applications are expected to be resilient so that they can connect to the dependent resource on multiple retries in case of connection loss. Docker contains inbuilt service discovery, services are registered and assigned an IP from the DNS automatically. During service registration, each service is registered with a set of internal IP for the container endpoints that are running the service. This makes it easy for any service to discover and integrate with any other service running on the same network by service name or IP address irrespective of the number of containers running for the application.

The following image shows the log for the preceding `docker-compose` using the `build` option:

```
PS C:\learningwsc\chapter11\docker-compose-build> docker-compose up -d
Creating network "dockercomposebuild_default" with driver "nat"
Building web
Step 1/6 : FROM microsoft/windowsservercore
 ---> b4713e4d8bab
Step 2/6 : LABEL Description ⌐¬⌐IIS⌐¬⌐ Vendor Microsoft⌐¬⌐ Version ⌐¬⌐10?
 ---> Using cache
 ---> 1564a5cd4960
Step 3/6 : RUN powershell -Command Add-WindowsFeature Web-Server
 ---> Running in 1b1eeebab1df

Success Restart Needed Exit Code      Feature Result
------- -------------- ---------      --------------
True    No             Success        {Common HTTP Features, Default Documen..


 ---> f4d245c62fb1
Removing intermediate container 1b1eeebab1df
Step 4/6 : COPY ./*.* c:/inetpub/wwwroot/
 ---> ee82411bb450
Removing intermediate container 96f782e73db9
Step 5/6 : EXPOSE 80
 ---> Running in e8d0e589f18b
 ---> 3c7492c9ee5e
Removing intermediate container e8d0e589f18b
Step 6/6 : CMD "ping localhost -t"
 ---> Running in 39d7772bf113
 ---> bf0aa8bc382e
Removing intermediate container 39d7772bf113
Successfully built bf0aa8bc382e
WARNING: Image for service web was built because it did not already exist. To
 build  or  docker-compose up --build .
Creating dockercomposebuild_db_1
Creating dockercomposebuild_cache_1
Creating webcontainer
```

Named volumes

You can also define named volumes apart from declaring them as part of the services as we saw preceding. The named volume can be used across services defined in the compose definition:

```yaml
version: '3'
services:
 db:
  image: microsoft/mssql-server-windows-express
  ports:
   - "1433:1433"
  volumes:
   - data-volume:c:\data
 cache:
  image: learningwsc/redis-server
  ports:
   - "6379:6379"
 web:
  build: .
  image: webserver:latest
  container_name: webcontainer
  ports:
   - "80:80"
  depends_on:
   - db
   - cache
  environment:
   - db_connection = db
   - cache_connection = cache
networks:
 default:
  driver: nat
  ipam:
   driver: default
   config:
    - subnet: 172.20.81.0/24
    volumes:
     data-volume:
```

Docker CLI options

docker-compose gives you lot of command line options to control the environment, you can see this information by running docker-compose - -help in the command line. We have seen the commands up and down which help setup an environment, in this section we will visit few more helpful commands which provide more granularized control on the environment:

```
Commands:
  build       Build or rebuild services
  bundle      Generate a Docker bundle from the Compose file
  config      Validate and view the compose file
  create      Create services
  down        Stop and remove containers, networks, images, and volumes
  events      Receive real time events from containers
  exec        Execute a command in a running container
  help        Get help on a command
  kill        Kill containers
  logs        View output from containers
  pause       Pause services
  port        Print the public port for a port binding
  ps          List containers
  pull        Pull service images
  push        Push service images
  restart     Restart services
  rm          Remove stopped containers
  run         Run a one-off command
  scale       Set number of containers for a service
  start       Start services
  stop        Stop services
  top         Display the running processes
  unpause     Unpause services
  up          Create and start containers
  version     Show the Docker-Compose version information
```

Start/stop services

Use the following command to stop all the services within a docker-compose environment:

```
docker-compose stop
```

To start the services, use the following command:

```
docker-compose start
```

```
PS C:\learningwsc\chapter11\docker-compose-build> docker-compose start
Starting cache ... done
Starting db ... done
Starting web ... done
```

To start/stop any one service within the compose definition suffix the name of service as shown following:

```
docker-compose start web
```

```
PS C:\learningwsc\chapter11\docker-compose-build> docker-compose stop web
Stopping webcontainer ... done
```

Building images

If there is a change in any service's docker file the image should be rebuilt, use the following command to rebuild the images defined using the `build` option in the `compose` file:

```
docker-compose build
```

The following command removes any intermediate containers why rebuilding the image:

```
docker-compose build --force-rm
```

Docker caches the intermediate layers while building the image to promote reusability, you can force docker to recreate intermediate layers while building an image using the following command. Obviously, this will increase the time to prepare the image:

```
docker-compose build --no-cache
```

The following command pulls the latest image used for the service named db:

```
docker-compose build --pull db
```

Creating containers

The following command helps in recreating the containers:

```
docker-compose create
```

Use the following command if you want the containers to be recreated even if their configuration and image have not changed:

```
docker-compose create --force-recreate
```

The combination given following builds the images and forces to recreate the containers:

```
docker-compose create --build --force-recreate
```

You can avoid the recreate of containers or rebuild of images by using the `--no-recreate` and `--no-build` flags accordingly.

Executing commands

This is an equivalent of `docker exec` command. Exec helps run arbitrary commands on your services. The following command helps attach a CMD to the running container:

```
docker-compose exec web cmd
```

Killing commands

To force shutdown the containers running in an environment run the command given following:

```
docker-compose kill
```

Pause or unpause

To pause or unpause containers running in an environment run the following commands:

```
docker-compose pause
docker-compose unpause
```

Scale

Scale helps you set number of containers for a service. For example, the following command creates 2 web containers and 3 db containers:

```
docker-compose scale web=2 worker=3
```

Cluster management

As you start running applications as containers, you might not just do away with one container host. To run contains in different environments like development, staging and production we will need more container hosts. In these circumstances, you would need a clustering tool which would abstract away the presence of multiple hosts and present you a single interface for managing multiple hosts collectively.

Docker Swarm is great tool to help you with docker cluster management. The cluster management and orchestration features are built into the Docker Engine using the swarm kit. Each Docker Engine running in a swarm cluster runs in a swarm mode. There are two ways to make run a Docker Engine in swarm mode, either you can initialize swarm or join the engine to an existing Swarm. A swarm is a cluster of Docker Engine (a cluster is group of machines or called nodes) where you can deploy containers. The Docker Engine and API contain methods to manage the cluster and perform activities like adding or removing nodes from the cluster or deploy services on the cluster. There is a difference in running a Docker Engine in swarm mode and without swarm. When we run a docker engine without a swarm mode we execute docker commands, but when we run the Docker Engine in swarm mode we orchestrate services. We can also run a hybrid docker engine by running docker commands and services on the same host. To use Docker Engine in swarm mode we should install the Docker Engine v1.12.0 or later.

Docker Swarm architecture

A node in a swarm cluster is any machine with docker engine installed and capable of hosting containers/services (When we run docker engine under swarm mode we often call applications as services). This is also referred as **Docker node**. A Docker node can be a physical machine or one or more virtual machines running on a physical host or cloud server. It is recommended to spread your docker nodes across multiple physical machines to provide availability and reliability for the applications running on the hosts. Docker Swarm environment consists of one or more manager nodes. To deploy an application on Docker Swarm we submit a request in the form of service definition to a manager node. Manager node performs orchestration and cluster management functions required to maintain the desired state of the farm. If there are multiple manager nodes in a swarm, the nodes elect a leader to conduct orchestration (Consul (`https://www.consul.io/`) is one of the framework which implements leader election strategy). Manager nodes assigns the task to worker node using unit of work pattern. A worker nodes receive the work from the manager nodes and report with the help of an agent running on each worker node. The worker node reports the manager node of the tasks assigned to it so that manager can maintain the desired state of the worker. The following image shows the swarm architecture with multiple managers and worker nodes:

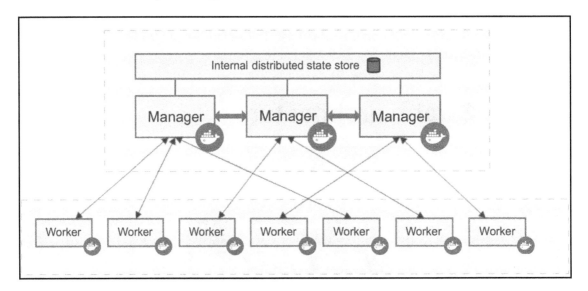

A Docker node can be configured to run as a manager node or worker node. A manager node can perform the functions of a worker node or it can be specially configured as an orchestrator only node. This is because all the docker nodes are running identical Docker Engine and each of those can be configured to perform any of the swarm roles on need basis.

A service is a task definition which is executed on the worker node is the primary unit of work. The task definition defines the image to use, ports and the commands to be executed inside a container. In the replicated services model, the manager creates *n* number replicas of the task, the *n* here is defined by the value of the scale attribute. For example, if you want two instances of web container and three instances of database container the manger replicates the task and assign to different worker roles. For global services, the swarm runs one task for the service on every available node in the cluster. Once a task is assigned to a node it cannot be moved to a different node. The swarm manager uses ingress load balancer for the services running on the worker nodes. Users or external component like load balancers can reach to any node in a swarm cluster irrespective of whether the node is running workloads. The port numbers are auto-assigned by the swarm manager from the range 30000-32767 if not assigned by the user. Swarm mode contains an inbuilt DNS which it uses to assign a DNS entry for every service running inside the swarm.

The IP address of the manager nodes is very critical, the remaining nodes in the cluster other than the manager nodes try to access the manager using the IP address. We should have always try to have a fixed IP for the manager. The following ports must and protocols should be enabled for communication among the hosts:

- TCP port 2377 for cluster management communications
- TCP and UDP port 7946 for communication among nodes

- UDP port `4789` for overlay network traffic

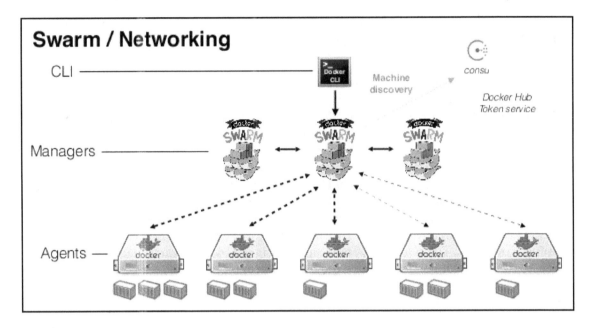

The preceding picture shows the communication model with docker swarm. We can use the same docker CLI to communicate with a swarm manager which assigns the task to any of the available agents. The agents report the task's status back to the elected manager.

Setting up a swarm cluster

There are a couple of ways of setting up a swarm cluster. You can create a cluster using any virtualized environments like Hyper-V, virtual box. The number of hosts running in a swarm cluster will be restricted to the host's CPU and memory capacity. Traditionally on premise environments are setup using multiple physical nodes. The second way of setting up swarm environment is by using hosted environments like Azure or AWS. In this section, we will learn to setup a hybrid cluster with Linux and Windows container host. On Azure there are two approaches for creating a swarm cluster, one way is to use any pre-defined ARM template like the one available here: `https://github.com/Azure/azure-quickstart -templates/tree/master/docker-swarm-cluster`.

This template deploys a swarm cluster on your Azure subscription with three swarm managers and a specified number of swarm nodes in the specified location of a resource group. The following diagram shows the cluster topology for the preceding template:

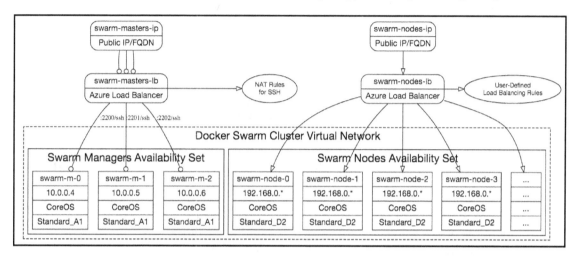

The swarm managers are part of an Azure availability set, which means each of them are on different fault domains; this increases the availability of the Swarm Manager. Further, they are load balanced using Azure load balancer. The load balancer is assigned a public IP address which can be used to assign tasks to the swarm manager. Similarly, the swarm nodes are also assigned to an availability set and an Azure load balance which is accessible using a public IP. This IP can be used to reach any services running on the swarm nodes. All the nodes in the cluster are in the same Azure Virtual Network, hence each node can access any other node in the network using internal IP. By default, the Azure VMs playing the role of swarm manager are assigned the private IP addresses 10.0.0.4, 10.0.0.5 and 10.0.0.6. Swarm manager co-ordinate using Consul agents to running in each manager to elect the leader.

Worker nodes are assigned IP address in the range `192.168.0.*`. The worker nodes are accessible via the manager nodes or by creating custom probes and load-balancers to the Azure load balancer. If you have notices the ARM template does not contain any windows server container host. While it is easy to add a new windows container host to the existing cluster, we will do it using a PaaS service provided by Azure called **Azure Container Service (ACS)**.

 The ARM template describe preceding works for Docker version v1.12, for which swarm was distributed as separate container. The template might require few modifications to make it work with versions higher than v1.12 for which Docker Swarm is inbuilt with Docker Engine.

ACS is an easy way to create a cluster of virtual machines on Azure that can host containers. ACS is so far, the simplest and most flexible way to run your containers on Azure. Why do we need a PaaS service like ACS? As organizations learn the benefits of containerization and look to scale at large in production soon they will also learn that it is tedious to create and manage large clusters. It might get difficult to add new nodes or manage the availability of the nodes using custom approach like the one described preceding. ACS is targeted to solve the preceding challenges by allowing the user to create simple or advanced cluster just by few clicks. In fact, using ACS you can build a cluster using Docker Swarm, Google Kubernetes or DC/OS:

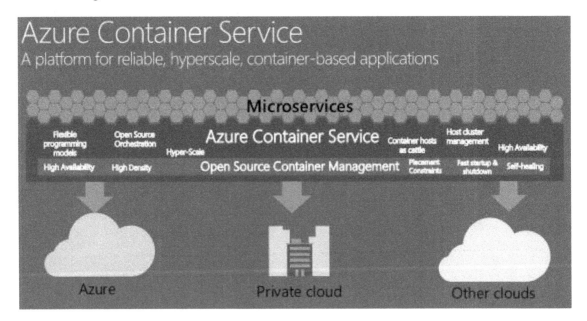

The following steps help you create a Swarm cluster on Azure using ACS. At this point the cluster is made up of Linux nodes only, we will learn to add windows container worker node to the cluster once the farm is successfully provisioned.

Generate SSH key

ACS supports only Linux workloads. Microsoft is working on the implementation of an enabling ACS for Windows Worker nodes as well. To connect to Linux worker node, we would need an SSH key. There are many ways to create a SSH key from a Windows machine, one such way is by using Git bash for Windows tool. You can down the tool from `https://desktop.github.com/`.

To generate SSH key, open the Git bash under elevated mode and run the following command:

```
ssh-keygen
```

By default, `ssh-keygen` creates the public/private RSA key in a `.ssh` folder in the user's directory. There will be two files created under this directory named `id_rsa` (private), `id_rsa.pub` (public). You can choose to override the file location or name, hit *Enter* to go ahead with the default naming and location. The system prompts you to enter the **pass phrase**, the pass phrase is like the password for connecting to the cluster, remember the pass phrase entered here as it will be used again while connecting to the Linux machine. Once done check the two files generated under `C:\users\{username}\.ssh`:

```
vism@sriks-machine MINGW64 ~
$ ssh-keygen
Generating public/private rsa key pair.
Enter file in which to save the key (/c/Users/vism/.ssh/id_rsa):
Enter passphrase (empty for no passphrase):
Enter same passphrase again:
Your identification has been saved in /c/Users/vism/.ssh/id_rsa.
Your public key has been saved in /c/Users/vism/.ssh/id_rsa.pub.
The key fingerprint is:
SHA256:TBtFeovnHGNLaJcvJLhdcZ+4C4MgNoONCxv5xsDQ4sk vism@sriks-machine
The key's randomart image is:
+---[RSA 2048]----+
|..          .o   |
|.o..        o    |
|o.B .     + o .  |
| E B * + * = o . |
|  . X = S % . o  |
|   o o = % = .   |
|    . o B o      |
|       + .       |
|                 |
+----[SHA256]-----+
```

Create swarm cluster on Azure Container Service

Swarm cluster on Azure can be created using Azure portal, Azure CLI or PowerShell. The CLI and PowerShell options can be used to setup Continuous Integration and deployment pipelines. The cost for running the cluster depends on the number and size of each machine selected for the farm. **Total Cost of Ownership (TCO)** can be derived by visiting the Azure calculator here `https://azure.microsoft.com/en-in/pricing/calculator/`. The swarm cluster consists of the following Azure resources:

- Virtual network
- Storage accounts
- Virtual machine scale set
- Public IP address
- **Network Security Group (NSG)**
- Network interface
- Load balancer
- Container service
- Availability set

Perform the following steps in order to create a cluster in Azure Container Service:

1. To create a swarm cluster login to Azure portal at `https://portal.azure.com`. Click on **+New** and search for **Azure Container Service**.

2. Click on **Azure Container Service** and then click on **Create**:

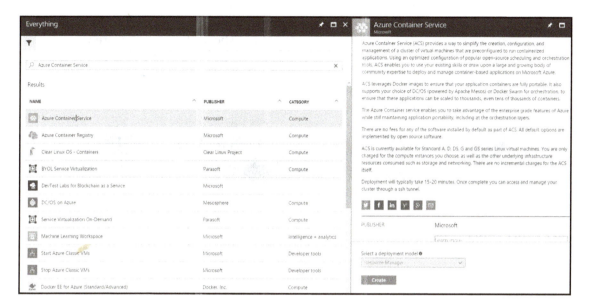

3. Select **Swarm** as the **Orchestrator**, and create a new **Resource group** as shown in the following screenshot and click **OK**.

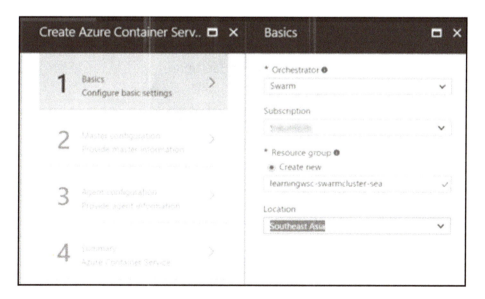

4. Select **DNS name prefix** for the cluster, this is used to prefix the nodes created as part of this cluster. Open the file `id_rsa.pub` from `C:\users\{username}\.ssh` in a notepad and copy the contents. Paste the copied contents to the SSH public key field as shown following. Here you can also select the number of masters required for the cluster. In this example, I'm using only one master, however you can select either 1, 3 or 5 from the list provided. **Enable** or **Disable Diagnostics** on the master node as required and Click **OK**.

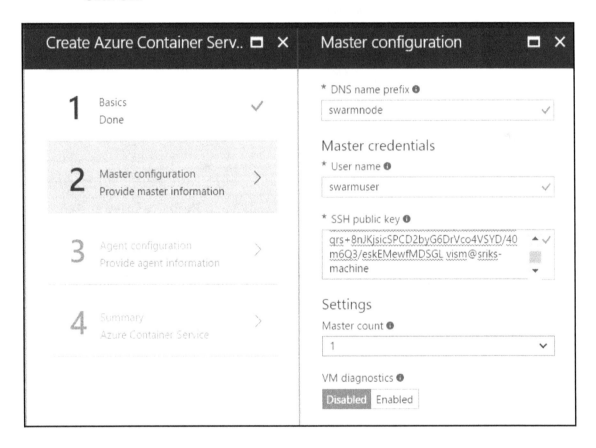

5. Select the number of agents and agent size as shown following and click **OK**.

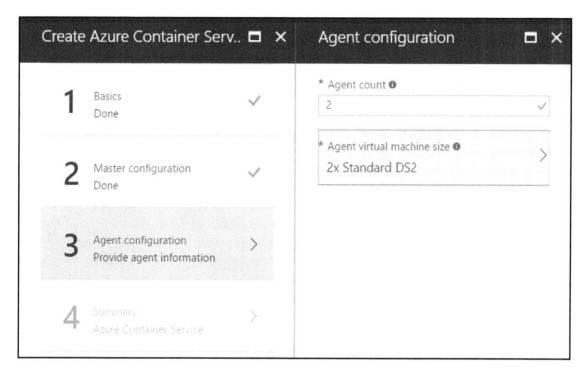

6. Ensure validations are successful as shown in the following screenshot:

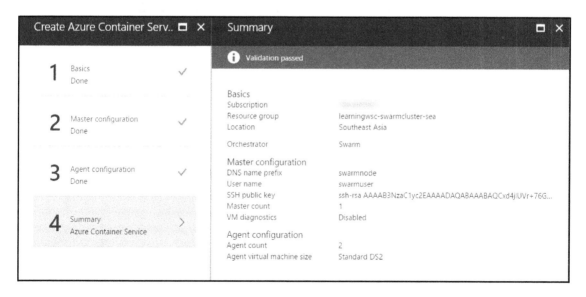

It takes several minutes to prepare the cluster. The following tile will show the deployed resources once the deployment is successful:

7. Post successful deployment, navigate to the `learningwsc-swarmcluster-sea` resource group and click on **Deployments section** | **Recent deployment Log**.

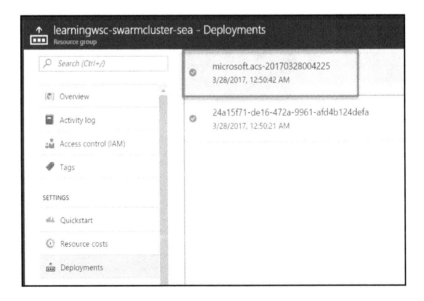

8. Copy the value from **SSHMASTER0** as shown in the following screenshot:

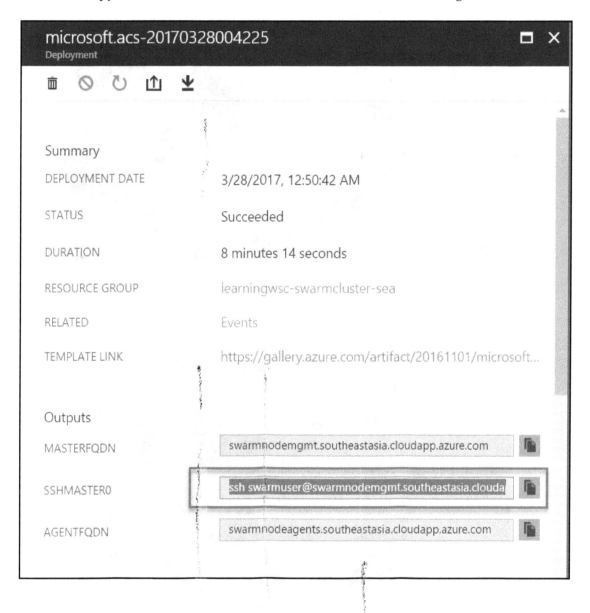

9. Open Git bash under elevated permission and paste the value as shown following. Enter the pass phrase chosen while creating the private/public key and hit *Enter*:

```
vism@sriks-machine MINGW64 ~
$ ssh swarmuser@swarmnodemgmt.southeastasia.cloudapp.azure.com -A -p 2200
The authenticity of host '[swarmnodemgmt.southeastasia.cloudapp.azure.com]:2200 ([52.187.30.107]:2200)' can't be established.
ECDSA key fingerprint is SHA256:yprsYt7CvRhi7fUquJjV7Dp+wbUtuCQN6TfhSeajLE8.
Are you sure you want to continue connecting (yes/no)? yes
Warning: Permanently added '[swarmnodemgmt.southeastasia.cloudapp.azure.com]:2200,[52.187.30.107]:2200' (ECDSA) to the list of known hosts.
Enter passphrase for key '/c/Users/vism/.ssh/id_rsa':
Welcome to Ubuntu 14.04.4 LTS (GNU/Linux 3.19.0-65-generic x86_64)

 * Documentation:  https://help.ubuntu.com/

  System information as of Mon Mar 27 19:21:25 UTC 2017

  System load: 0.31              Memory usage: 1%   Processes:       93
  Usage of /: 5.7% of 28.80GB    Swap usage:   0%   Users logged in: 0

  Graph this data and manage this system at:
    https://landscape.canonical.com/

  Get cloud support with Ubuntu Advantage Cloud Guest:
    http://www.ubuntu.com/business/services/cloud

New release '16.04.2 LTS' available.
Run 'do-release-upgrade' to upgrade to it.


The programs included with the Ubuntu system are free software;
the exact distribution terms for each program are described in the
individual files in /usr/share/doc/*/copyright.

Ubuntu comes with ABSOLUTELY NO WARRANTY, to the extent permitted by
applicable law.

swarmuser@swarm-master-B633E6FA-0:~$
```

10. We are now connected to the master node on the swarm cluster. Run the following command to get the information about the swarm cluster:

```
swarmuser@swarm-master-B633E6FA-0:~$ docker -H 172.16.0.5 info
Containers: 0
 Running: 0
 Paused: 0
 Stopped: 0
Images: 0
Role: primary
Strategy: spread
Filters: health, port, dependency, affinity, constraint
Nodes: 2
 swarm-agent-B633E6FA000000: 10.0.0.4:2375
  └ Status: Healthy
  └ Containers: 0
  └ Reserved CPUs: 0 / 2
  └ Reserved Memory: 0 B / 7.145 GiB
  └ Labels: executiondriver=<not supported>, kernelversion=3.19.0-65-generic, operatingsystem=Ubuntu 14.04.4 LTS, storagedriver=aufs
  └ Error: (none)
  └ UpdatedAt: 2017-03-27T19:36:36Z
 swarm-agent-B633E6FA000001: 10.0.0.7:2375
  └ Status: Healthy
  └ Containers: 0
  └ Reserved CPUs: 0 / 2
  └ Reserved Memory: 0 B / 7.145 GiB
  └ Labels: executiondriver=<not supported>, kernelversion=3.19.0-65-generic, operatingsystem=Ubuntu 14.04.4 LTS, storagedriver=aufs
  └ Error: (none)
  └ UpdatedAt: 2017-03-27T19:36:49Z
Plugins:
 Volume:
 Network:
Swarm:
 NodeID:
 Is Manager: false
 Node Address:
Kernel Version: 3.19.0-65-generic
Operating System: linux
Architecture: amd64
CPUs: 4
Total Memory: 14.29 GiB
Name: 5b301e7adc64
Docker Root Dir:
Debug Mode (client): false
Debug Mode (server): false
WARNING: No kernel memory limit support
Experimental: false
Live Restore Enabled: false
swarmuser@swarm-master-B633E6FA-0:~$
```

11. You can notice that there are two worker nodes running of type Ubuntu 14.04.4. The operating system of the master is Linux. Now let us add a Windows worker node to the preceding cluster. Click on the `learningwsc-swarmcluster-sear` resource group and then click on the **Overview** section. Click on the + symbol at the top to add a new resource to the existing group as shown in the following screenshot:

12. Search for resource **Windows Server 2016 Datacenter - with containers**. Select the **Windows Server 2016** machine with Containers and click **Create**. Select the basic configuration as shown following; ensure using the existing resource group. Remember the username and password selected here, we might use to configure the firewall rules in the next section.

13. Use the default settings for the remaining options or change as per requirement and click on **OK** to start the deployment. Azure creates a new Windows machine and adds it to the existing resource group under the same virtual network. Click on the **Virtual Network** resource on the swarm cluster resource group to see the details of the virtual network as shown in the following screenshot:

Login to the windows machine using the RDP client and credentials as configured while creating the machine. Open a PowerShell command line window under elevated permissions and run the following commands to configure the firewall ports:

```
netsh advfirewall firewall add rule name="docker daemon"
dir=in action=allow protocol=TCP localport=2375 enable=yes
netsh advfirewall firewall add rule name="docker overlay1"
dir=in action=allow protocol=udp localport=4789,7946 enable=yes
netsh advfirewall firewall add rule name="docker overlay2"
dir=in action=allow protocol=tcp localport=7946 enable=yes
```

The Windows machine should be added to the existing swarm cluster my notifying the master node. In order to do that we should make the Docker service on the windows machine start listening on port `2375`. Let us kill the existing docker service by killing the process `dockerd.exe` by navigating to **Task Manager** | **More Details** | **Details**. Right-click on the process named `dockerd.exe` and click **End Task**, also delete the file `docker.pid` under `C:\ProgramData` (Remember, `ProgramData` is a hidden folder in Windows Operating System). Run the command `ipconfig` on Windows host and note the IP address of the machine.

Run the following command to add the windows node to the swarm cluster. In the following command `10.0.0.5` is the IPV4 address of the windows node and `172.16.0.5` is the private IP address of the master node. To obtain the IP address of the master node visit virtual network section of the swarm cluster as shown in the preceding image:

```
dockerd.exe -D -H 10.0.0.5:2375 --cluster-
store=consul://172.16.0.5:8500
--cluster-advertise=10.0.0.5:2375
```

To check if the connection is successful switch back to the Git bash command line connected to the master node and run the following command once again.

```
docker -H 172.16.0.5 info
```

This time around you should see three nodes and one among them will be a Windows node running operating system Windows Server 2016 datacenter:

```
Nodes: 3
 swarm-agent-B633E6FA000000: 10.0.0.4:2375
  └ Status: Healthy
  └ Containers: 0
  └ Reserved CPUs: 0 / 2
  └ Reserved Memory: 0 B / 7.145 GiB
  └ Labels: executiondriver=<not supported>, kernelversion=3.19.0-65-generic, operatingsy:
TS, storagedriver=aufs
  └ Error: (none)
  └ UpdatedAt: 2017-03-27T20:33:12Z
 swarm-agent-B633E6FA000003: 10.0.0.7:2375
  └ Status: Healthy
  └ Containers: 0
  └ Reserved CPUs: 0 / 2
  └ Reserved Memory: 0 B / 7.145 GiB
  └ Labels: executiondriver=<not supported>, kernelversion=3.19.0-65-generic, operatingsy:
TS, storagedriver=aufs
  └ Error: (none)
  └ UpdatedAt: 2017-03-27T20:33:18Z
 windowsnode: 10.0.0.5:2375
  └ Status: Healthy
  └ Containers: 0
  └ Reserved CPUs: 0 / 2
  └ Reserved Memory: 0 B / 14.7 GiB
  └ Labels: executiondriver=, kernelversion=10.0 14393 (14393.729.amd64fre.rs1_release_in
3), operatingsystem=Windows Server 2016 Datacenter, storagedriver=windowsfilter
  └ Error: (none)
  └ UpdatedAt: 2017-03-27T20:32:48Z
```

Run the following command to get list of images available on the cluster:

```
swarmuser@swarm-master-B633E6FA-0:~$ docker -H 172.16.0.5 images
REPOSITORY                    TAG       IMAGE ID       CREATED        SIZE
microsoft/windowsservercore   latest    4d83c32ad497   2 months ago   9.56 GB
microsoft/nanoserver          latest    d9bccb9d4cac   2 months ago   925 MB
```

Run the command given following to create a Linux container and a windows container correspondingly on the swarm cluster:

```
docker -H 172.16.0.5 run --name hello-nginx -d -p 80:80 nginx
docker -H 172.16.0.5 run --name windowscontainer
microsoft/windowsservercore tasklist
```

The swarm manager picks up the node based on the base OS image, Linux for Nginx and Windows for Windows Server core intelligently. The output from the containers spun from the preceding commands is shown in the following screenshot:

Following is the response from Windows Container:

```
swarmuser@swarm-master-A0331446-0:~$ docker -H 172.16.0.5 run --name hello-nginx -d -p 80:80 nginx
2909980987bb9812db9e119c121378781b2da8375b65ba7455eb074339aff633
swarmuser@swarm-master-A0331446-0:~$ docker -H 172.16.0.5 run --name windowscontainer microsoft/windowsservercore tasklist

Image Name                     PID Session Name        Session#    Mem Usage
========================= ======= ================ =========== ============
System Idle Process              0                           0          4 K
System                           4                           0        136 K
smss.exe                      5228                           0      1,172 K
csrss.exe                     6116 Services                  4      4,120 K
wininit.exe                   5204 Services                  4      5,240 K
services.exe                  4564 Services                  4      5,976 K
lsass.exe                     5524 Services                  4     10,328 K
svchost.exe                    880 Services                  4      9,076 K
svchost.exe                    664 Services                  4      6,908 K
svchost.exe                   5048 Services                  4     10,764 K
svchost.exe                   2228 Services                  4     11,468 K
svchost.exe                   4204 Services                  4     25,860 K
svchost.exe                   4076 Services                  4      9,844 K
svchost.exe                   1792 Services                  4     15,192 K
svchost.exe                   5332 Services                  4      5,428 K
CExecSvc.exe                  3320 Services                  4      4,592 K
svchost.exe                   5992 Services                  4     12,784 K
tasklist.exe                  1036 Services                  4      7,532 K
DeviceCensus.exe              4420 Services                  4        616 K
CompatTelRunner.exe           4756 Services                  4      6,100 K
conhost.exe                   1696 Services                  4      5,804 K
WmiPrvSE.exe                  2544 Services                  4      8,232 K
```

Docker Swarm features

Docker Swarm is not the only cluster management tool available in the market; there are few more famous ones like Kubernetes, Mesos and DC/OS. There is an inclination towards swarm given its nativity, seamless integration capabilities with the docker engine and standard Docker API.

The following are few salient features of Docker Swarm which makes it more prominent among the other cluster management tools.

- The existing Docker CLI can be used to setup Docker Swarm or Docker Engines to deploy applications, this eliminates the need to learn a new tool or language to manager group of Docker nodes.
- Nodes in a Docker Swarm are not specialized which means any node can perform the role of Manager or Worker because they all use the same Docker Engine.
- Docker Swarm also has inbuilt resiliency, if you desire to have 10 replicas of a container the manager always checks for the desired state. The manager will create new containers instantly in the event of any crash. The same applies to the worker nodes, if any of the worker nodes crash, the new service requests are automatically redirected to the available nodes and redeploy the crashed containers on stable nodes.
- Swarm supports overlay network. The manager can automatically assign IP address from the overlay network when it initializes or updates any container.
- Swarm managers assign a unique DNS name to each service running in the cluster, this helps in querying any container running in the swarm through the embedded DNS server.
- Swarm supports performing updates to the running services in an incremental manner, you can control the delay between service deployments and also roll-back to a previous version of the service in case of failures.

Kubernetes is another way of creating and managing container clusters, Kubernetes an open-source system for automating deployment, and management of containerized applications. Kubernetes is built by Google based on their vast experience on running containers in production environments. Like Swarm's worker nodes, Kubernetes runs its containers on nodes called Kubernetes nodes, each node consists of atomic units called as **Pods**, and each pod is a single atomic unit of deployment. Each Pod can host up to five containers, containers running in a Pod share the IP. Pods in a Kubernetes cluster can talk to each other as well.

Services running in Kubernetes cluster are addressed by name; services are assigned to Pods in round-robin fashion. **Replication Controllers (RC)** are like Swarm managers which instantiate the pods, control and monitor the pods for a service, provide fault tolerance. We can create a Kubernetes cluster using ACS, for detailed steps visit `https://docs.microsof` `t.com/en-us/azure/container-service/container-service-kubernetes-windows-wal` `kthrough`. The following picture represents Kubernetes architecture at a very high level:

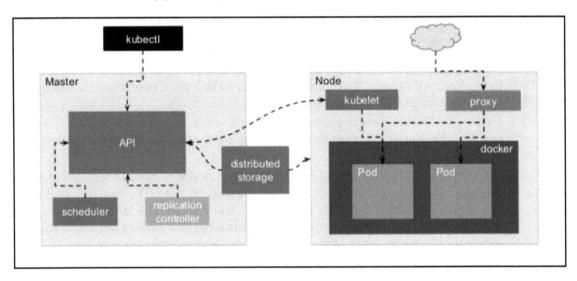

DC/OS is another container clustered management tool which can be used with ACS. Unlike Docker Swarm or Kubernetes there are many tools available which work on top of DC/OS cluster and help in managing schedules and executing compute workloads, one of such tools is Marathon. For more details on creating a DC/OS cluster on ACS visit `https://docs.microsoft.com/en-us/azure/container-service/container-service-meso` `s-marathon-ui`.

Summary

`docker-compose` is a command line tool for defining and running multi-container dockerized applications. `docker-compose` uses a single file to define a multi-container environment. A `docker-compose` file should be saved with extension `yml` or `yaml`. We can compose container environments using services, networks and volumes in a `docker-compose` file. `docker-compose` CLI tool should be available on the container host to run the commands. `docker-compose` gives you options to build images, create volumes, port mappings, define dependencies among components and so on. `docker-compose` CLI contains commands to manage environments, services or containers. The CLI cane used to setup number of containers for each service. Service Discovery and Registration come out of the box with `docker-compose`. Docker Swarm is one of the many tools available to manage cluster of containers. The cluster management and orchestration features are built into the Docker Engine using the swarm kit. Docker Swarm uses identical machines with Docker Engines installed to under different role configurations like manager and worker Nodes. Azure Container Service helps you quickly setup container clusters with windows and Linux machines as nodes. ACS can also be used to deploy Google Kubernetes or DC/OS farm setups using Windows Docker hosts.

12
Nano Server

You should know by now that the industry is up for a major shift on how we provision environments, it is time to divide and rule, split your application into multiple sustainable containers and scale at large using cutting edge cloud hosting providers. Well, we might have solved large part of the virtualization problems; there is still an unsolved problem. Containers live on a host and Windows Server 2016 is a bulky OS. There might be few features of the server which you might not even care, but you might have to regularly patch them and maintain the server, or worse the host restarts kill the application(s). So, why can't we just have what we need for the application to run? Bare minimum features which reduces the surface area, less maintenance and less fuss. You will be amazed to know that Microsoft is also thinking on the same lines. Microsoft's new Nano Server, the topic of this chapter is a much scaled down version of the Windows Server to server the ever-increasing needs of higher density and more efficient OS resource utilization. In this chapter, we will learn to play with Nano Server on cloud or on premise environments, deploy purpose built applications, remote management and automation. The following topics will be discussed in this chapter:

- A brief introduction to Nano Server
- Benefits of running workloads on Nano Server
- Provisioning Nano Server on Azure and Windows 10
- Package management
- Deploy .NET Core applications on Nano Server
- Configuration management using PowerShell DSC, Chef
- Technology roadmap

A brief introduction to Nano Server

Modern data centers would need a highly-optimized server platforms to run distributed applications cloud based apps or containers based on MicroServices architecture. The existing server platforms are powerful yet bulky, have large surface area (more ports open and the VHD Size) and demand more reboots for patch updates. Sometimes you are forced to reboot the server for patch updates which are not used at all which impacts the application's up times. With Windows Server 2016 Microsoft has added another installation option called Nano Server which greatly reduces the server footprint and solves the ports and reboot problems, specially designed to run on private clouds and data centers. The Nano Server installation option is available for Standard and DataCenter editions of Windows Server 2016. Nano Servers are fast and powerful with remote administration capabilities at the same time they are meant for tailored applications.

Nano Server is the new headless deployment option which comes with Windows Server 2016. Nano Server is a deeply refactored version designed to provide lightest, fastest sever configuration with lesser patches, reboots, better resource utilization and tighter security. Nano Server does not have a GUI and no RDP hence the only way to manage a Nano Server is by using Remote Administration via PowerShell or WMI. There is also a web based management tool for remote administration. Nano Server also comes with complete 64-bit support and no 32-bit support. Nano server also does not support windows installer. Nano Server has 93% lesser VHD Size, 92% fewer critical security advisories and 80% fewer reboots than the Windows Server.

Microsoft's vision for optimized server is not of today's; Window Server 2003 or Windows NT was the first full blown server operating system from Microsoft with fancy GUI. As the UI's were becoming fancier, consuming more CPU cycles and memory it defeated the whole purpose of the server operating systems. Server operating systems are meant to be used for production, highly sensitive and optimized workloads which should be available all times to the customers and most of the times remotely administered. Fancy UIs, animations and corresponding drivers or roles negatively impacted the server performance. With Windows Server 2008 Microsoft released additional installation option called Server Core. It was an installation time decision whether to go for full GUI version or Server Core. Server Core came with reduced code base, no GUI and lesser surface area reducing the chances of attacks. Server Core version in Windows 2008 came with lesser roles or features and only had those which are of more interest for the server administrators, roles or features like say the GUI layer were completely removed, users were yet allowed to install the required roles like IIS, Domain Controller, DNS using remote administration tools.

This was very like Nano Server we see today but back then the need for management experience was given the top priority over server optimization thus the server core was not well received. With the release of Windows Server 2012 and R2 Microsoft announced 3 installation options one with full blow GUI which has similar experience as of a desktop operating system, the second option came with minimum server interface like **Microsoft Management Console** (**MMC**) and Server Manager but no windows explorer and the last option was the server core with no GUI absolutely and severely refactored. Server Core option in Windows Server can be remotely managed using graphical user interface like MMC, Remote Server Administration Tools from your client machine without impacting the resources on the server.

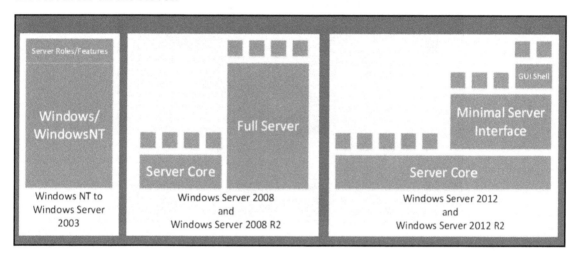

Nano Server is built from bottom up; it just has the bare minimum set of features (just enough OS) which are required for the cloud or on premise data centers. With enterprises thinking at large scale compute on cloud and resource optimization this change will be very well welcomed. Nano Server contains reduced attack surface and servicing requirements and they can also inter-operate with existing workloads.

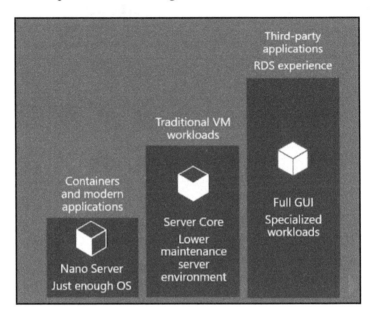

Windows Server 2016 comes with three installation options as shown previously, the Nano server option contains just enough OS tailored for modern container applications. The server core version which was part of the earlier Windows Server versions is still part of Windows Server 2016 which can be used to run traditional workloads with lower maintenance. GUI version can be used to run third-party, legacy workloads which need UI based management capabilities. Nano server comes with minimum roles and features that are required for running workloads on cloud like clustering, DNS, Storage (SoFS), IIS, Core CLR, and ASP.NET 5 and most importantly everything which is not required lives outside the server and should be installed via remote management tools. This is a drastic change when compared to Server Core because in a Server Core or Full blows Server OS the driver files for all the roles are on the server irrespective of whether the feature is installed or not, this increases the security risks and patching required for each of those roles or drivers. Nano Server also comes with PowerShell core which is a refactored version of PowerShell and runs on top of .NET Core.

Benefits of running workloads on Nano Server

Let us look at some of the core challenges that Nano Server solves when compared to server core or the GUI version.

Live migrations

Managing a cluster of Windows Server Machines is a trivial task, when one is asked to migrate say 10-20 servers across geographical boundaries, then this is one hell of a task. Each Windows Server machine roughly takes around 4-5 GB of space with all the roles installed. Live Migrating 10-20 servers demands huge bandwidth, we are transferring almost 1 TB of data for just migrating 20 servers across the globe. Often to overcome this, server administrators deploy new set of servers in the new location and migrate the workloads instead, but this too involves cost overheads and downtimes to the application. Using Nano Server Live Migrations will be easy and fast because each server takes just about 400-500 MB of storage space.

Zero footprint

Nano Server comes with what is just needed, any server roles or optional features are not available on the server unlike other server operating systems. This makes the server lean and thin and reduces the area that can be attacked. More features or roles mean more open ports with reduced features we can only open those ports which are required for the application to run. Any additional software packages should be pulled and installed using the package management tools.

Package management

Package management (also known as **OneGet**) is a pretty famous package management tool which is available on Windows 10 and Windows Server Operating Systems like 2012 and above. The expectation with Nano Server with a disk space of 440 MB of disk space is to start small and then add only the features/components that you will use. The package management provide for Nano Server is completely different from the other operating systems. The following image shows the package management architecture and provider list for Nano Server. By default, Nano Server comes with `PowerShell Get` and the other providers can be installed on demand:

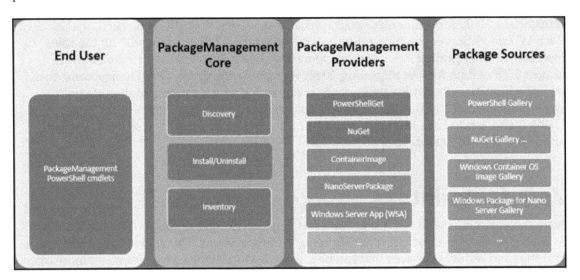

Reboots

Every time there is a critical update patch the host should be restarted, typically reboot times for a server operating system is for about 2-3 minutes. A server gets restarted typically once or twice a month, which means the down time per year for any server is approximately 1-2 hours/20-30 reboots just for update patches (excluding the time it takes for updating the system with new patch) apparently, that is a very huge number. Nano Server comes with a promise of 80% fewer reboots. This is mostly attributed to the refactored version, less drivers or roles and no support for 32-bit software.

Provisioning time

Provisioning a new server operating system takes about 3-4 minutes even on a cloud provider like Azure. Nano Server boots in just five seconds on a high-end host, we can setup a cluster in couple of minutes, how great is that. The following table shows a comparison on number of reboots, open ports and VHD Size for different versions of operating systems, clearly Nano Server Stands out:

Windows Server 2016	Nano Server	Windows Server Core	Full GUI Server
Reboots	3	6	11
Patches	2	8	23
Ports	11	26	34
VHD size	440 MB	6.5 GB	10.4 GB

Server management

The good news is that you do not have to be a PowerShell expert to manage a Nano Server. All the existing MMC tools, Hyper-V tools can still be used to manage Nano Server. Any existing scripts written using WMI version 1 or 2 can still be re-used on Nano Server. Microsoft has plans to update the existing platforms like the Ibiza portal and Azure Stack to act as web interfaces for Nano Servers on Cloud and on premise environments respectively. You can configure the server using PowerShell desired state configuration.

PowerShell core

Nano Server includes PowerShell core by default on all Nano Servers. PowerShell core is optimized version of PowerShell which runs on optimized windows server editions like Nano Server and Windows IoT Core. There are few limitations for PowerShell core when compared to PowerShell on Windows Server with Full GUI, we will learn the differences in the next section.

Provisioning Nano Server on Azure

There are several ways to create a Nano Server, using PowerShell or by using the Azure Portal. In this section, let us learn to create a Nano Server using Azure Portal.

1. Login to **Azure Portal** and Click on the **Virtual Machines Section** (one without the classic option).
2. Click on + to add a new Virtual Machine
3. Search for **Windows Server 2016 - Nano Server**

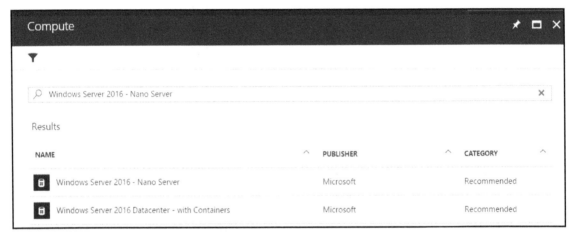

4. Select the first option and click on **Create**.

5. Select the **Basic Settings** and click **OK**.

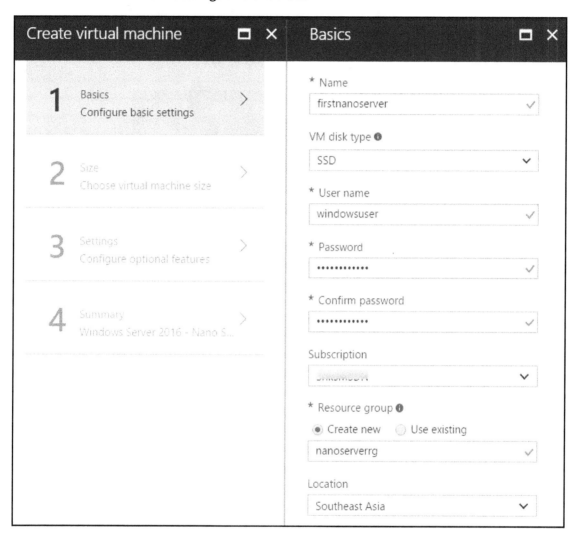

6. Choose any VM size, here I have chosen **DS2_V2**.

7. The most important step is to configure the Network Security Group to allow PowerShell Remoting because RDP is not supported on Nano Server. There are two options to run WinRM, over HTTP (5985) or HTTPS (5986). For production scenarios, it is always recommended to use WinRM via HTTPS. Select **Virtual Network** | **Create new to create a new network**.

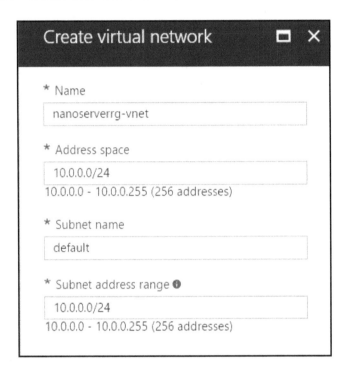

8. Click on **Network Security Group** (firewall) option, and then click on **+Add inbound rule**. Select WinRM from the service dropdown, assign name and priority to the firewall rule and click **OK**. You can as well remove the RDP Rule by clicking on the ellipses, and then clicking on remove as it will not be used for Nano Servers.

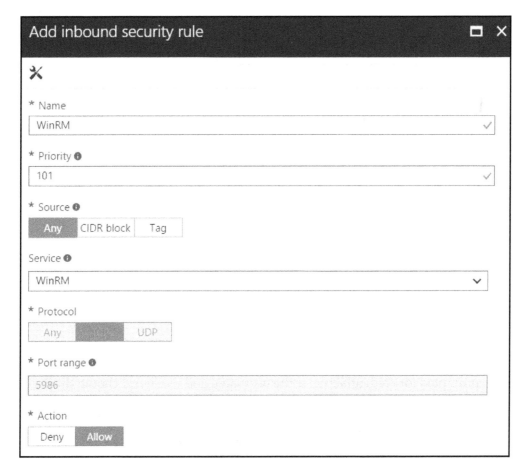

9. Click **OK** on the **Network Security Group** and then click on **OK** to jump to the summary section.
10. Ensure all the validations pass and then click on **OK** to create the server, this might take a couple of minutes.

11. Once the VM is created pick the public IP address from the portal from following the section:

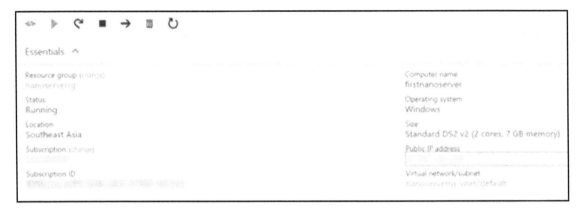

12. Run the following commands in a PowerShell command window (elevated mode) to setup WinRM for your client:

```
Start-Service WinRM
"Public IP for Server"
```

13. Now you can connect to the Nano Server using the following commands. When prompted for credentials enter the username and password chosen during VM creation.

```
$cred=Get-Credential
Enter-PSSession -ComputerName "Public IP for Server"
-credential $cred
```

The image shows that we are now successfully logged in the server and are connected via the Windows Remote Management Console. Execute the following script given to get the list of processes running on the server:

```
Get-Process
```

```
PS C:\windows\system32> Enter-PSSession -ComputerName              -credential $cred
[                ]: PS C:\Users\windowsuser\Documents> get-process

Handles  NPM(K)    PM(K)     WS(K)    CPU(s)     Id  SI ProcessName
-------  ------    -----     -----    ------     --  -- -----------
      0       6      768      1992      0.00    356   0 csrss
      0       5      912      4276      0.00   1140   0 EMT
      0       0        0         4                0   0 Idle
      0      18     4232     11960      1.16    432   0 lsass
      0      50    43772     59388      3.58   1084   0 Microsoft.Azure.Agent.Windows
      0       8     1848      5468      0.09    412   0 services
      0       2      324      1148      0.00    260   0 smss
      0      14     4488     13356      0.09    524   0 svchost
      0       8     1612      6144      0.05    528   0 svchost
      0      13     1832      6560      0.05    580   0 svchost
      0       7     1420      6400      0.11    672   0 svchost
      0       7     1328      5552      0.13    704   0 svchost
      0      14     7776     13024      0.06    728   0 svchost
      0      18     7268     16580      0.33    772   0 svchost
      0      17     3284      9600      0.02    812   0 svchost
      0      35     6796     17260      0.08    852   0 svchost
      0      26     3728      9864      0.06    988   0 svchost
      0       0       80        80      1.31      4   0 System
      0       4      680      3640      0.02    308   0 WaSvc
      0       7      748      4052      0.05    384   0 wininit
      0      41    37080     61764      1.77   1488   0 wsmprovhost
```

Provisioning Nano Server on Windows 10

Nano Server can be deployed on Windows 10 machine with Hyper-V installed. Microsoft provides evaluation version of Nano Server image which is valid for 180 days that can be customized as per needs. The ISO for Windows Server 2016 can be downloaded from https://www.microsoft.com/en-us/evalcenter/evaluate-windows-server-2016. Click on **Register** to continue and login with **Windows Live** account, fill in the registration form.

The portal shows three download options as shown in the following screenshot:

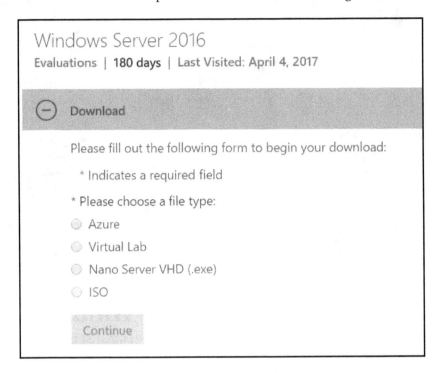

The Nano Server VHD (.exe) is the easiest option to quickly setup Nano Server on Windows 10. This contains a ready to use VHD which can be mounted using Hyper-V manager. Click on **Nano Server VHD** option and select **continue** to download the EXE version, this would download a EXE by name NanoServerDataCenter.vhd.exe of size 120 MB. The EXE when installed extracts the VHD file to C:\Windows Server 2016 DataCenter Nano VHD\ folder by default, the size of the VHD is 554 MB.

Let us now create a Virtual machine using this VHD and Hyper-V manager. Hyper-V manager can be installed from **Control Panel** | **Programs** | **Turn on or off Windows Features** option:

1. Open Hyper-V manager and select **New** | **Virtual Machine** from the Actions menu on the right-side.
2. Click **Next** on the **First Wizard** step, choose a name and location for the VM as shown in the following screenshot:

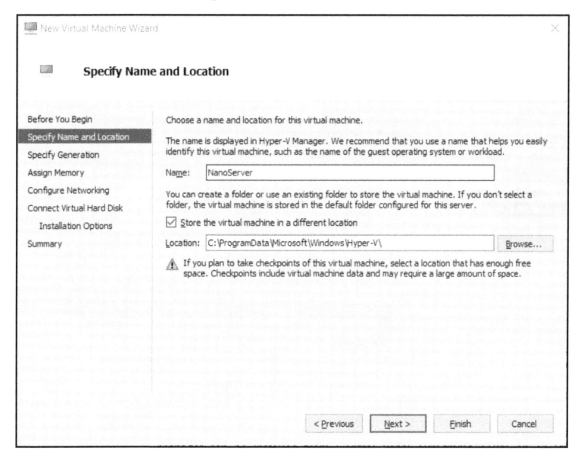

3. Click **Next** and select **Generation 1** in the **Specify Generation** step and click **Next** to continue.
4. Specify the **Startup memory** as 1024 MB or you can increase as per your requirements and click **Next** to continue.

5. Select **Not Connected** in the connection section and click **Next** on the **Configure Networking** Section. The virtual machine we are creating here using the VHD will not be connected the internet or intranet as a result, to connect the Virtual Machine to internet visit `https://docs.microsoft.com/en-us/virtualization/hyper-v-on-windows/quick-start/connect-to-network`.

6. Select the VHD file from the extracted location as shown in the following screenshot:

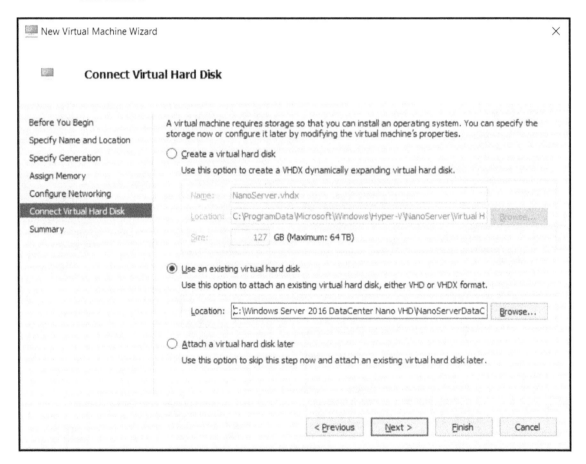

7. Click **Next**, and then click **Finish** to create a new Virtual Machine using Nano Server VHD.

8. Click on the Virtual Machine and then click on **Start** to start the VM.

9. You will be prompted within a login prompt; since we do not have a password we should go to the recovery console to reset the password. Hit *F11* to reach the recovery console.

10. The following screenshot shows the Nano Server recovery console, the recovery console only supports basic keyboard functions. Keyboard lights, 10-key sections, and keyboard layout switching such as *Caps Lock* and *Num Lock* are not supported. Users can view or update the firewall rules, network configuration and reset WinRM configuration using recovery console.

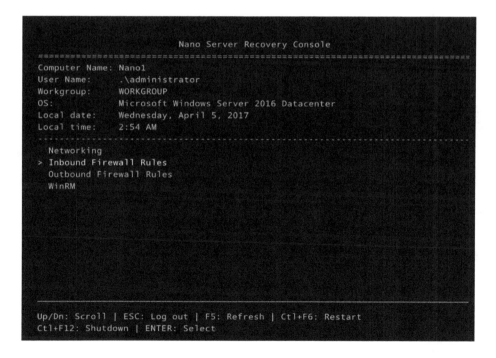

11. Open a new PowerShell window as administrator and run the following command to remote login to the Nano Server. In the following command, `NanoServer` is the name of my virtual machine and `162.254.245.92` is the IP address of the virtual machine running on my desktop:

```
Set-Item WSMan:\localhost\Client\TrustedHosts
-Value 169.254.245.92
Enter-PSSession -VMName "NanoServer" -credential
169.254.245.92\administrator
```

Package management

As we have learnt earlier Nano Server does not come with roles or features that are required in the server. In this section, we will learn to install roles on VM which is connected to Azure and create a custom VHD with roles already installed. Nano server comes with online package repository which allows us to connect to any online repository, install and download roles and features that are available. In order to connect to online package repository, the server should be connected to the internet, in the next section I will show you how to install packages on servers not connected to the internet.

As a first step let us get the list of package providers supported on Nano Server, run the following command from WinRM session connected to Nano Server on Azure:

```
Find-PackageProvider
```

```
[         ]: PS C:\inetpub\wwwroot> Find-PackageProvider

Name                  Version      Source           Summary
----                  -------      ------           -------
nuget                 2.8.5.205    https://onege... NuGet provider for the OneGet meta-package manager
ps1                   1.0.0.210    https://onege... package source list provider for the OneGet meta-pa...
DockerMsftProvider    1.0.0.1      PSGallery        PowerShell module with commands for discovering, in...
ContainerImage        0.6.4.0      PSGallery        This is a PackageManagement provider module which h...
PowerShellGet         1.1.2.0      PSGallery        PowerShell module with commands for discovering, in...
NanoServerPackage     1.0.1.0      PSGallery        A PackageManagement provider to Discover, Save and...
GitHubProvider        0.5          PSGallery        GitHub-as-a-Package - PackageManagement PowerShell ...
MyAlbum               0.1.2        PSGallery        MyAlbum provider discovers the photos in your remot...
OfficeProvider        1.0.0.1      PSGallery        OfficeProvider allows users to install Microsoft Of...
ChocolateyGet         1.0.0.1      PSGallery        An PowerShell OneGet provider that discovers packag...
GistProvider          0.6          PSGallery        Gist-as-a-Package - PackageManagement PowerShell P...
GitLabProvider        1.3.4        PSGallery        GitLab PackageManagement provider
WSAProvider           1.0.0.4      PSGallery        Provider to Discover, Install and inventory windows...
TSDProvider           0.2          PSGallery        PowerShell PackageManager provider to search & inst...
Oinstall              2.12.1       PSGallery        Zero Install is a decentralized cross-platform soft...
AppxGet               0.1.0.1      PSGallery        Powershell Package Management (OneGet) Provider for...
```

Notice most of the famous package providers are supported on Nano Server, let us install the `NanoServer` package provider by running the following command. With the Windows Management Framework 5.0 preview, Microsoft released a PowerShell module called OneGet. OneGet is the new way to discover and install software packages from around the Web:

> **Install-PackageProvider NanoServerPackage**

`NanoServerPackage` internally depends on NuGet provider so you will be prompted to download the dependent packages as well. Once installed you can import the package any time using the following command:

> **Import-PackageProvider NanoServerPackage**

The following command shows the package providers installed on the machine:

```
Get-PackageSource
```

```
[              ]: PS C:\inetpub\wwwroot> Get-PackageSource

Name                        ProviderName      IsTrusted  Location
----                        ------------      ---------  --------
PSGallery                   PowerShellGet     False      https://www.powershellgallery.com/api/v2/
NanoServerPackageSource     NanoServerPac...  False      http://go.microsoft.com/fwlink/?LinkID=723027&clcid=0x409
```

Run the following command given to see the packages available as part of
NanoServerPackage:

```
Find-NanoServerPackage -Name *
```

```
[              ]: PS C:\inetpub\wwwroot> Find-NanoServerPackage -Name *

Name                                             Version         Culture          Description
----                                             -------         -------          -----------
Microsoft-NanoServer-FailoverCluster-Package     10.0.14393.0    cs-cz, de-de,... Includes Failover Clusterin...
Microsoft-NanoServer-Compute-Package             10.0.14393.0    cs-cz, de-de,... Includes Hyper-V and NetQoS...
Microsoft-NanoServer-DCB-Package                 10.0.14393.0    cs-cz, de-de,... Includes Data Center Bridgi...
Microsoft-NanoServer-SCVMM-Compute-Package       10.0.14393.0    cs-cz, de-de,... Includes services for monit...
Microsoft-NanoServer-SCVMM-Package               10.0.14393.0    cs-cz, de-de,... Includes services for monit...
Microsoft-NanoServer-DSC-Package                 10.0.14393.0    cs-cz, de-de,... Includes PowerShell Desired...
Microsoft-NanoServer-SoftwareInventoryLogging-P... 10.0.14393.0  cs-cz, de-de,... Includes services and tools...
Microsoft-NanoServer-SecureStartup-Package       10.0.14393.0    cs-cz, de-de,... Includes support for BitLoc...
Microsoft-NanoServer-OEM-Drivers-Package         10.0.14393.0    cs-cz, de-de,... Includes basic drivers for ...
Microsoft-NanoServer-Containers-Package          10.0.14393.0    cs-cz, de-de,... Includes services and tools...
Microsoft-NanoServer-IPHelper-Service-Package    10.0.14393.576  cs-cz, de-de,... Provides tunnel connectivit...
Microsoft-NanoServer-Defender-Package            10.0.14393.0    cs-cz, de-de,... Includes Windows Defender w...
Microsoft-NanoServer-IIS-Package                 10.0.14393.0    cs-cz, de-de,... Includes Internet Informati...
Microsoft-NanoServer-Storage-Package             10.0.14393.0    cs-cz, de-de,... Includes services and tools...
Microsoft-NanoServer-Guest-Package               10.0.14393.0    cs-cz, de-de,... Includes drivers and integr...
Microsoft-NanoServer-ShieldedVM-Package          10.0.14393.0    cs-cz, de-de,... Includes Host Guardian Serv...
Microsoft-NanoServer-DNS-Package                 10.0.14393.0    cs-cz, de-de,... Includes Domain Name System...
Microsoft-NanoServer-SNMP-Agent-Package          10.0.14393.576  cs-cz, de-de,... Simple Network Management P...
Microsoft-NanoServer-Host-Package                10.0.14393.0    cs-cz, de-de,... Includes drivers and servic...
```

The following command installs IIS on Nano Server:

```
Find-NanoServerPackage *iis* | install-NanoServerPackage
-culture en-us
```

Restart the server using the following command:

```
restart-computer
```

The following command creates a new site under IIS and set the physical path location:

```
cd\
md mysite
Import-module iis*
New-iissite -Name mysite -BindingInformation
"*:80:mysite" -PhysicalPath c:\mysite
```

If we browse by using the public IP or DNS Name of the Nano Server, we should see the default IIS page. Ensure the Nano Server contains the inbound security rule for port 80 open. After you have installed the package you can list by using `Get-Package` cmdlet or uninstall a package by using the `Uninstall-Package` cmdlet.

Installing packages on a server connected to Internet is easy as you have seen. In some enterprises, the machines in private data centers are not connected to internet due to security reasons, in such cases we must perform an offline installation of roles or features in Nano Server. There are a couple of ways to do this; one way is to create a custom image. If you are planning to build a farm or a cluster of hundreds of Nano server machines seemingly this is the best option, it allows you to create a custom Nano Server image with the required software installed which can be re-used to create any number of Nano Server machines. To create a custom Nano Server image, we should download the Windows Server 2016 ISO. You can download the 6.5 GB ISO image from `https://www.microsoft.com/en-us/evalcenter/evaluate-windows-server-2016/`. In the following section, we will build a custom Nano Server image with IIS installed and create a virtual machine using the custom image:

1. On a Windows 10 machine, right-click the downloaded ISO file and say **Mount**.
2. Open the mounted disk in **Windows Explorer** and copy the contents of `d:\NanoServer` to a separate folder on the host like `c:\nano`. Here `D:\` drive is where the ISO is mounted on my machine.
3. Open a new PowerShell windows under elevated permissions and run the following command to import the image preparation module for Nano Server.

   Import-Module C:\nano\NanoServerImageGenerator.psm1

4. The following command creates a new Nano Server image using standard edition. In the following command, media path points to the drive where the ISO is mounted, `BasePath` will be used to store temporary files, `TargetPath` is where the result is stored and package option mentions the package to be installed on the server:

```
New-NanoServerImage -Edition Standard -MediaPath D:\
-BasePath C:\Nano -TargetPath c:\nano\nanowebserver.vhdx
-DeploymentType Guest -ComputerName nanowebserver -Storage
-Package Microsoft-NanoServer-IIS-Package -verbose
```

5. Enter the administrator password when prompted. The image preparation takes a couple of minutes, the following image shows the verbose log and the progress indicator:

6. After successful completion the `.vhdx` file should be available at `c:\nano\nanowebserver.vhdx`. Let us create a new virtual machine using this `.vhdx` file and the steps as mentioned in the section *Provisioning Nano Server on Windows 10*

7. As shown, I'm attempting to create a new virtual machine using Hyper-V manager and the `.vhdx` file created previously:

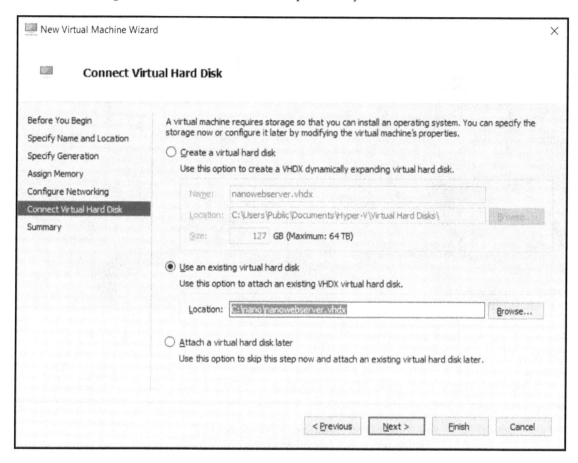

8. Ensure the machine is running and WinRM is configured on the virtual machine.
9. Login to the machine from a PowerShell window using WinRM command shown:

```
Set-Item WSMan:\localhost\Client\TrustedHosts -Value
<<IP address of the VM>>
Enter-PSSession -VMName nanowebserver -credential
<<IP Address of the VM>>\administrator
```

10. You can now manage IIS using PowerShell commands, enable/disable IIS features, create websites, app pools, certificates and so on using the PowerShell cmdlets. The following image shows few commands used to create a default website:

```
[nanowebserver]: PS C:\Users\administrator\Documents> cd\
[nanowebserver]: PS C:\> dir


    Directory: C:\


Mode                LastWriteTime         Length Name
----                -------------         ------ ----
d-----        4/5/2017   10:03 AM                inetpub
d-----        7/16/2016   5:20 AM                Program Files
d-----        7/16/2016   5:09 AM                Program Files (x86)
d-r---        4/5/2017   10:20 AM                Users
d-----        4/5/2017   10:17 AM                Windows


[nanowebserver]: PS C:\> Import-Module iis*
[nanowebserver]: PS C:\> md test


    Directory: C:\


Mode                LastWriteTime         Length Name
----                -------------         ------ ----
d-----        4/5/2017   10:24 AM                test


[nanowebserver]: PS C:\> New-IISSite -Name TestSite -BindingInformation "*:80:TestSite" -PhysicalPath c:\test
```

Let us image you have a set of Nano Servers running and you are asked to install a new Package like IIS or DSC, the above method would not help. For such cases, we can move the packages folder to the remote virtual machine and perform and offline installation. The following line creates a PowerShell session which will used to copy files to the remote server.

```
$session = New-PSSession -VMName nanowebserver
-Credential nanowebserver\administrator
```

Next, let us copy the packages folder from the host machine to the remote machine using the following command. The packages folder contains the `.cab` file one for each package as shown in the following command. These files can be found under `D:\Nanoserver\Packages` inside the ISO file when mounted:

```
copy-item 'C:\nano\packages' -Destination c:\nano -recurse
-ToSession $session -verbose
```

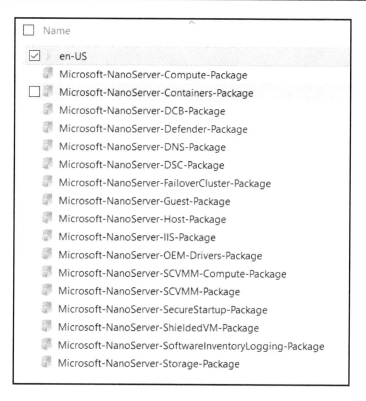

Now remote login into the virtual machine and run the following commands to install the IIS package on the Nano Server:

```
dism /online /add-package /PackagePath:c:\nano\Microsoft
-NanoServer-Storage-Package.cab
dism /online /add-package /PackagePath:c:\nano\Microsoft
-NanoServer-IIS-Package.cab
```

 For more information on managing IIS on Windows Server 2016 - Nano Server please visit
https://technet.microsoft.com/en-us/windows-server-docs/get-star
ted/iis-on-nano-server#application-development.

Deploy .NET Core applications on Nano Server

Nano Server can be used to host ASP.NET Core applications. In this section, we will be using VM created in Azure to host an ASP.NET Core application. Before proceeding we would need a published version of ASP.NET Core application, this can be copied from `c:\learningwsc\chapter12\sampleaspnetcoreapp`. The following steps are valid for Nano Server created On-Premise or Azure:

1. Open a PowerShell windows under elevated mode and run the following command to create a new PowerShell session to the Nano Server:

```
$ip = "<<IP Address of Nano Server>>"
Set-Item WSMan:\localhost\Client\TrustedHosts -Value $ip
$cred = Get-Credential
$session = New-PSSession -ComputerName $ip -Credential $cred
```

2. The following image shows a successful connection to server:

3. Run the following command in the remote PowerShell mode to open a firewall port to let IIS listen for incoming traffic on port `TCP/8000`:

```
New-NetFirewallRule -Name "AspNet5 IIS" -DisplayName
"Allow HTTP on TCP/8000" -Protocol TCP -LocalPort 8000
-Action Allow -Enabled True
```

4. Run the following commands to install `NanoPackage` provider and Windows packages:

```
Install-PackageProvider NanoServerPackage
Import-PackageProvider NanoServerPackage
Install-NanoServerPackage -Name Microsoft-NanoServer
-Storage-Package
Install-NanoServerPackage -Name Microsoft-NanoServer
-IIS-Package
```

5. Restart the Nano Server by running the following command:

```
Restart-Computer -Force
```

Now if you visit the `http://<<IP Address>>` you should see the default welcome page for IIS. Installing ASP.NET Core and .NET Core at this point is a manual step. We must download and install the .NET Core Windows Hosting Bundle from `https://go.microsoft.com/fwlink/?linkid=844461` on a normal machine like Windows 10.

Run the following commands from Windows 10 machine to copy the ASP.NET Core module and corresponding configuration file to the Nano Server:

```
Copy-Item -ToSession $session -Path 'C:\Program Files\IIS
Express\aspnetcore.dll' -Destination C:\windows\system32\inetsrv\
-Force Copy-Item -ToSession $session -Path 'C:\Program Files\IIS
Express\config\schema\aspnetcore_schema.xml' -Destination
C:\windows\system32\inetsrv\ -Force
```

To install ASP.NET Core and .NET core on Nano Server copy the installation scripts from `c:\learningwsc\chapter12` to `c:\` and run the following commands:

```
Invoke-Command -Session $session -FilePath C:\
Install-AspNetCore.ps1
Invoke-Command -Session $session -FilePath C:\
dotnetcore.ps1
```

Copy the application artifacts from `c:\learningwsc\chapter12` to `c:\sampleapp` and run the following command to copy the same to the Nano Server:

```
Copy-Item -ToSession $session -Path "C:\sampleapp\"&grave;
-Filter "*" -Destination
c:\PublishedApps\AspNetCoreSampleForNano\sampleapp\
-Recurse -Force
```

Run the following command to create a remote session to the Nano Server and create a new site in IIS for the published application on a different port than the default web site. Ensure port 8000 is open on the Nano Server to access the portal:

```
Enter-PSSession -Session $session
Import-module IISAdministration
New-IISSite -Name "AspNetCore" -PhysicalPath
C:\PublishedApps\AspNetCoreSampleForNano\sampleapp\
-BindingInformation "*:8000:"
```

Run the following command to overcome a known issue running .NET Core CLI on Nano Server:

```
New-NetFirewallRule -Name "AspNetCore App Port 81 IIS"
-DisplayName "Allow HTTP on TCP/81" -Protocol TCP
-LocalPort 81 -Action Allow -Enabled True
```

The published website will be accessible using `http://<<IP Address>>:8000`.

Configuration management using PowerShell DSC

Desired state configuration is an essential tool for configuration, management and maintenance of Windows Server. PowerShell DSC is a declarative way of configuring servers, upon configuring the desired state of the server using simple PowerShell cmdlets, DSC will just *make it so*. PowerShell DSC facilitates standard server configurations like roles/features, file system, users/groups, and software updates. PowerShell DSC on Nano Server is an optional package. Working with DSC is a two-step process, first we create a PowerShell DSC script which gets converted to MOF File. The step in the configuration process is to use the MOF file to configure the server. PowerShell DSC can be run locally on the Nano Server or from a remote host.

The following steps describe setting PowerShell DSC on a Nano Server:

1. Connect to a Nano Server using WinRM from a PowerShell Window under elevated permissions.

2. Run the following commands to install the DSC Package on Nano Server (Assuming `NanoServerPackage` is already install, if not visit the *Package management* section):

```
Import-PackageProvider NanoServerPackage
Install-NanoServerPackage -name Microsoft-
NanoServer-DSC-Package -Culture en-us
```

3. Run the following command to see the list of commands supported by PowerShell DSC on Nano Server:

```
Get-Command -Module PSDesiredStateConfiguration
```

```
[          ]: PS C:\> Get-Command -Module PSDesiredStateConfiguration

CommandType     Name                                  Version    Source
-----------     ----                                  -------    ------
Function        Configuration                         1.1        PSDesiredStateConfiguration
Function        Disable-DscDebug                      1.1        PSDesiredStateConfiguration
Function        Enable-DscDebug                       1.1        PSDesiredStateConfiguration
Function        Get-DscConfiguration                  1.1        PSDesiredStateConfiguration
Function        Get-DscConfigurationStatus            1.1        PSDesiredStateConfiguration
Function        Get-DscLocalConfigurationManager      1.1        PSDesiredStateConfiguration
Function        Get-DscResource                       1.1        PSDesiredStateConfiguration
Function        New-DscChecksum                       1.1        PSDesiredStateConfiguration
Function        Remove-DscConfigurationDocument       1.1        PSDesiredStateConfiguration
Function        Restore-DscConfiguration              1.1        PSDesiredStateConfiguration
Function        Stop-DscConfiguration                 1.1        PSDesiredStateConfiguration
Cmdlet          Invoke-DscResource                    1.1        PSDesiredStateConfiguration
Cmdlet          Publish-DscConfiguration              1.1        PSDesiredStateConfiguration
Cmdlet          Set-DscLocalConfigurationManager      1.1        PSDesiredStateConfiguration
Cmdlet          Start-DscConfiguration                1.1        PSDesiredStateConfiguration
Cmdlet          Test-DscConfiguration                 1.1        PSDesiredStateConfiguration
Cmdlet          Update-DscConfiguration               1.1        PSDesiredStateConfiguration
```

In the earlier section, we have installed IIS on the Nano Server now let us add a default `Index.html` page to the Nano Server using PowerShell DSC. The following script shows the PowerShell DSC script for adding a `Index.html` page:

```
Configuration NanoConfig
{
  Import-DscResource -ModuleName 'PSDesiredStateConfiguration'
  Node '<<IP Address>>'
    {
      File Folder
      {
        Ensure="Present"
        DestinationPath="c:\inetpub\wwwroot"
        Type="Directory"
      }
      File HomePage
      {
```

```
            Ensure="Present"
            DestinationPath="c:\inetpub\wwwroot\index.html"
            Contents="<h1> Hello from Nano Server !! </h1>"
            Type="File"
            DependsOn="[File]Folder"
        }
    }
}
NanoConfig
```

In the preceding command, we are ensuring the IIS default root folder exists and create an `Index.html` file in the root folder. If you notice the file creation step depends on the folder check. PowerShell DSC allows you to declare dependencies among the installations or configurations. Replace `<<IP Address>>` with the IP address of the server and save the preceding script under `c:\nanoconfig.ps1`

Exit from the WinRM session and execute the following command to create an `MOF` file for the preceding configuration. `MOF` file is a special type of file which the DSC Engine understands. Each `MOF` file targets a specific node or server. We will run this configuration by using from the host machine or a remote machine which is connected to the Nano Server:

```
PS C:\> ./nanoconfig.ps1

    Directory: C:\NanoConfig

Mode                 LastWriteTime         Length Name
----                 -------------         ------ ----
-a----        08-04-2017     01:54           2942          .mof
```

The preceding command creates a `.mof` file under `c:\NanoConfig`, the folder name here is inferred from the name of the configuration. Run the following command to apply the DSC configuration on the Nano Server (again replace the IP address with IP address of the Nano Server):

```
$cred = Get-Credential
Start-DscConfiguration -Path 'C:\NanoConfig\' -ComputerName
'<<IP Address>>' -Credential $cred -Verbose -Wait -Force
```

The following image shows the configuration verbose log. Even though the sample achieves a simple configuration, PowerShell DSC fits for all types of needs and can be used to configure large number of servers at once. DSC also takes care of drift management using the *Push or Pull Model*. For example, if someone updates the contents, `Index.html` manually in the next run of DSC configuration (which happens automatically) DSC ensures the file contents are intact. DSC Clients can be configured to pull the configuration from a web server on regular basis:

If we browse the IP address of the Nano Server using a web browser, we should see the default HTML page as shown:

Hello from Nano Server !!

The following DSC features are not available on Nano Server yet:

- Decrypting MOF document with encrypted password(s)
- Pull Server—you cannot currently set up a pull server on Nano Server

Nano containers

Till now we have been learning about Nano Server which is an installation option with Windows Server 2016. Windows Server 2016 contains two types of base images, `windowsservercore` and `nanoserver`. In the previous chapters, we have learnt to build applications using Windows Server Core as base image, in this section we will learn to use Nano Server base OS image to create containerized applications which are much smaller and easily manageable. Nano Server containers can be created on Windows Server 2016 with Full GUI, Windows Server core or even Nano Server versions. The following steps show setting up Docker and Nano Server:

1. Run the following command to create a WinRM session to Nano Server. Login with the Windows Login credentials when prompted:

   ```
   $ip = "<<IP Address of Nano Server"
   $cred = Get-Credential
   Set-Item WSMan:\localhost\Client\TrustedHosts -Value $ip
   Enter-PSSession -ComputerName $ip -Credential $cred
   ```

2. Few critical updates are required to install Windows Container features on Nano Server. These updates can be installed by running the following commands:

   ```
   $sess = New-CimInstance -Namespace
   root/Microsoft/Windows/WindowsUpdate -ClassName
   MSFT_WUOperationsSession
   Invoke-CimMethod -InputObject $sess -MethodName
   ApplyApplicableUpdates
   ```

3. Reboot the system once the updates are installed using the following command:

   ```
   Restart-Computer
   ```

The following commands use the OneGet provider PowerShell module to install Docker. The provider will enable the container feature on the Nano Server and install Docker, this too requires a reboot:

```
Install-Module -Name DockerMsftProvider -Repository
PSGallery -Force
```

The following command installs the latest version of Docker:

```
Install-Package -Name docker -ProviderName DockerMsftProvider
```

The image given later shows Docker running on a Nano Server virtual machine. The following command downloads the Nano Server container image from Microsoft Docker Hub:

```
Docker pull Microsoft/nanoserver
```

Unlike Microsoft official repository for Windows Server Containers there is no such official repository for Nano Server Containers yet.

 For more information on Microsoft Nano Server base OS image for Windows Containers visit
https://hub.docker.com/r/microsoft/nanoserver/.

```
[          ]: PS C:\> docker info
Containers: 0
 Running: 0
 Paused: 0
 Stopped: 0
Images: 0
Server Version: 17.03.1-ee-3
Storage Driver: windowsfilter
 Windows:
Logging Driver: json-file
Plugins:
 Volume: local
 Network: l2bridge l2tunnel nat null overlay transparent
Swarm: inactive
Default Isolation: process
Kernel Version: 10.0 14393 (14393.953.amd64fre.rs1_release_inmarket.170303-1614)
Operating System: Windows Server 2016 Datacenter
OSType: windows
Architecture: x86_64
CPUs: 2
Total Memory: 7 GiB
Name: nanowebserver
ID: J234:S3GT:UNAA:AUZK:PANE:AGHL:DQH5:LYDB:BKUF:777I:3YLV:TGCH
Docker Root Dir: C:\ProgramData\docker
Debug Mode (client): false
Debug Mode (server): false
Registry: https://index.docker.io/v1/
Experimental: false
Insecure Registries:
 127.0.0.0/8
Live Restore Enabled: false
```

Summary

Nano Server is the new headless deployment option which comes with Windows Server 2016. Nano Server is a deeply refactored version designed to provide lightest, fastest ever configuration with lesser patches, reboots, better resource utilization and tighter security. Nano Server does not have any GUI component, the only way to manage Nano Server is by using Windows Remote Management. Nano Server has 93% lesser VHD Size, 92% fewer critical security advisories and 80% fewer reboots than the Windows Server. Nano Server can be provisioned on Azure or on-premise environment by using the Nano Server installation ISO, VHD options. Roles and features live outside Nano Server, so they should be downloaded from Internet or copied to the Nano Server. Microsoft has also release a custom image builder for Nano Server. Nano server comes with online package repository which allows us to connect to any online repository, install and download roles and features that are available. Microsoft also released a Nano Server base OS image for Windows Containers called `microsoft/nanoserver` which can be used on all deployment options of Windows Server including Nano Server. Nano Server supports server configuration tools like PowerShell DSC, Chef, and Puppet.

Index

C

D